D1481473

The subjects of this book

Russell George, age 67
indecent assaults on little girls

Wilfred Johnson, age 58
indecent assaults on little boys

Billy Atkinson, age 37
sexual assaults on women

Graham Davis, age 20
buggery with adolescent boys

Nat Burke, age 45
persistent importuning of males

Harry Mills, age 45
indecent exposure

Charlie Cox, age 37
living on immoral earnings

Andrew Brown, age 36
rape (for which he is serving four consecutive life-sentences)

'It is impossible to overpraise Mr. Parker's skill as an interviewer . . . empathy of this order is a rare phenomenon. This book should be obligatory reading for every judge and magistrate before whom these unfortunates appear'

Anthony Storr in *The Sunday Times*

Tony Parker, a sociologist, has specialized in the study of criminal cases in depth. His five books, of which *The Courage of his Convictions* was a landmark, are based on the criminal's own tape-recorded words.

Tony Parker

The Twisting Lane
some sex offenders

Panther Modern Society

The Twisting Lane

A Panther Book

First published in Great Britain by
Hutchinson & Co (Publishers) Limited 1969
Panther edition published 1970

*Printed in Great Britain by Cox & Wyman Ltd.,
London, Reading and Fakenham, and published
by Panther Books,
3 Upper James Street, London, W.1*

for Douglas Gibson, adviser and friend

Those who pursue me taking a twisting lane
To find themselves immediately alone
With savage water or unfeeling stone,
In labyrinths where they must entertain
Confusion, cripples, tigers, thunder, pain.

W. H. AUDEN: For the Time Being

Contents

Introductory Note

The material in this book consists of edited transcriptions of
tape-recordings made over a period of eighteen months with
eight people, each of whom has been convicted for sexual
offences of a different kind. Real names and place names and a
few minor details have been altered to protect anonymity.
None of them is representative of a type, only of himself.
These are personal statements made at unknown cost and with
inestimable bravery and to try adequately to thank those
who made them by allowing themselves to be subjected to
persistent questioning is beyond my power; I can only state
my respect and admiration for their courage and dignity.
There are no insights or interpretations offered other than
theirs. I am not competent to make any of my own.
I have omitted most of my questions and allowed what they
said to stand in the way that they said it, hoping it will convey
at least something of who and what and how they are.

T.P.

This Other Life

Russell George

The forty-one miles of motorway featureless, a hard swathe of white concrete unreeling endlessly over the rain-drenched December countryside, and the angry afternoon gale-wind lashing and buffeting south-west to north-east at right-angles straight across it. The car at sixty persistently gliding out of the fast lane, across the middle, veering into the slow, then lunging violently back towards the fast in the temporary haven of cuttings through hills, and bursting out once more at the end of them back into the noise and shove of the wind. Mud spray from the mumbling clusters of over-taken lorries straggling up the long climbs, wipers steadily whirring and clicking, sweeping the windscreen clear, obscured, clear. Flash of headlights from behind caught in the mirror, a hooting black Jaguar swamping past, ripping importantly on into the distance through its own accom-panying cascade. Direction signs huge as posters, white on blue, chronographers of distance and of time: Brompton thirty-five miles, twenty-six miles, fifteen miles, nine.

Eventually at last the count-down markers before the junction: three hundred yards ahead, two hundred, one. A sharp swing off the wide carriageway, round and down through the group of artificially landscaped hillocks and into the trunk road, the swishing stream of traffic overhead high on the motorway fading away at the back with the recession of the embankment. A pleasantly quiet road now, the wind less difficult and the rain blowing in light curtains across the ribbed brown earth of the bare winter fields.

Slowly through small villages, past an old country church and a derelict wooden barn. On past two petrol pumps de-serted in front of a combined grocer's and off-licence and

post-office. Right at the next cross-roads, then left in two
hundred yards at the wooden finger-post pointing to Far-
dale. Half a mile further on, and left again into an
unmarked by-road almost concealed with high hedges: un-
metalled, wide enough most of the time for one vehicle
only, winding falling rising for four miles like a piece of
string dropped over the undulations of the land. Foliage
overgrowing both sides, an unbroken thicket of hawthorn,
brambles, wild privet, ivy, willow bushes, holly, pollarded
stunted limes, rotten paling fencing held together by rusting
strands of barbed wire. A tiny meadow on a hairpin bend
at the bottom of a hill, a lightning-struck tree naked in the
middle of it, bare branches against the black-clouded sky,
an arthritic hand. Steep rises and bends, puddles and pot-
holes, mud and loose gravel at dank corners unpenetrated
by the pale daylight....

A twisting lane, long, unused, and nearly unusable, going
nowhere.

But suddenly over the crest of a small hill it widens and
comes out into the open past a line of tall copper beeches,
running straight on to the narrow gravel path that neatly
fringes Ambergrove Green. An unexpected community of
twenty houses and a shack for the village store. Total population thirty-four. A scattering of dwellings irregularly
grouped round half an acre of smooth grass, some of them
visible only as smoking chimneys behind wattle fences and
wooden gates, a few more with flat roofs, plate-glass picture
windows and well-kept open lawns set with miniature
spruces and standard roses, with white-washed rocks as
frontage marks. In the summer a modest beauty spot, not
quite worth a special visit, but known to a few off-track
wanderers. Here and there a house to let in August perhaps
for someone wanting a quiet simple holiday. But through
the winter the inhabitants mostly keep themselves to themselves. Elderly people nearly all: a retired headmaster and
headmistress in 'White Gables' with their retired school-
mistress daughter, a lady in the big red brick bungalow
called 'Flanders' with only eleven Schipperkes as companions.

Unnoticed at first along the east side of the green a brief
terrace of two-roomed cottages, farm-labourers' homes

once, with low front doors opening straight into the down-stairs room. Sitting in a fireside chair in Number Five, prod-ding the logs in the grate with a poker to bring up a blaze, a man turning his face sometimes to glance out of the window at the dark blue rainfull sky, the glitter of the flames catching his glasses at an opaque angle then and giving him two huge round crimson eyes. An aquiline nose, thin lips, the age-lines carved deeply down his cheeks from temple to chin; a high domed bald head fringed with a fluff of grey hair round the back and sides. Straight-backed and upright, a wiry body in a roll-necked canary yellow pull-over, long-legged whipcord trousers, soft brown leather casual shoes.

Speaking quietly, from time to time lapsing into silence and staring motionless into the fire. A former area manager of the National Coal Board, and after a lifetime's work now pensioned and retired. Russell George, expatriate Lancas-trian in a strange southern county, a widower living alone and keeping himself to himself mostly: now seventy years of age.

—It doesn't look like it's going to stop raining this side of Christmas does it? And they say the south has better weather than t'north! Well, I don't know, ever since I've come down here it's been bloody awful it has. Like ruddy Manchester all the time it is, winter and summer, rain rain rain, I've never seen nothing like it, seems to do nowt else. Well I suppose it's got to leave off sometime though, hasn't it? Have you finished your tea, will you have another cup? A biscuit then?

All right I'm ready to make a start if you are. See how far we get, shall we? You'll not want to stop too long each time, I know, you've a long journey back haven't you? If I ramble too much you must stop me, because there's not a lot of people you can talk to down here.

Well I was born in 1898 in Lanarkshire. But I'm not Scot-tish, my parents were English people, my father was work-ing up there in one of the mines. I was the fifth child, there was a brother and then four sisters before me; Malcolm, Elizabeth, Joan, Mary and Eileen – though for some reason she was never called anything else but 'Lena'. There was about two years between each of us, more or less: and then four years after me there was two more girls again, Dora and Barbara, but that wasn't till later, after we'd moved down into England, I'll be coming to that of course at the time.

I don't remember anything much before I was about five. My father had quite a decent job for those days, he was a mechanical engineer, what used to be called the 'engine-wright'. I know in Scotland we used to live in a sort of big block, more or less a tenement place it was, up on the fourth or fifth floor, with only three rooms if I remember, and an outside washplace at the end of the stone landing. And then there was this wide spiral staircase with like an iron balus-trade round a courtyard in the centre of the block. You had to go out on the landing to the wash-house when you got up in the mornings and at night before you went to bed: in the open it was, not protected from the weather or anything, and very cold in the winter. Not much else I can recollect about it I don't think – oh yes I remember the bed, my mother's and father's, one of those sort you fold up into a recess like, in the wall of the living-room during the day.

Chiefly I remember things more clearly from when I was five or six onwards, when we'd come down to live in North-umberland where my father had got a new job. They were all privately owned, the coalmines in those days of course: and he went to work for a man who owned the mine in one of the little villages in those parts. He not only owned the mine but all the houses as well, there'd only be about twelve of them, little cottages in a terrace very much like this, grey stone with slate roofs, then the mine-shaft a few yards away up at the top of the street. And then, at the end the other way, three bigger houses standing on their own; one for the owner, a smaller one for the pit-manager, and then a smaller one still for the chief engineer, which was my father.

Mind you, it was quite a big house for those days you know, four rooms downstairs and the same again on top. I don't suppose what my father earned would sound much to people now, I expect it couldn't have been above five pounds a week – but with the house thrown in rent free and a new suit every year from the company and things like that, he'd be considered well off. He was a strange sort of man my father, at least I always found him so; very remote and austere, never had much time for people outside, and never much to say for himself at home either. When he was younger, he'd had some kind of an accident, fallen getting off a moving tram in Glasgow and banged a nerve in his head or something, and it'd left him with a very bad speech impediment. Perhaps that's why he never talked much, because it was difficult to him.

My mother she was more or less the same sort of person too as he was, another very quiet one. A rather gaunt, sallow-complexioned woman, sewing or dress-making in the evenings, one bottle of stout with her supper on Saturday nights, and that was about all she had in the way of excitement. A strange pair altogether when I think back on them: one thing for instance, when you went to bed no one ever came up and tucked you in or gave you a kiss, it was just 'Off you go to bed now, Russell, mind you wash' and that was it. And then you lay in the dark until you went to sleep. Right up at the top of the house I was, in a little kind of an attic with a sloping roof.

Russell? Well that was after one of my uncles, my mother's brother. I can remember him coming to see us once, he was a soldier in a red jacket with white trimming on it and a big helmet. It must have been during the Boer War, he was just going out to South Africa; I think he got killed there, anyway I don't remember ever seeing or hearing of him again.

A lonely little boy I'd say, always very lonely: my memories of that house are of a big cold place with dark wallpaper, dim candle lights, never any laughter or fun in it, and sitting nearly every evening at the table doing my sums from school. But school I liked, I was quite good at it, especially arithmetic; right from being very young, I'd always enjoyed that. I have done all my life, mathematics, taken a real pleasure in it. I enjoyed drawing too – not art-drawing, but diagrams of how things worked, what different pieces of machinery looked like, and I wasn't satisfied until I'd drawn them very very precisely and accurate, and exactly as they were. I suppose it was what they call technical drawing nowadays. I must have been quite bright I think, because when I was about ten I was sent to another school in the town which must have been at least twelve or thirteen miles away. There was no buses in those days so I had to walk about three miles every morning to the station to catch the train, and then walk the same back again at night.

I never had any friends when I was a little boy: I've never had any since for that matter, but living so far away from the school there was never any question of making friends with any of the boys there because it was too far for them to come home with me to play. And going to the town school I got to know none of the village children either. We weren't let play with them much anyway, since they were mostly the mine-workers' children and we were the family of one of the bosses. My father went to work in a suit and a bowler hat, so that made him a different class of person, you see – and I was brought up to look at it that way too; that was the start of it, of my snobbishness which I've had ever since. I've always had the tendency to think myself a cut above other people, based on absolutely nothing. A right snob I've been all my life.

Well, as I said, I was good at school and well behaved and quiet at home and well behaved there too since we children were always kept in our place by our parents. My brother of course he was a lot older than me; by the time I started at the town school he'd gone off working in the Midlands somewhere. He began with a horse and cart, and he finished up a big draper with six or seven shops of his own. He took my sisters into his business looking after the shops for him, one by one as they got old enough; they all worked for him right through until they retired, and none of them ever got married.

The only person I had as a playmate as a child was the older sister next to me, Lena; I liked her, I got on very well with her indeed. We had quite an understanding of each other, at night sometimes she'd come upstairs into the attic and get into my bed, or we'd run about chasing each other in the dark. There was nothing sexual in it, in fact I never knew anything whatsoever about sex until I was seventeen and a half – but that's running on a bit, so I'll leave that subject till later. But there was something about Lena that I really loved when I was a kid; the quiet way she talked, but always with a bit of a twinkle in her eye, the way she moved – she was very neat and graceful. Sometimes when we were romping around in the bed with the light still on I'd catch sight of different parts of her body, and I did, I liked the way she was made. In fact I often used to wish I was a girl, like her, instead of a boy. I had the idea my mother favoured all the girls more than she did me, and it must be because there was something wrong with the way I was made myself, ungainly and awkward, and not like Lena at all.

I wished very often at that age I could be a girl. It used to take me in some funny ways. I'd never urinate standing up for instance, I always had to sit down and do it like a girl did. And when she was a schoolgirl Lena started taking a great interest in dressmaking, and I'd ask her to let me try the clothes on that she'd made so that she could study what they looked like and see if there were any alterations needed making. Coats, dresses, underclothes, everything: I enjoyed parading about for her in them, until one day all of a sudden she burst out giggling and said I looked daft; after that I never did it again.

The word I used about my father – 'austere' – that was the word that summed up the whole of my childhood, really, I think. I don't know what other people's was like of course so it's difficult to compare, but certainly I always knew I was missing something. I felt life ought to have more in it somehow than just school and going home and sitting quietly reading until it was time for bed. I know what it was all right, though I wasn't conscious so much at the time what it was that I was short of: it was love. I was never ill as a child, so there was no occasion that I was ever petted or made a fuss of: though I doubt if there would have been even if I had, since the whole family never went in for demonstrations of affection of any sort. For instance I never saw my father and mother kiss each other or put their arms round each other, nothing of that kind at all.

There was just once I think, out of my whole childhood, one incident I look back on when anyone ever mentions the subject of love: about the only time I ever had any idea at all what it meant. I must have been about eleven or twelve I suppose. One of my aunties, one of my mother's sisters, had come to stay with us for a few days. In the evening everyone was sitting round quiet as usual and I was reading a book in the corner on my own; and I suddenly felt very lonely and miserable and I started to cry – about nothing, of course, as it seemed to everyone else. My mother didn't like that sort of thing at all, and she told me very sharp it was past my bedtime, to get on upstairs and get to sleep. 'Off you go now, mind you wash, good night.' I went up to bed like I was told, and not long after I'd put my light out my auntie came up to me. She didn't say anything, just sat on the side of the bed in the dark, and then suddenly she wrapped her arms round me and cuddled me against her breast. She opened her blouse and took out her breast right out for me, and rocked me against her until I dropped off to sleep. She never said a single word the whole time and neither did I; it was as if she knew what I wanted and decided for once to give it to me – a few moments' mothering so that at least I'd have had the experience of it, I suppose. That isolated incident, that was it: that was the first and only time I've ever known what it was like. Years ago, sixty years nearly, and I can still feel the warmth and softness of her breast now.

Well then it came to what, when I was thirteen I should think; that was the next thing, leaving school. In those days that was the leaving age, and I started work when I was thirteen years and one day old, in the machine repair-shop at the pit-head. Seventy-five per cent of the haulage underground was done by ponies, but there were a few machines to be attended to, for ventilation and that sort of thing. I'll say this for my father, he gave me a very good training, he was always taking me along to the pit even when I was still at school and showing me how the different engines worked; how to operate the screwing and drilling machines and so on, so that by the time I actually started work I could do lathe-work and all that, and I was a good deal further-on than most boys of my age. He had one of the very early motor-cars too, a Stanley Steam Car it was, and he taught me all the ins and outs of that as well.

He was keen I should follow after him and one day get a job like his; he was very proud of having risen to it by his own efforts and without much education. About the only books we ever had in our house were ones to do with mining-engineering, and I used to study them and try to follow them even before I could hardly understand the words. I was always mechanically-minded, right from being very young.

That and my natural aptitude paid off and soon he was able to leave me more or less in charge of the repair shop on the surface while he looked after things underground, even though I was only a lad. I kept on with my studies at night school after I'd started work, I used to go three evenings a week to college in the town. It was hard though, keeping up schooling after a hard working day, walking to the railway station for the train, and not getting back before ten or half past at night, and then having to be up again at six the next morning for work. There was some certificate or other I took, I think it was City & Guilds or whatever the equivalent was in those times: I know it was a four-year course combining engineering, mechanics and heat; and anyway eventually I passed it.

But by then the war was on, and so after a time I was called-up into the Army. I didn't mind about going, I don't think I gave it much thought one way or the other, I wasn't very patriotic or anything like that. It was inevitable, when you got to a certain age you went like everyone else did, and that was all there was to it. But I was one of the lucky ones, I didn't get put in the infantry, because of the specialized knowledge I had. They gave me a trade test and I was sent down to London to be an instructor in the Royal Army Service Corps, teaching men how to maintain vehicles. After six months I was put up to sergeant, and then I was sent to France to a big Army car depot in Paris. I was in Etaples and Amiens too, but I never saw any of the fighting. I was always miles behind the front except when the Germans made that last big push which nearly won the war for them, but the guns in the distance was about all I ever heard.

When it came to the Armistice, the officer I worked for asked me did I want to get out of the Army and go home, but I said I didn't mind stopping-on for a bit. I liked the life, the independence it brought, and being able to spend all my time with machinery and cars and things. I was in Paris right through the Peace Conference of 1919, in charge of the servicing of all the vehicles for the different diplomats who came there for it. One of them was Paderewski, he was the Polish Prime Minister leading the Polish delegation. He gave a concert once while he was there. It was a great experience to see him and hear him; he played the Moonlight Sonata of Beethoven, that was the first time I ever heard it, and it was what started me off on the liking for classical music that I've had ever since.

It was while I was in Paris during the war that I had my first sexual experience: somehow I'd got to seventeen and a half without having anything happen to me of that kind and never even giving it a thought. I used to go a lot to a kind of club for Allied soldiers, and there was a Frenchwoman there, one of the volunteer helpers, and I think she rather took a fancy to me. I wasn't a bad-looking young chap, and tall for my age, five foot ten and a half. She was a widow, a lot older than me, thirty-nine or forty perhaps she must have been, and one day she asked me round to her flat for tea. When I went there was a big chasse-lounge thing by the window, and I hadn't been there more than ten minutes before she'd got me on to it and was egging me on to take her clothes off. I was a rotten lover I can tell you that, totally inexperienced, really green; and what's more I couldn't get any kind of an erection at all, I was completely impotent. She did her best, but it was just useless, an absolute fiasco all round.

But it didn't put her off though; she kept on asking me round to her flat, dressing herself up in a négligé and doing everything she could to get me going. But the fact of the matter was I simply didn't want it or like it: the only time I got even a very small erection was once when she climbed on top of me and did everything herself. I couldn't get over the feeling which I had all the time that it was somehow wrong way round, I ought to have been the woman and have things done to me. Anyway after a few weeks eventually she gave up, it must have been too frustrating for her. She didn't ask me round to the flat no more. And I can't say it worried me because it didn't, I just hadn't got any taste for it at all.

I stayed in Paris until 1920 I think it would be, and then I was demobilized and sent back home. Straight back to the village, straight back into my old job at the pit. And in a couple of years it seemed as though the war'd never happened and I'd never been away from home. Work and study again, that was my life, more or less all together; nothing changed, nothing changing and nothing ever going to change. I began to get quite a collection of diplomas and things for exams I'd passed, and by 1922 or so I was workshop foreman, and then assistant engineer underground. As I say, I liked the work – and so long as I was working with some kind of machinery I was happy.

The thing that appealed to me was that it was exact: you knew how it was going to behave, and if you studied it you could make it behave how you wanted to. All through my life I've had this knack of being able to look at a machine that was broken and being able to tell what was wrong with it even before I started to take it apart. I was completely at home with it, I understood it: so long as you got this right and that right and the other right, you knew exactly where you were. Precision, attention to detail – that was all that mattered: get everything in order and you were away. That's always been me: I never do anything simple like even writing a letter asking the coalman to call without first drafting it out carefully beforehand.

Then it would be about 1926 that for the first time I started going out with a girl. She lived at one of the farms a mile or two further down the road, she was the farmer's daughter, the youngest of about six. I can't remember the exact circumstances I met her in, but I used to go to see her on my motor-bike and sidecar which I'd bought for myself second-hand. She led a hard-working life herself too. Sunday afternoons I'd go and talk to her in the dairy where she was milking the cows, and they had one of those big churns for making butter which she used to make me turn for her by hand while we chatted. I said to her one afternoon, 'One day I'm going to electrify this damn thing for you!', and I did, I got it fixed up with a motor and working on its own.

Her name was Margaret. She was a big strong girl, quite good looking, long hair down her back to her waist and blue eyes. She was like me, not very talkative, so we suited each other. She wasn't very passionate or much interested in sex either, and that suited me too. In 1926 there was the strike and all the pits closed down. We weren't off work of course, the maintenance staff, we had to try and keep things going, see to the ventilation plant, keep the haulage roads clear and so on. All the same, it did mean I had a good deal of free time, and she and I used to go out on the motor-bike together, exploring the countryside. Altogether we were courting for about two years I'd say, something like that.

Her sister had a boy-friend too, and sometimes the four of us would go out together, he had a motor-bike and a sidecar as well. We decided one week-end we'd go and have a few days in the Lake District, and when we got there we started looking round for somewhere to stay, and I think it was Keswick we ended up in. He went into this sort of boarding-house place to see if they'd got any rooms, and when he came out he said it was all right, they'd two double rooms and he'd booked them for us. He and Margaret's sister kept giggling about it all the time, and it wasn't till we got back to the place in the evening he told us what he'd fixed up. Of course I'd been expecting he and I would share one room and the girls the other, but what he'd done was booked us in as two married couples. Well, Margaret and I decided we'd just have to accept it; her sister and boy-friend were obviously determined they were going to sleep together, so we didn't have much choice.

When we got into bed we made love together a bit, but it was still the same thing as before with me. I couldn't do it, I was still impotent. I thought Margaret would give me up then, but she didn't, it didn't seem to bother her in the slightest. When we got back home I began to feel really awful about it. We'd slept together, and that was something to my way of thinking was quite wrong for people who weren't married. So I asked her if she would marry me, because I thought it was only right we should. She agreed, and we went and asked her father's permission: he said yes, he thought it'd be a very suitable match, and that was it, we got married in the autumn of that year. Quite a do the wedding was, we both had large families, everybody treated it as a big event. I can't say I was madly in love with her, nothing of that kind; but I liked her well enough and she probably felt the same for me too. We had a bit of a honeymoon, I forget where it was, Whitley Bay I think – bed was no good there either – and then afterwards we went to live in a house of our own her father gave us on some of his land.

I carried on working just the same in the pit with my father. Then after two years we had our first baby, Donald; and a year or two after that we had our second son, Stephen. What sex-life there was between us was very rare, I was still impotent and used to ejaculate far too quickly, at least according to what you're supposed to do that I've ever read about the subject. So the fact we managed to have two children was more a matter of good luck than good management. But that was one of the nice things about Margaret, she never complained, she was really as little interested in the subject as I was, and that kind of thing was never a problem between us at all.

By the time Stephen was born, which would be in the thirties, obviously I needed more money than I was ever going to be able to earn in a small job like the one I had with my father, and I started to look for something better. It didn't take me long to find it either: I was very experienced, and very well qualified too, as I've told you. I moved into the Lancashire coal-field, and I got a job in a pit near Wigan at much better pay. We bought our own house there: things were a bit of a struggle at first, but we kept going, and I did well in my job and got the usual annual increases in salary, so we were improving all the time.

When the 1939 war came coal-mining was one of the most important industries there was, and I got given more and more responsibility. I was always widening my experience: with the result that after the war, when the Labour Government brought in the nationalization of the mines, I was in on the ground floor of it and able to take advantage of the big opportunities that there were available. I got into a good job with the Coal Board, and eventually I went right up to area manager, responsible for everything to do with the mechanical side of about half a dozen pits. I was earning very good money, I had a company house and a company car, the boys were at the best schools there were in the district, everything was just right for me. I was in a good pension scheme too – something else that I'd got in on at the beginning of nationalization – and I don't think there was anything I wanted that I hadn't got, or couldn't get. Holidays abroad we had – Spain, Italy, France – and what I had I'd worked for, I'd earned it by my own ability and skill.

The only thing was, I'd no social life and no friends at all, and we'd quarrelled with all my wife's family too by then. This was nobody's fault but my own. I was a real cantankerous sort of person, always arguing with people and disagreeing with them; and the manner I had with it didn't help either. At work I'd no idea of tact at all. At the Coal Board meetings of area managers for instance, I was perpetually criticizing other people's ideas and suggestions, and telling them they were bloody fools. So they were, a lot of them; but it didn't make folk like me any better when I told them they'd no idea how to do their jobs properly. I think I'd have got the sack many a time if I hadn't been so good at my job.

Even when there was a chance of any social side, I never bothered to take advantage of it. Golf, for example, I used to play a lot of that; I liked the fresh air and the exercise, and the way you could think it out all very carefully, what would be the right club to use for each particular shot depending on the distance and the lie of the ball and all that sort of thing. I got my handicap down to twelve, which wasn't bad for an amateur. But the thing was, you see, I'd never play with anybody else: I always used to go round the course on my own, I couldn't stand to have anyone with me, we'd only play a few holes and then I'd start criticizing and telling them what they were doing wrong. Or I didn't like the way they talked, or the way they dressed, I always thought they weren't in my class: the snobbishness thing that I was telling you about before. So I just had no friends, not one. But I didn't mind, I never made the faintest effort to get any, I wouldn't put myself out to be civil or pleasant to anyone.

When the boys got older and grew up, they both married early and set up homes of their own. Donald, he always took after me, he'd got the mechanical turn of mind too. When he was just over twenty, he got himself a good job with a big firm of civil engineering contractors; he took a degree which they paid for him to study, and he's been with them ever since and doing very well he is, I wouldn't be surprised if he didn't eventually get a directorship one day. But Stephen, now he was completely different, just the opposite – always very artistic right from when he was young, and still is. I don't know where he gets it from: but he's done very well himself in the commercial art world. Now he does a lot of designing for television and that sort of thing. Fine boys both of them are, nice families of their own, good jobs, they're well breeched, as they say, for the rest of their lives. What was I saying, yes about them moving away from home and getting married: well after that my wife and I, naturally we had to move into a smaller house; we got a nice bungalow on the outskirts of Preston.

We're getting on now, this is bringing us up to about 1959, 1960. And it was then that I had my accident in the mine, entirely my own fault, there was no one else to blame but me, and being the sort of person I was. There was a very complicated new type of coal-cutting machine that was going to be installed for a trial in one of the pits I was in charge of, and it was my responsibility to check it thoroughly and make sure it was working as it should. On the surface – that was where it had to do with me, and after that, when it was installed, I had nothing else, no cause even to think about it. So I checked it through very carefully and passed it, and that should have been it.

But of course no, that wasn't good enough for me. The next morning after it had been installed, a Saturday it was, I thought to myself 'I'll just go down and have a look at it, make sure the people underground know what they're doing and have put it in right' – so down I went, completely unofficially on my own, not telling anyone where I was going. I'd no right to go down there, no right at all. I had a look at the machine, I couldn't find anything wrong or anything I could criticize: so finally just to make doubly certain I threw the switch and started it up.

And that was it: I was bending down watching it, and before I knew where I was it'd caught me, the flap of my jacket hanging open I suppose or something like that. That I wasn't killed was just a sheer fluke, that's all. I was lying there unconscious for something like two hours I believe, before anyone found me and got me out and I was taken to hospital. I had my shoulder smashed, my forearm broken, my upper arm broken in two places, my hip broken, my thigh broken, and my knee-cap as well. A right mess I was in. Over six months I was in hospital as a result of it, as a result of my own pig-headedness, nothing else. Lying in plaster all down this side almost from my head to my foot, and my leg up in one of those what do they call them, Thomas's splints? Agony it was, real agony: not so much the physical pain, I was tough and I could stand that, but the mental agony of being helpless, having to lie there like a child all that time and knowing there was no one I could blame for it only myself. And up till then I'd never had a single day off work with illness my whole life. Sometimes I really thought I'd go mad I did. A terrible patient too, of course, always swearing and cursing at the doctors and nurses, telling them they didn't know what they were doing, why weren't they getting me back on my feet again, and all the rest of it.

Anyway, gradually, I did begin to get better. They used to send me along to the physiotherapy classes then to do exercises to help get my limbs and my muscles working again. I didn't like any of the other patients there naturally; to my mind they weren't making any real effort to get themselves right. I used to really despise them for the pathetic attempts they were making on those fixed-bicycle pedalling things, ladders for climbing and other bits of apparatus. I made up my mind I was going to get myself discharged before any of them, and I used to stick at the exercises, on and on, driving myself all the time however painful it was.

Well, eventually I did it, I got myself right – or as right as I ever will be. My hip's pinned together still, and it could easily go again at any time, it'll always be like that; and this leg's two inches shorter than the other one, I have to wear this special built-up shoe. As a matter of fact I ought to wear a surgical boot on it, but I won't. Because I'm too vain, I suppose – but I'd sooner put up with it and ignore it as much as I can. I've trained myself to walk without hardly a limp; I'm just not going to have anything as conspicuous as a boot whatever they say, I can get by. Stubborn, you see.

I got myself out of the hospital, and I insisted to the Coal Board I could go back to work. They wanted me to retire a few years early, I was sixty then, on medical grounds. But I knew if I did that it would mean a reduced pension for me, and anyway I wanted to hang on and retire at the proper age. I knew too that if I did take a medical retirement, I wouldn't do very well on compensation. They have a sort of price-scale at the Coal Board, so much for the loss of an arm, so much for a leg and so on. I went into it, and I found out that my compensation would come out at something like £8,000 all together – but then it'd be assessed by an arbitration tribunal, and at very best I'd be held responsible at least 80 per cent myself, so I'd only get a very small sum at the finish.

I was lucky because nearly all my job by that time anyway was administrative, supervision, paper-work and so on, so what physical incapacity I had wasn't going to prevent me working. I managed to hang on until the end of my time nearly, and I retired just a bit early in 1961.

We sold the bungalow at Preston, and bought ourselves a nice little bungalow up on the Fylde coast, a few miles out from Blackpool. I must say I found retirement very hard after fifty years: I just finished work on the Friday night as usual, and then on the Monday morning instead of going off to work all I had to do was sit and twiddle my thumbs. For someone like me, used all my life to being active and working, it was a real problem: and it took me a long time to settle down to it, especially as I'd no outside interests. I used to take the wife out for rides in the car, we'd sit somewhere quiet and secluded and look at the sea or read the papers, but it was very hard and boring, it really was. I felt absolutely lost. Her mother came to stay with us for a while, but she'd only been there a few months when she was taken into hospital: we'd go and visit her every day, but three months later she died.

Then the next thing that happened was that Margaret herself took ill, and then she had to go into hospital too. It wasn't long before the doctors told me what it was, it was cancer and at the most they said she'd only got about three months herself to live. We'd arranged to go to Italy the next year for our holidays, so I had to go on pretending about it, talking to her about getting the tickets and so on. Suddenly she seemed to rally; they often do I'm told, and for a few days I really began to think she might be getting better.

But that was the end of it, it was only about a week after that that she was dead. I was sixty-four then, so we'd had just over a year of my retirement, that's all.

After she'd gone I lived for a while on my own in the same house; then eighteen months ago I sold up and came down to live in London with Stephen and his wife in their flat. I stopped with them until last August, then I came across this place, saw this cottage was going, so I took it and here I am. It's just about my mark this is, it suits me perfect – very peaceful and out of the way, nice and small and easy to keep clean. In a few months the spring will be coming, then the summer after that. I should imagine it'll be quite pretty round here in the summer, I'm looking forward to seeing it. I don't suppose there can be all that many years left for me now.

But when you're getting on you seem somehow to enjoy things more, because you know they aren't going to last, and so that makes you appreciate them while you can. The birds in the trees, the sunrise on a frosty morning, all little things like that. They're the things that matter, you feel you're going to enjoy them while you're still alive.

So there you are then, that's it, that's what you might call the biography of me I suppose – or at least the outward details of it, the events and mileposts and things that a stranger looking at it might see. Nothing very outstanding or spectacular, just a plain existence of an ordinary man. If you didn't know any better.

But all the time as well, right through it all for forty years or more now, there's been this other life.

—Six convictions altogether, for indecent assaults on little girls. Eventually I ended up in prison for it – and the only wonder was that it didn't come much earlier than it did. The times I've done it and not even been reported, let alone caught for it and charged. It could easily have been sixty convictions; double that even, and that's no exaggeration.

Always the same age group, six to eleven: no younger and no older, outside those limits it didn't appeal to me at all. Playing about with them with my hands under their skirts, tickling their bottoms, getting them to let me take their knickers down. No more than that, I never tried to rape them or have intercourse with them: I couldn't have done, I was impotent as I've told you. But I did get sexual satisfaction out of it: I'd sit them on my knee and play with them, and at the same time I was able to masturbate myself without using my hands. Five, ten minutes at the outside, then I got my ejaculation and that was it.

*   *   *

Outside, the winter afternoons nearly always windy and raining week after week, and over the green the reddening, deepening, darkening sky. Inside by the fire the old man talking, a voice sometimes soft and sometimes like gravel and sometimes trailing away, the towering pillars of his silences rising up like pylons into the scudding clouds.

A whole lifetime of work, my job, my position, my family, my home: all put in the balance over and over again, ready to be thrown away and lost for the sake of the ten minutes every now and then that I had to have, fumbling about with some little girl. Mad, I must have been mad. And you know I never even thought about it, about what I was doing, all the time I kept it right at the back of my mind. I didn't take it seriously; I never expected anyone else to either. I didn't worry about it so I didn't think they should, I couldn't even see it was any concern of theirs. It was just a little fault I had, nothing serious, not even worth talking about.

I lied to people, deceived them, said it wasn't important and anyway I wouldn't do it again – though I always knew perfectly well that I would. Nobody ever suggested to me I ought to try and do something about it, have treatment or something like that – but if they had, I wouldn't have paid attention to them, I wasn't prepared to discuss it even. My wife, Margaret, you know, she was a real Trojan about it. All those years it went on and she knew it, she knew it was happening, but she still stuck by me. I wish ... well, it's too late now, she's gone.

It didn't start until quite late on in my life really: a few years after we were married, when I'd be coming up to round about thirty. She had a large family, several brothers and sisters, and they were married too with families, most of them had small children. There used to be family parties and things, everyone getting together at Christmas, and when we went to them I used to find myself being more and more attracted to those that were little girls. I was always picking them up, giving them rides on my shoulders, talking to them, sitting them on my knee bouncing them up and down.

Everybody used to say it was because Margaret and I had two sons and I hadn't got a daughter of my own; and perhaps it was that at the beginning. But as these little girls got older, my nieces and their friends, I got more and more keen on them, I used to look forward to the occasions when I'd have an excuse for being with them, and then when I got there I'd be spending nearly my entire time picking them up and carrying them about, and taking them into different rooms so I could have them for a few minutes on my own.

After a while it got so noticeable that their parents began to get a bit uneasy about it, and Margaret would say to me afterwards, 'I don't think you ought to do that so much, Russell, Annie and Joe are getting a bit worried about it' or something like that. I'd just pass it off, laugh and make a joke out of it, saying it wasn't doing any harm, I was just very fond of the kids, that was all.

It's not easy for people in the same family of course to start making accusations, is it, about that sort of thing, about one of their own relatives? I was always very sly about it, I'd wait until I was on my own with the child and its parents were out of the room, and even then I never used to do very much in case it might say something afterwards.

But one Christmas I think it was, I did, I did go too far. It might have been because I'd had a bit too much to drink or something like that, but anyway I took one of my nieces who was about six and quite a big girl, I took her upstairs into one of the bedrooms and I was sitting with her on my knee and I had her knickers down. The door opened and her father came in. There it was, he'd caught me right at it, there was no chance of passing it off as a joke that time. He didn't say anything at all, just took her up in his arms and carried her out without a word, went downstairs and told his wife to get her hat and coat on, they were going home.

After they'd gone there was a bit of an embarrassing scene, nobody really wanting to talk about it in front of the others, my wife very upset when she finally found out what had happened and all the rest of it. When we got home ourselves she tried to face me with it, ask me exactly what it was, why her brother-in-law and his wife had left like that in the middle of the celebrations – but I wouldn't talk, I insisted it was a lot of fuss about nothing, he'd got hold of completely the wrong idea. Putting the blame on him in fact, though of course he'd been absolutely in the right and every reason to be angry about it.

Well, it went on that way for a good few years. All I ever did was with the children in the family whenever there was a get-together; and only with the little girls after they'd reached that certain age. Very irregular, perhaps no more than two or three times a year, just when the occasion arose. But naturally it got talked about in the family, first this child and then that, and their parents talking amongst each other I suppose. Anyway in the finish it got to where none of them would come to our house with their children; and then they wouldn't go to each other's houses if they knew beforehand I was going to be present. Or if they came unexpectedly and found I was there, they wouldn't stop, they'd make some excuse and go home again.

I think my wife never did take it seriously, she let me convince her there was nothing in it for any reasonable person to worry over. That wasn't her fault, because I was always so insistent about it myself. Absolutely adamant I was – and we never talked about that sort of thing much between us anyway, sex. I think she really did in her heart put it down to me missing having a daughter of my own, and she thought perhaps if we had one ourselves everything would be all right then. But we had sex between us very rarely: it wasn't that we weren't fond of each other, but neither of us had much interest in it and it was never very enjoyable. We didn't use contraception ever but she conceived no more after the two boys.

By the time we were both fifty there was no more hope for another child for us anyway; and by then, too, things had got so bad with the families that I was getting no opportunities at all for what I wanted to do. If I wanted it, I'd have to go out and look for it – so in due course that was what I did. On Saturday afternoons I started going into the

nearest town and hanging round the toy departments of the
various stores, keeping my eyes open for little girls on their
own or perhaps with a friend of their own age, then getting
up behind them and feeling at their bottoms under their
clothes.

A lot of them of course they didn't like it and they'd
move away. But there were some, a lot more than you'd
expect in fact, who didn't mind and would let you go on
doing it. When I found one of that sort I'd start chatting
to her, ask her where she lived and if she'd like me to take
her home in my car, or perhaps come and have a ride round
in it and I'd buy her some sweets. If she would, then I'd take
her out of the town, off the road into the woods somewhere
and play about with her for a bit, ask her if she'd let me
look at her knickers and that sort of thing, were they very
tight and could I pull them down and so on. Ten minutes
perhaps at the outside before I'd ejaculate, and then immediately I lost interest: I'd drop her off near her home,
give her a few sweets or a sixpence and that was the finish
of it.

I'd never try and see her again or make any arrangements
for meeting another time. The next week it'd be a different
child, perhaps even a different town I'd go to round about
the district, so as to make sure I wouldn't get caught. I
hadn't a hope of avoiding it eventually, and I don't know
what made me think I had; but all the same I went on a fair
number of years before I was. Then one little girl who'd
seemed quite willing enough at the time, unknown to me
she must have taken my car-number when I was driving
away from her, and she told her parents who took it up with
the police, and they traced me and took me to court over it.
A lot of parents won't bother, out of consideration for the
feelings of their child, but these ones did. The police told
me they'd had quite a few reports of the same thing going
on in the town for a long while, but they couldn't get any
clear enough evidence against me. Either the parents didn't
want to rake it all up again in their child's mind, or the
children themselves weren't too sure whether it was me or
not after the passage of time. And of course I denied everything, I insisted this was the first and only time it had ever
happened.

The outcome was I got away with a fine, I think it was £5, something like that. There was a bit got put into the local paper about it, but I just shrugged it off. If anyone at work read it, they certainly didn't mention it, probably because they weren't exactly on very good terms with me, as I've told you. Margaret of course was terribly upset, she said we'd have to leave the district and go and live somewhere else. And I said all right, if that was how she felt about it, if it'd make her any happier that's what we'd do.

One way and another time went on, we looked at a few houses now and again but the price wasn't right or they were too big or too small, I always found some objection to them. I didn't honestly see why we should move just for what I thought was a trivial little reason like that. I didn't care what the neighbours thought, it didn't worry me at all; if they were going to think things, let them – that was my attitude, and the same for the people at work.

Incredibly, really, I don't think it was more than three or four days after I'd been fined than I was at it again, back in the town hanging round the toy departments until I found another little girl who'd come in the car with me. But once more, I was never caught for a long time, and Margaret was probably of the opinion it'd just been a passing incident and it had died down. It's true it did die down sometimes, maybe for up to six months at a stretch. I used to think myself that as I was getting older perhaps the desire for it was fading away. Then back it'd come again; and I'd give no thought to the consequences, off I'd go. And as for the children, the little girls, what it might be doing to them, it never entered my mind, not once.

The second time I was caught there'd been this quite long period since the previous occasion, and again there was the usual trouble for the police of trying to get children to come forward and make a positive identification. Once more all I got was a fine, I think it was £20 that time. The usual business, a paragraph in the local paper; but Margaret was really insistent then that we'd got to move, so I didn't argue any more about it, I said all right we'd go somewhere else and I'd make a fresh start.

Being an area manager with the Coal Board it wasn't essential for me to live in one particular town any more than in five or six others which would suit me equally as well, so there was no difficulty there. The boys were grown up and married by this time, so we took the house in Preston that I told you about.

For a few months there were no incidents, everything was going nicely, until about the summer I should think – and then it started all over again. We used to go at weekends over to the holiday places, Blackpool, Morecambe, Southport. There was ample opportunities there for me. I'd drop the wife off to do some shopping, and I'd go wandering round the pier and amusement arcades until I found a suitable little girl who was agreeable to me doing things to her. A lot of them were only there just that week for their holidays perhaps, so the chances of them reporting it and me getting caught were less than ever. The wife knew nothing of it, of course, in fact I don't know that she even suspected.

There was one funny thing about it you see, that I suppose used to make her think it was all right and I was over it. It was that the little girls always had to be fully dressed with skirts and coats on. Sometimes if the weather was nice we'd be sitting out on the sands in deck-chairs, and perhaps some little girls in bathing-costumes or with those like little romper-pants on would come and start playing near us. Margaret would say, 'Do you think we ought to go and sit somewhere else?' And I'd say, 'No, why should we, we're all right here, nothing's worrying me.' It was true: a half-naked child or one in a bathing suit had no effect on me at all, I wasn't the least bit interested, I wouldn't have looked twice at one. Always this thing of having to get my hands under their clothing, secretive, feeling what they'd got on, that was it.

As I say, she could see it didn't disturb me, and that must have helped her on towards believing what she wanted to believe all through her life, that what I did was no more than what I said it was. 'An unfortunate little habit' – that was one of my phrases whenever I referred to it, and she always persuaded herself it couldn't be more than that.

What might have happened eventually then I don't know. But anyway the next thing was the accident, and of course that put a stop to my activities for quite a long time, over a year or more. I even started to think myself that that was probably the finish of it too. But it wasn't, in fact after I recovered and got back to work things went very rapidly then from bad to worse. I was in more trouble, up in front of the court again. This time I had a solicitor. Living in a different place from where I'd been on the other occasions, for some reason they hadn't got my previous convictions, and of course I didn't say anything about them myself. The solicitor put forward a case based on my accident, that it'd upset me and made me forget myself; I think all they'd actually caught me for on this occasion was interfering with a little girl in a shop somewhere, and I'd been seen and reported by one of the assistants. Anyhow all that happened was that I was bound over.

Then in double quick time it happened again, I was caught once more, I'd been seen driving into the woods with a child, and the police came and caught me there. This time it was a £50 fine; and once again the way it took Margaret was that she thought the only thing to do was move. This tied in with the business over my retirement, it all came together more or less at once, so we moved over to the bungalow at Blackpool. I was really at a loose end, really desperate then, no work, nothing to occupy myself with, it was dreadful.

When Margaret's mother came to live with us, it wasn't long before she had to go into hospital. Every afternoon we used to go up and see her, and more times than not I'd started getting really fidgety and I'd say, 'I'm just going out for a breath of air, I'll be back in half an hour.' And straight away I'd go out, get in the car, drive around the town while the children were coming out of school until I found one who agreed to come for a ride with me.

I'd take her down a lane somewhere, the usual business, ten minutes that's all; then straight back to the hospital. Walk in completely unconcerned, pick up Margaret and take her back home. Every day it got to be, I'd lost all sense of proportion, all reasoning power, everything. It got to the stage too that I was behaving without any thought at all as to the consequences, not even bothering any more if anybody should see me while I was doing it. Side-roads that people were walking up and down, pub car-parks, I just didn't bother to be careful any more. Once I picked up two little girls together, and that time I went further than I'd ever done: as well as playing about with both of them I exposed myself to them as well. They started giggling, and one of them said 'Oh what a little one, I've seen much bigger ones than that' – and that really upset me. I never did that again, because of course it confirmed what I've always thought myself, that I was exceptionally small made.

My wife's mother died, then the wife herself took ill, and while that was going on the sexual needs that I had, they died down too, and I didn't go out looking for girls or anything. Then she went, and a few months later back it came once more as bad as ever, even worse. Living on my own, nothing to do, nothing to think about, missing Margaret; and the only outlet I had of any kind, this thing. Caught again, I had to be, didn't I, doing it so much and not caring where or who with or how.

A solicitor again, I wasn't short of money; and the story this time was about how my wife had only recently died, it'd thrown me off my balance. Another fairy-tale. Well I got a big fine this time, and a real stiff warning from the magistrate with it: this was the very last chance, he said, and the next time it didn't matter what the excuse was or my age or anything; it'd be prison.

And did it make any difference? Not the faintest. It can't have been above a week I should think before I was back at it again. I was so well known round the district by then, I was, I was notorious, that's the only word for it. About another three months, and then this time they'd really got me: one charge, and about another six or seven they were ready to prove right up to the hilt.

There was just nothing to be done then, I knew what was coming. And it did. I was tried, found guilty, and remanded into Strangeways for a month to await sentence.

And you know, that was the first time ever that it really came home to me, when I finally found I'd got myself put in prison. Oh, what a place, I'd never seen anything like it, you couldn't believe such things existed. Dirty, old-fashioned, hot, packed with people: locked-up hours and hours on end, three to a cell, no toilets, you all had to use a bucket. Three beds in a space about this big, two of them bunks and I had the bottom one, and in the night the man above me kept urinating in his sleep and it all poured down all over my

face ... oh dear oh dear, oh dearie-me, I can't describe it,
I can't find words for it, I really can't.

I knew there was no question of sticking it out, I couldn't
do it at my age, it just wasn't going to be possible. What
was I going to get? Six months at the very least, perhaps
nine months or even a year. I've always been the sort of person if he makes up his mind to something he'll do it, and I
thought, 'Well this is the finish, there's no point in it, there's
nothing to go on for, there's no Margaret to go back to – so
if they put me back in here I'll set my mind to finding a
way of ending it and polishing myself off.' It wasn't self-
pity. I didn't cry or anything like that: I just thought it out
and decided that was the only logical thing to do.

And then, about ten days before I was due back up in
court to hear my sentence, they came and said there was a
visitor for me; it was my son Stephen. How he'd found out
I was there I don't know because I certainly hadn't told him
and I couldn't think of any one else who could have. He
said to me, 'Well Dad, what are we going to do?' I just
shrugged: I knew what I was going to do, but there wasn't
any point in having a discussion about it. Anyway, then he
went on and told me that he'd taken some legal advice down
in London where he was living, he'd got a barrister who was
prepared to come up to Manchester and take the case for
me – and that if I'd have treatment from a psychiatrist,
they thought there was a good chance of the court agreeing
to it so long as I was under proper supervision.

To be honest, it just seemed to me to be utterly pointless;
as far as I could see there was nothing a psychiatrist or anyone else could do for someone at my age, it was only going
to be a big waste of money all round. But he wouldn't give
up, Stephen: he talked and talked to me, and eventually
more to shut him up than anything else I said all right I'd
give it a try – but I didn't think the judge would listen to it
as it was anyway.

But surprisingly, he did. Stephen's counsel put it all to
him, how there was a psychiatrist in London who'd said
he'd take me on, either in hospital or as a private patient;
and there was a probation officer willing to have me under
his supervision as well. On top of that, Stephen and his wife
were prepared to have me live with them in their home.

Naturally the judge looked a bit sceptical first of all, but this barrister he really put everything he'd got into it, presented it like a whole neatly wrapped-up parcel – and the judge said eventually all right, perhaps it was worth taking a chance. But he made it quite plain at the same time he wasn't going to have any back-slidings – one little incident, any suggestion I wasn't going to co-operate in having the treatment or not do what the probation officer said, and that'd be the end of it and he wouldn't listen to any excuses.

It was a marvellous thing, you know, was what Stephen and his wife did. She was his second wife, and they'd got two small children of their own, and one of them a little girl. My other boy Donald, his wife wouldn't have me in her house not for the last twenty years, she'd never let me anywhere near her children; and she still won't to this day. You can't blame her: and you couldn't have blamed Stephen's wife if she'd felt the same. Anyway, there it was; they were prepared to have me, and they did.

I came down to London, the probation officer he was a nice young chap, very helpful; and the psychiatrist, well at first I didn't know at all what to make of him. I'd never met one before, but I gather they're all pretty much the same. They let you do all the talking and they just sit and listen. He said I could either go into a hospital he was connected with under the Health Service, and stop there for three or maybe four years; or I could go to him as a private patient more or less every day of the week, and in that case it'd take perhaps only eighteen months to two years.

I thought well I could afford it, I'd nothing else to spend my money on, both the boys had got enough of their own without having to bother about how much I was going to leave to them – and at my age, every month was worth almost like a year to everybody else. So I said that's what I'd do, I'd pay for it and have it privately and get straight on with it.

To someone like myself, all that long life behind him, no friends and making a point deliberately of not being talkative with anyone, it wasn't easy by God; it wasn't easy at all. He just left me, you see, left me to do everything for about the first whole year, and himself he never said a word. I had to sit there in a chair and try to talk – about myself,

with him out of sight behind me and me just looking at the
wall. I had to sweat it out like that, on and on and on, time
after time. There were days when I couldn't get a word out,
not a thing: I'd sit wriggling about in downright misery, not
knowing why I'd come or what I was supposed to be doing
or anything. So I'd just talk about that, tell him all about
that, how confused I was and scared.

And I was scared. It's a very painful experience to someone who's not normally an introspective sort of person, believe me. Some afternoons I'd get as far as his front door
and stretch my hand out to ring his bell and I couldn't do it,
I'd start shaking and sweating, and I'd have to walk away
again down the street and smoke a cigarette, and then force
myself to go back. That was the one time in life I think
when this stubbornness, this obstinacy I have, really paid
off. I'd say, 'Well, I've started, and I'm going to go through
with it, I've never started anything yet that I haven't finished.' And that's how it was.

I did, I had some narrow escapes too. Going to a psychiatrist every day, even that's not a full-time occupation, and
I used to go down into Oxford Street into the big stores and
start wandering round. Then after a bit I'd find myself in
the toy department of course, watching a little girl, trying to
pick out one who was on her own; and then seeing one and
edging all the time a little bit nearer and nearer to her, until
I was close enough to start stretching out my hand.

But somehow, right at the very last moment then I'd always manage to stop myself. I'd turn round and walk away,
out of the department, out of the store, up into Hyde Park,
anywhere, anywhere as far away as I could possibly get.
And the reaction, I'd be exhausted with it, I could hardly
stand up; I'd go straight back to Stephen's flat then, I was
finished for the day. But I always managed to bring myself
to tell the doctor about it at the next session; I went over
and over it in detail, talking it out of myself, talking it out
all the time. Till eventually I got to the stage of not wanting
to do it much at all, just wanting to talk about it
instead; and that was how it went on then, and the worst
was over.

After about a year he said I only needed to see him three
times a week, so I did that for six months; and then he said

it only needed to be twice a week. It wasn't long after that I saw this cottage: it's not impossible to get up and down to London from here in the car, and there was nothing else for me to do except a bit of gardening and pottering about. So I discussed it with him, with the psychiatrist; and with the probation officer, and no doubt they discussed it with each other – and anyway, they said it'd be all right. So I came here. Then it got down to once a week with the psychiatrist, then once a month: and then eventually at last he signed me off.

So there it is. There's two little girls live next door, two more in that house over the other side of the green. It's all gone, finished now, it doesn't mean a thing. Don't ask me to explain it, I couldn't tell you; how something like that which can dominate your whole life can become at the finish so unimportant not only does it not worry you, you even begin to wonder how it ever could have – whether it was you, that person who spent so much of his time and thoughts on it, or whether it wasn't perhaps somebody else you once read about somewhere, maybe in a book.

What a difference: what a difference it makes when it's gone. It's like a dream. In a way your life's empty; mine is, it's very empty since Margaret's gone. It's such a big regret to me she couldn't have been with me now, she couldn't have lived just that few years longer to share what I have, to get some kind of reward for all she went through – the peace of mind, perhaps, of knowing the settled state I've come to at the last. A Trojan you know, a real Trojan she was, a wonderful woman to put up with all that. But perhaps it's as well in a way, because she'd have had to see the other part too, wouldn't she, all that went before, and the imprisonment. That would have caused her such pain, and it was bad enough for me, but it would have been unbearable for her.

—What to say now … I don't know, I really don't, not where others who are like me are concerned. There's no way of recognizing them is there? Homosexuals, I believe a lot of them can recognize each other and if they want to talk about it and discuss it they're fairly sure the other one will understand. But this thing of mine: you can't look at a

man and say, 'Oh yes, he's another one the same as me.'
They don't have badges, they don't talk about it – in fact if
they were like me, they'd deny it right up to the hilt even
when you held the proof up for them right in front of their
eyes. And the children too, the dreadful things it must do to
them . . . and you never even give it a thought.

And yet if only it could be got over. . . . If only you
could, you know, get them to see there is something the
matter with them, but that it's something there's treatment
for, that it can be cured. So they don't have to go on all
through their lives, bringing misery to those who are near
and dear to them, and all the shame. It doesn't have to be a
complete waste for everyone, like my life was. They don't
have to end up at seventy like me, looking back knowing it
was all thrown away and when they're gone they're gone,
and there's nothing anyone will ever remember them by. I
do, I do wish somehow that that could be said.

A Malady Come Upon You

Wilfred Johnson

A month after the season had finished the holiday resort was characterless, uninhabited and depersonalized with the colourful summer-thronging crowds gone from the streets and cafés and amusement arcades. Along the concrete promenade with its decorated lamp-posts and regularly spaced shelters and benches there was no one to be seen; the steep flights of steps and the sloping paths coming down from the cliffs were deserted, and between them the formal flowerbeds were now only empty and unplanted bare patches of soil. Over the lines of abandoned beach huts and shuttered refreshment stalls a ragged group of mute seagulls flapped and dipped hungrily and the distant pier unused and silent stretched out like an atrophied arm into the sea.

In the honeyed afternoon sunlight he stood by the balustrade of the sea-wall, staring intently at the glittering white-flecked waves of the grey North Sea heaving slowly one after another to break hissing and frothing on the beach below. A small frail man of sixty with dark green eyes in a thin and troubled face, and the collar of the military-looking macintosh the prison had lent him for the day turned up against the breeze from off the water which blew through his short-cropped and neatly parted greying hair. His hands resting on the wall, he stayed for a long time silent, looking at the pastel colours of the sand and sky, breathing the salt-fresh air and watching the ocean's endless sullen surge.

—The sand, he said after a while, it looks like brown sugar, doesn't it, don't you think it does? Barbados Muscavados, 'brown moist', that's what they used to call it if I remember, in the trade. Oh this is a lovely scene isn't it, all very peaceful, so beautiful, it really is.

Do you believe in God? No? I do. I'm sure there must be a god somewhere, you know. I don't see how else you can explain it otherwise – that you should say a prayer and then that it should come exactly true. I did, yes, I prayed last night before I went to sleep: that today would be nice and sunny, that it'd be a happy day and we'd get on well together, and we could be somewhere quiet and peaceful where we could have a good long talk. I never expected the seaside though you know, somehow I hadn't thought of that, that's made it even better still. So it's all turned out like I hoped, just like I prayed it would; absolutely perfect in every way. He answered my prayer, I'm quite convinced of that.

It was good of them to let me come out with you wasn't it? I've never heard of that being done before, somehow in prison you never expect they might let you out for a day. Three years is a long time to spend locked up in a place; and you completely forget what it's going to be like outside, you've put all thoughts of it out of your mind. I was a bit frightened at the idea, yes, I thought it'd be too overwhelming for me somehow, with all the bustle and the people and the noise. That was why it was such a good idea to come here. Look – not a solitary soul in sight is there, anywhere? We might almost be the only people left in the world, mightn't we, it'd be funny that, wouldn't it, if we were? When we went back into the town we found everyone had vanished and there was no one left but us. What should we do then? Sometimes the mind runs on like that, doesn't it? Mine does, does yours? I often think it's going to happen you know, everyone wiped out in a war perhaps, and I'd be the only one left alive.

It wouldn't be too difficult for me, having no one to talk to; I wouldn't miss other people, I don't think, very much. There's often no one at all that I talk to anyway. You can't, you see, in prison: it's not possible, it's too much of a risk. All the other prisoners talk: they boast, even, a lot of them. Because to their way of thinking they've got something to boast about I suppose; big robberies they've done, safe-breaking, smash-and-grab, wages-snatches, cleverly worked-out frauds. They can't be all that clever though can they, otherwise they wouldn't be in prison for it? But it's

funny, that aspect of it never seems to cross their minds.
They concentrate on the jobs they did without being caught
for, or the big ones they're going to do when they eventually get out. 'Next time it'll be different, I'll be more careful, I definitely won't get caught again' – that's what they
all say.

There's a man like that I walk round with on exercise;
he's in for what they call 'kites', dud cheques you know,
that sort of thing. Always describing the details of it, how
he does it, the ones no one's ever found out about, the
marvellous living he was making at it before a little bit of
bad luck brought it to an end. 'And in the future I'll never
be any different,' he says, 'only much shrewder, they won't
get a chance to catch up with me next time.' A nicely spoken
man he is too you know; well I suppose you've got to be,
haven't you, for that sort of thing? I quite like him, he's
honest according to his own lights anyway about himself
and what he is, he never pretends.

But the thing I like most about him is that he doesn't
ask me any questions about myself. He never has done, not
once in three years. Perhaps he's not interested, perhaps he
doesn't care. Now and again though I suddenly get the feeling he's going to: I'll be lying in bed one night and it comes
over me like that, out of nowhere, and I start thinking he's
going to ask me about it the next day. I'm sure he is, I'm
convinced of it. He's going to turn round to me and say 'Oh
by the way' – that's how he'll put it – 'oh by the way,
you've never told me before, but just exactly what are the
details of your own particular case?'

I get so frightened you know, really terrified. I convince
myself that he'll say it, that he's going to come out with it;
I'm certain he is, and I feel myself starting to sweat all over.
Then for the next few days, perhaps for a week even, I
won't walk round with him, I make some excuse like I'm
not feeling very well, I'm not up to walking round with him
on exercise. I go off out of sight somewhere on my own then
where he can't see me, keep right out of his way until the
feeling's worn off again.

You just can't risk it you see, you never can. All your time
in prison you're scared to death that someone's going to find
out. You know from how you hear them talk when there's

some sort of similar case reported in the papers, and they all start discussing it among themselves. 'Make a note of his name,' they say, 'so that if he ever turns up in here we'll know who he is, we'll see he gets what he deserves.' The way they talk, the way they look; they mean it all right. In fact there's instances I've heard of where it's actually happened, someone like that's been set on by the others; and the screws won't lift a finger to help them either you know, they feel the same way about it themselves. As soon as something starts they don't interfere to try and break it up or go to the man's assistance, they just turn their backs and walk away.

You wouldn't get a chance to explain it to anyone, you couldn't tell them anyway how it was because they wouldn't listen, and even if they did it'd make no difference. In their eyes it's absolutely contemptible. And they're right you know. It is: it is contemptible, there's no other word you can use for it, really there isn't, not when you come to think about it.

*   *   *

Wilfred Johnson. Date of birth: 19th April 1908. Address: 'Rosecot', Field Bank, Walthorpe, Sussex.

16.6.1945. Kent Magistrates' Court. 6 months' imprisonment. Indecent assault on boy aged 10.

29.8.1951. Sussex Quarter Sessions. 2 years' imprisonment. Indecent assault on boy aged 8. Two other charges concerning boy aged 9 and boy aged 11 taken into consideration.

22.7.1953. Sussex Quarter Sessions. 21 months' imprisonment. Indecent assault on boy aged 11 and boy aged 10.

11.3.1957. Sussex Quarter Sessions. 8 years' preventive detention. Indecent assault on boy aged 10, boy aged 8, two boys aged 9, one boy aged 11.

18.8.1965. Sussex Quarter Sessions. 5 years' imprisonment. Indecent behaviour with boy aged 12, boy aged 11, boy aged 9.

—The first thing I remember must have been in the war, I think, the Great War, when I was about seven I suppose, and there'd been a house bombed in Golders Green. At least I think it'd been bombed but I couldn't be sure; my sister who was two or three years older than me, she was always a great one for a lark and a joke you know, she might have been pulling my leg. It was a rare event of course in those days, a house being bombed, not like the Second War. 'Come on, Wilf!' she said, 'we'll go and see if we can find it,' and the two of us went off, it was miles and miles from where we lived. There wasn't all that much to see now I think about it when we got there. I know it was very late when we got back, our mum didn't know where we'd been and she was getting really worried about it. But Sally she couldn't have cared less, anything with a bit of excitement or fun in it always appealed to her.

My father was often away at sea during the Great War so my mother was having a hard time of it nearly always. No, he wasn't a sailor, he was a kind of a clerk on board ship, looked after the book-keeping and stores and that sort of thing. I believe he was called a 'ship's writer', something like that. Of course at school with the other kids, I always told them my dad was a sailor. I remember I was very disappointed when he came home on leave and he didn't have the outfit, bell-bottomed trousers and all the rest of it that I thought a proper sailor should have.

There were three children actually all together; as well as my sister I had an older brother, his name was Harold. He was my father's favourite, my brother was. They used to spend a lot of time together when he was at home, going out a lot and that sort of thing. There was something about Harold, I don't know what it was: he was quite studious I think, and my father was always saying he'd go a long way in life.

I remember the shortages too in the war, how our mum sent Sally and me out once round the shops to see if we could find a pound of sugar anywhere, I think it was three-pence she gave us for it. She was really delighted when we found a shop that had some and brought it back. I was fairly clever at school, I know I got some sort of a scholarship when I was ten or eleven, to go to what would be the equivalent of a grammar school up in Edmonton somewhere. But I never stopped at one school long, we were always moving about; my mother was a very restless sort of a person, adventurous you might have called her almost. She'd

say, 'Oh I'm fed up of living in this place, let's move somewhere else,' and the next week we'd be gone. Flats, parts of
other people's houses, a little detached house of our own I
remember once: south London, north London, we must have
had a dozen different addresses at some time or another. But
she always seemed to make friends wherever she went, she
was never short of company: of course she was a very gay
and lively woman in those days, and very good looking. She
had beautiful long brown hair which she wore sometimes
up and sometimes down to her waist, whatever the fashion
decreed at the time. Lovely grey eyes, a nice wide mouth, a
slender figure, only about five foot two she was; what you'd
call 'petite', that'd be the word. And she played the piano a
lot, and had a nice singing voice, and a very good dancer
too, very light on her feet. It wasn't surprising everyone
liked her. Originally she was of Austrian descent, her great-
grandfather on her mother's side, something like that. She
came from a very well-educated family, sensitive well-bred
sort of people they were with good educations, and talented
at music and things like that. When she was younger I can
remember she used to give what they called 'musical evenings' – a few friends in, and she'd play the piano and sing
for them. Not jazz, you know, but good stuff, classical music.
It was from her I got my own love of it. I can't stand this
present-day 'pop' stuff, but really decent music – Ivor Nov-
ello, Irving Berlin – I'm very fond of all that.

    We hadn't a lot of money ever and I've known her cut up
one of her own skirts to make a little pair of trousers for me
when things were hard. 'I don't need this old thing,' she'd
say, 'I can find a much better use for it for something for
you.' And perhaps it'd been only the week before, you
know, that she'd got it for herself. But she never complained,
she always did it with a laugh and made light of it. A really
lovely person in every way, the best sort of mother anyone
could ever wish for, she was.

    She wasn't happy though; she can't have been with my
father, not for years. When he was home there was always
terrible rows. My brother would come running into the
room. 'A-B-U,' he'd say, 'A-B-U!', and then he'd run out
again. 'Another Bust Up', that was what it meant. And I'd
go down to wherever they were – and if I saw my mother

crying I wouldn't hesitate for one moment, I'd set on my
father and pummel him like that with my fists; only eight
or nine years old I'd be but I'd really go for him, I would.
I could never bear to see her cry. Sometimes I think I could
have killed him, I honestly would have tried to kill him
you know, I was so wild about it. I hate people rowing: I
did then, and I always have done, right through the rest of
my life, it upsets me terribly.

Of course looking back on it now later in life, I can see
he wasn't really all that bad a person as I used to think he
was when I was a child. It was something in him, just an
unfortunate habit he'd got that he couldn't keep his eye off
the ladies. My mother used to get so jealous always, I think
she used to be quite unreasonable about it sometimes. We'd
all go out for a walk, or shopping or something like that,
and when we got back she'd burst into tears and say she
didn't like the way he'd been looking at one of the girl shop
assistants perhaps; his eyes all over her she'd say, and asking
us to back her up and say that we'd noticed it too.

With him being away a lot I suppose he might have got
the taste for it when he was in the different ports and places.
Other women, that's what started it all. When he came home
he was always pacing up and down, he couldn't hardly bear
to be in the house sometimes, he was so bad-tempered. Till
eventually mother would say to him, 'Oh go down to the
docks,' she'd say, 'see if you can't find yourself another
ship, I know you don't want to be here with us.' He always
wanted to return to the water, so off he'd go: we wouldn't see
him again for months and months until he came back then
from his trip. While the war was on I think, sometimes he
was away for perhaps as much as a year at a time. I was
never sorry really myself to see him go. He was a bit too
heavy-handed for my liking, he'd hit you first and ask questions afterwards, you know how I mean? I got quite a few
tannings from him, usually for very trivial things.

I know at the finish it got just too much for both mother
and father, they couldn't get on at all together, and they
had a legal separation. That was not long after the war was
over, about 1921 perhaps or 1922, when I'd be about fourteen. In fact that's right, it was just when I was fourteen,
because I know I had to leave school then and get a job to

help out with the money. My brother he'd gone off somewhere working, I think it was up to Birmingham or some
place like that, and we didn't see him any more. He got
married and settled down and had a family of his own. He's
done very well for himself ever since; at least he seems to
have done, whenever I've seen him, which hasn't been a lot
of course in the last twenty or thirty years. But I don't
think my mother minded all that much as long as she'd got
me. I was always her favourite, I know that. You can tell it
from the way a person looks at you, I think, can't you? A
child's always very sensitive to things like that.

And myself, I was glad to leave school, I preferred being
at home. I had a terrible squint, all the other kids used to
call me 'Boss-eye' and things of that sort, they can be very
cruel, children, can't they sometimes? My mother was very
good about it, she used to comfort me – and at the same
time she never tried to make me go to hospital and have
something done about it, which I was terrified of. She'd
say, 'It's all right, Wilfred, you don't need to, it makes no
difference to me.' In fact I was over thirty before I sum-
moned up the courage to have it done, and in all that time
she never tried to push me into it, not once she didn't.

The first job I had was in a grocer's shop, a kind of general
assistant and delivery boy. Fifteen shillings a week I was
earning, my mother was very glad of it. She got some kind of
an allowance for me and my sister from my father, he
always paid that regular, but even so there wasn't a lot
to go round. But things were a lot better and more settled
then, my mother certainly seemed to be happier and not so
restless. We lived in one place for a long time then, a little
house we had in Lewisham just big enough for the three of
us and she made it into a very nice home. We were used to
dad being away anyway, so we didn't mind much that he
wasn't there – and he still used to come and see us, you
know, from time to time. In fact him and mother got on
much better after they were separated, they remained quite
friendly really all the time right up to when he died, not
long before the Second War.

I liked the grocer's, I've always thought that was an
interesting sort of trade. Nice clean work, isn't it, with food-
stuffs and packages and things? I've often wished since I'd

stayed there. You never know, things might have turned
out that little bit different for me if I had. They were good
people to work for too. I had a bit of an accident while I
was there, hurt my foot when I was knocked down by a bus.
I was off for three months with it, and eventually I got compensation, from the insurance you know. I believe it was a
hundred pounds – a huge sum in those days. And this firm
kept my job open for me until I got back. I was with them
quite a long time, seven or eight years. Then my sister got
married and went away too, so that only left me and my
mother, and I wanted to get a better job because she was
ill; more or less a permanent invalid from then on she was.
I always wanted to try and do the best I could for her and
have her looked after properly. She was treated for years
and years for pernicious anaemia, that's what they thought
it was – and it was only right at the end they discovered it
wasn't that at all, it was a cancer, and a very bad one; and
of course it was too late to do anything about it by that
time. But she was a brave woman, she never made a fuss of
herself, she used to spend all her time taking care of me.

She never remarried, she never wanted to, she didn't believe in that sort of thing. She was like a wife to me really.
In fact better than a wife because I'd known her all my life
you see, and you can't get any closer can you to anyone
than that? You're longer with your mother than anyone,
aren't you, even your wife? Oh a lovely relationship we had
together all those years, never a cross word between us,
nothing; it was just perfect. Real pals we were, we neither
of us wanted anyone else, you know, at all. I was a great
home-bird myself, I didn't really have any other friends
except her. She was my best friend and I was perfectly
happy like that – great friends we were, real chums. She
understood me and I understood her, our minds always
seemed to be in keeping with each other. We could sit for
hours in the evening, you know, in the same room, never
talking: we never needed to talk about things, each one
knew at once what the other was thinking; and that's a
wonderful thing when it's like that.

I had a little Austin Seven in those days, we used to go out
for a run every single weekend without fail – Brighton,
Margate, Hastings, all sorts of places – once we even went as

far as Portsmouth we did, and then the car broke down on the way back and we had to spend the night pulled up at the side of the road! She had a canary in a cage she was very fond of, she'd never be parted from it, so that had to come everywhere with us on the trips too. And still the same sort of venturesome person she was, always. 'Where should we go today, Wilfred?' she'd ask me, and I'd say, 'Well how about Birchington, do you think the car'll make it as far as that?' and she'd say, 'Well come on, let's give it a try shall we, eh?' So we did. A really great sport she was, ready for anything. She'd make up sandwiches for the day for us, we'd pack all our things in, the canary as well, and away we'd go. Oh some very happy times we had, really happy times.

I'm only sorry you can't meet her, you'd have loved her, really you would. Well there it is, she's gone now, and that's the way it is, isn't it? But you can imagine, I expect, being a married man yourself: what it would be like after years and years of happy marriage if your wife was to die. It's like the end of your own life somehow, a light going out, you can't ever really grasp it, what it means that a person's gone for good; not when you've been like we were you can't. Everything to each other, everything. Very wonderful it is, of course, too, when you look back on it, lots and lots of happy memories, places you've been together, things that you've seen. A dear soul she was in every possible way. An angel, in fact, that's what I think, that's the word I'd use for her, it's the only word there is. Life with her was marvellous, it really was, and I look back on it as something very beautiful. There's a lot of people would think there was something strange about a man feeling like that about his mother. But that's because they've never experienced anything like it themselves.

Perhaps you think me foolish, soft like, to go on like this about her. But I want you to know me as I am, you see, there's nothing I want to hide from you, nothing I wouldn't say. And it is true that my life virtually ended for me when she went; it left a great sort of gap in the world for me that could never be filled. My sister's said to me that I've got to get over it; but it's easier for her I suppose isn't it, with a husband and family of her own? And she never saw her like I did you know, she wasn't there herself at the end. But I was; I was with her when she died, I saw her in such pain she was trying to get out at the bottom of the bed, and I had to lift her up and put her back on her pillows again. And then soon after, she just put her hand gently over mine and gave a big like a sigh it was, and then she died. Silly, isn't it, a grown man in tears, I do beg your pardon, I'll just blow my nose. But it's nice to talk to someone about her, after all this time. It still feels almost like last week you know, just as recent as that. I can hardly believe it myself that so much time has gone past since she went: it's quite a long time now, nearly twelve years.

*   *   *

From far along the promenade the faint yelping of an approaching dog; louder and nearer, and then still yapping unceasingly as it came by with its head down and went on towards some vague aim a long way ahead, a portly Cairn terrier scampered past and disappeared into the distance.

—Poor old chap, I wonder where he lives, he looks a long way from home doesn't he? Well I know where I live; and I suppose now you ought to be taking me back, shouldn't you? Not a minute later than five o'clock I had to be in, they said. Will you come again? Oh good, yes I'd like that very much. Perhaps next time we ought to get down to facts hadn't we, really try and talk about my cases and things of that sort? Yes, I think I'd like to try, I really would, yes.

*   *   *

—I remember every single little detail of that day we had together last month, you know – the sunshine, the sea, that lovely old church we stopped to have a look at on the way back. It was just the sort of day my mother would have liked if she'd been alive. Afterwards when I was in my cell thinking about it, it reminded me of her favourite piece of music, the one she used to like to play on the piano. It was called 'A Perfect Day'. I can see it clearly in my mind's eye now, an old-fashioned cover it had, a drawing of a country scene. She used to prop it up in front of her while she played, though I'm sure she didn't need it you know, she must have known every note of it off by heart.

Today's not so nice though is it, all this rain; I think the winter's here all right now, don't you? We were very lucky with that other day weren't we? An Indian summer wasn't it, that's what they call it, yes. Well never mind, it's nice in your car, we're all right up here on the cliffs, warm and dry and no one to disturb us. It was jolly cold though, down there on the shore, wasn't it? I couldn't have stood longer than ten minutes of that, could you? No. It's good of them at the prison to let me out a few times with you, they're not all bad people in those places. That assistant governor, Mr. Whitaker, he's a nice man, the sort of person you could talk to if you got the chance. But there's so many isn't there, so many prisoners I mean? It's all the staff can do most of the time just to remember people's names. He did talk to me once a year or so ago, Mr. Whitaker; and what he said to me was true all right. 'You know, Johnson,' he said, 'the other side of that wall at the bottom of the yard there, there's rows of little wooden crosses in the ground, just with names on them that's all – and one of them one day's going to have your name on it, if you don't try and do something about yourself.' He meant well by it, he said it kindly; it wasn't his fault what happened after that.

I put my name down for the doctor from the Home Office and when he came I was called up to see him. You wonder where they get some of them from, don't you? To my mind he wasn't like a doctor at all. It was a hot day but somehow you don't expect a medical man to be sitting in his shirt-sleeves and braces do you, chain-smoking all the time? Even though it's only prison, that sort of thing doesn't seem the right kind of behaviour for a doctor. A great big man he was, more like a publican than anything else, very loud-voiced and rude. 'Well come on, what do you want?' he said. When I told him I wanted to try and have something done about my trouble, he looked at my record he'd got in front of him and he said, 'Oh yes,' he said. 'Well, it's taken you long enough to come round to it, hasn't it? Twenty years or more, and then you suddenly turn up today and say you want to try and do something about it. Why haven't you thought about this before? Why haven't you tried to get

treatment for yourself while you were out, instead of waiting till now? Anyhow,' he said, 'there's no treatment we can
give you, so you're wasting my time.'

Even if it's true, I think he could have put it over in a
different way. I don't think it's much help to someone, that
sort of attitude, is it? In a sense he's right I suppose; I mean
it is up to me really when I'm out, you can't argue with that.
There's been times when I thought I would, I'd put my
mind to it when I was released and see if there was anything
could be done. But when you get out your mind doesn't
work like that. First of all you're glad to be free and all
you want is a few days to settle down, get back into the
swing of things. It does take time to get accustomed to it.
When I came out from my P.D. for instance, all the tele-
phone-boxes had been altered, you needed completely different coins for them. Trivialities of that sort, it's very
unsettling until you get used to it. You're all the time wondering what the next surprise is going to be, how you're going
to explain it to people when they give you a funny look
because you don't know.

And there's so many things to get on with; you've got to
fix up for milk to be delivered, get your clothes in order,
have your shoes mended, think about finding a job – dozens
of things to occupy you. So you push everything else to the
back of your mind. You think, 'Well, I'll just get myself
organized, start earning some money again, that's the first
thing.' And the weeks pass, time goes on, you still haven't
got round to it, to thinking about yourself. In fact you don't
even really want to think about it; you can't face going
along to your doctor and telling him what it is or anything
of that kind. Then you start a job and you think, 'Well, I'll
be all right now I'm working.' That's how it goes on; six
months'll pass, a year, sometimes even two years before you
begin getting yourself into trouble again. And there you are,
it's happened, and it's too late.

—Last time I think we were mainly on my childhood days,
weren't we? I'd been telling you about my father leaving
home, my brother and sister getting married and so on, yes.
I'd be in my early twenties then. In every way just an ordinary sort of young man, except I wasn't much for the social

life or other people, I'd sooner go about with my mother
like I told you. There was nothing of importance in those
days of my life at all. Just long happy years, me and my
mother together on our own. The car I told you about didn't
I, the little Austin Seven we had? Yes. I know what it was,
the new job that I took – that was it wasn't it, where we
left off?

Well I got the job like I told you, because there was more
money in it than the grocery trade. It was with a retail wine
merchants, they had a big chain of places all round south
London. Selling in a shop, delivering orders in the van, that
sort of thing mostly. Altogether I must have been with them
eleven or twelve years. I think it was while I was there I
first developed my taste for drink. Not a lot, I wasn't a heavy
drinker or an alcoholic, nothing like that – but just at weekends I'd take home a bottle of wine or a half-bottle of whis-
key at trade price. I was never one for going in pubs; instead
my mother would cook a nice meal and we'd have a drink
with it. She never touched it herself. I used to enjoy it but
it wasn't a problem, though; I don't want to give you that
impression. In the week when I was working I never drank
at all, and as I say at weekends it was not a large quantity.
I wouldn't be incapable, nothing of that sort. But I got used
to it, that was the point; and later on in life that turned out
to be not a very good thing.

I wish I could remember some occasion or incident from
those times that was particularly memorable that I could
tell you about; but I can't. An even, regular sort of life, a
steady job, no excitements or troubles. Looking back on it
I'd say it was perfect contentment; both of us happy, devoted to each other. I used to think it would go on for ever
just like it was. The only thing that worried me was my
mother's health; it was never good, often she'd have to stay
in bed for days at a time and I'd have to look after her,
do all the housework and shopping after work and so on.
But I never minded; after all when she was well she gave up
all her time to looking after me, didn't she?

When the 1939 war came I got a low medical grading
because of the injury to my foot. We were both glad of that
because it meant I wouldn't have to go away in the Army
or anything. But then when they brought in the direction of

labour later in the war I had to change my job and go and work for a ship-building firm, marine engineers they were, down in Sheerness. It was just about possible from where we lived in London for me to travel up and down each day. It meant a long journey, but it was better than having to leave home. I was very worried about mother in the bombing, but she bore up bravely you know, she was wonderful. Sometimes I'd say I wanted to get her away, out into the country somewhere where I'd know she'd be safe. But she wouldn't hear of it. 'This is our home,' she'd say, 'and this is where I'm going to stay.' It was on the outskirts of south London so it was never too bad.

Round Sheerness was very nice in the summer, and I began to take an interest in all the little boats that there were lying about. Some of them were going very cheap indeed: towards the end of the war there was hardly any private sailing, people weren't so much interested in it as they are these days. I bought myself one of those very small sort of cabin boats, just about big enough for two people, and I spent most of my spare time on the engine getting it back into running order. I never went far out to sea in it, only round the coast or up some of the little inlets and creeks and places of that sort. It was a hobby for me at weekends. I often used to try and persuade my mother to come down there with me for a bit of a sail, but she never would, she didn't fancy the idea.

And that was when my first trouble came on. There were always lots of kids about in the boat-yards, asking could they help you, would you take them out in your boat for a ride. One Saturday afternoon there was two of them, two little boys, I said all right they could come out with me because they'd helped me push my boat down into the water from the shed. A very hot day it was. They went over the side for a swim. They'd no costumes on. When they got back in the boat they were running about skylarking and laughing. And I did you know, I must admit I did go so far as to forget myself, I laid hands on them. Nothing serious, please don't think that, I didn't attack them or anything of that kind. Only playing about, touching them, that was as far as it went. They didn't object, they didn't complain, it was a harmless bit of fun you might say. It never crossed my mind they hadn't liked it, they seemed willing enough.

That was why it was such a surprise to me the next week-end. I was down there again tuning up the old engine, and these two plain-clothes policemen came into the shed. They asked me exactly what it was had happened the Saturday before, and I told them. I didn't hide anything, I told them just how it was; no more and no less. They weren't even boys that I knew, I hadn't made arrangement to see them again, nothing of that sort. But they'd told their parents I suppose about it. Anyway there it was, that was it. The police took me to court straight away for it, and I was given six months.

I couldn't believe it at first, I really couldn't. Six months, just like that; no other inquiries, nothing. The magistrate said, 'There's too much of this sort of thing going on, I'm going to put a stop to it.' Being near the end of the war as it was, I suppose they were short-handed, they wouldn't have time for probation reports and so on; in fact they didn't seem to be even thinking of probation at all for my sort of case.

Before I knew where I was I found myself in Canterbury prison, sewing mail-bags. Thirty-seven I think I was then, or thirty-eight. To end up suddenly one day like that in prison, you don't believe it could happen to you, especially when you've lived all your life in an ordinary respectable manner. There wasn't one person I knew or had ever heard of who'd been convicted before.

As for my mother, well, she simply couldn't grasp it at all. She came to see me when I was due for a visit, even though she was very ill – she'd gone to live at my sister's, they brought her and took her back all the way in the car. She cried, she looked terrible, she did. 'What is it, Wilfred?' she kept asking me. 'What's it all about, what's happened?' What could I say to her? As soon as I started trying to explain she said, 'I don't believe it.' She wouldn't listen, she just couldn't believe it at all. She wrote me some lovely letters you know, while I was inside, never blaming me or anything; just saying I must look after myself and not to worry about her, and when it was over we'd forget it for ever.

I looked at it the same way too – it was just something

that had happened that there was no accounting for. I'd done wrong, it was no use pretending about that: but I was being punished for it, and it was up to me afterwards to see it didn't happen again. I think one of the things was that it had never occurred before, you know: it'd come on me suddenly, without any warning at all. A hot day, two little boys on the boat without any clothes on: I couldn't think what had possessed me.

When I came out there was no question of me going back to the same job, the people at work would know all about it, it would be too embarrassing, I couldn't face that. We didn't know what we should do really. Then one day my mother said she thought the best thing would be if I was to get away, make a completely fresh start, widen my horizons and that sort of thing, make a new life for myself altogether. My brother-in-law had a bit of influence with one of the shipping lines, so he put in a word for me and got me a job as a steward on a cargo vessel. It had a few passenger cabins, but chiefly it took engines and machine tools to different places round the Mediterranean, and then loaded up with fruit, oranges and lemons, for the journey back.

When I got used to it I quite liked the seafaring life. I think I probably took to it because it'd been in the family, hadn't it, with my father? We went to some nice places, Gibraltar, Valencia, Barcelona, Majorca, Malta, and on all round the Greek islands; some lovely places there are round there, you know. Each trip would take almost a month to the day, then I'd be home for a few days, and then off again once more. It was ideal for me really, took me right out of myself; there was no trouble of any kind. I could look back on the incident I'd been to prison for as something completely in the past. Once in Barcelona I met a girl, Spanish she was, very bright and jolly, working as a waitress in a café. I even thought sometimes if I got to know her better I might bring her back to England with me and marry her; we struck up quite a correspondence between us for a few months. But I was never on a ship that did that particular run again, so I didn't get the opportunity to see her any more, and it just fizzled out. A pity that was, I think, looking back on it; a nice woman of that kind might have made all the difference to me, you know.

Altogether I was at sea for just about two years, ending up with a very long trip over to Singapore and Hong Kong. That meant I was away for four months or more, it was a long time, my mother wasn't very keen on it at all, she missed me terribly. I missed her too, and after another long trip like that I decided to give up the life then, and come back. We bought a house, a cottage it was – well, more of a what you might call a prefabricated bungalow really; one of those summer-places, you know what I mean, two rooms, made of corrugated iron and asbestos mostly, a wooden roof and an Elsan out at the back, and a stand-pipe for water just over the road. It wasn't meant for living in all the year round. One of my uncles had it originally, and he sold it cheap to us for somewhere to live. 'Rosecot' it was called – it's a terrible name isn't it? I can't think why we've never changed it, we often used to have a laugh about it and say anyone would think that it must be very picturesque with a name like that. Actually it's in a field at the end of a road all on its own, near a little village on the coast. Not a proper holiday place, more like somewhere people go out of London at weekends to be on their own. It has electric light, we had that put in; and over the years from time to time I've cleared a bit of ground round it and laid out a sort of garden.

Yes, it's still there, I've still got it. Really ramshackle it must be now, I don't like to think of it. When I went back after my P.D. there was great holes in the roof, all the fencing down, everywhere overgrown with grass and weeds; it was in a shocking state, it broke my heart to see it, it did. But in those days I'm telling you about now, when my mother and I first took it over, we got it really nice; painted it up, put up an archway of roses round the door to fit the frame – it was a real home it was, and we had many happy years there. It could be a bit bleak in the winter, but in the summer it was very nice, really lovely.

When I saw it that first time it made up my mind: I didn't want to go to sea any more. I wanted to stop there with her. But we hadn't been in it very long before she took very ill; I couldn't look after her and do a job as well, so she had to go back and stop with my sister again for a while. I'd got a fairly decent job as a site-clerk with a small firm of builders in the locality; I used to go up to London to see her every week on the Saturday. But the rest of the week was awful, down there in that place on my own without her, I never knew what to do. And I did the very thing that was worst for me: I started to drink.

I used to spend all the Sundays drinking, not eating, not caring about anything at all except trying to forget how lonely I was. Not in pubs mind you, I was never one for that. Instead I used to buy one or sometimes two bottles of the very cheapest wine there was, British stuff which was made out of I don't know what, rough and raw tasting, but it had a terrific kick with it, you could get yourself almost unconscious on a couple of bottles of that.

There were several boys from round the district, you know, from the village and other houses scattered about, and they took to coming along on Sunday afternoon, giving me a hand with the garden, doing odd jobs for me for a few coppers or a drink of lemonade, something like that. I knew it was wrong of me to encourage them to come there, they were upsetting me, I could feel it: but that only made me drink the more, to try and suppress these feelings that I had.

But it was no use, it didn't make me feel better, it made things worse; in fact it got to the stage I was doing things I'd never have dreamt of if I'd been sober. I suppose you could say it was weakness on my part; well it was, I should have had more sense, more will-power, shouldn't I, told them to clear off and go right away. But I didn't. There was things went on, childish things, really stupid, no way for a grown man to behave at all. I don't know what it was, why I should want to carry on with them as I did. Sitting them on my knee, playing silly games with them, you wouldn't believe anyone could be so stupid as to do it. On and on, these boys coming, bringing their friends with them; they talked about it among themselves I suppose, they knew where they could go and get a sixpence anytime if they wanted one.

So that was it again, exactly the same thing; one of them must have told his parents about it eventually and they brought in the police. I was really for it that time, a second conviction; and up at the Assizes too, in front of a judge. He didn't say much, there wouldn't be much he could say

would there? Two years, I think that was all he said when
he'd heard the evidence, just 'Two years' like that.

I felt dreadful about it. All that time, you know, that I'd
gone away to sea to get away from it; the new home we'd
made, a job I'd not long started with the building people.
My mother, she was too ill to be told about it for quite a
long while, my sister and her husband had to break it to her.
Though once again, you know, she was marvellous; wrote
to me regularly, said it would be all right again when we got
back together in our own little house. I don't know how she
stuck it, I honestly don't, it just shows you what kind of a
mother she must have been, doesn't it?

Two years in Pentonville that time, a dreadful place; the
only thing that kept me going was I'd made up my mind it
was the very last time ever. I was forty-five, by the time
you've got to that age you're no longer a young man. You
know it's going to be the turning-point, it must be. I put it
all down myself to the drink. And while I was in prison I
wasn't drinking of course, so I knew I could do without it
if I really put my mind to it.

When I came out in 1952 I really thought things were
going to be different. I got my mother back in the little
house, for a short while I thought it was going to be all right,
I'd turned the corner. Well, I have to admit it to you— I
wasn't better, in fact I was worse. That same year when the
autumn came on and mother was still ill, I took her back to
my sister's again – and then I was back straight away in the
same thing, down at the bungalow, drinking and having
boys in at the weekends. I don't think I was out a year
that time before I was caught. I thought it was going to be
a really long sentence then, at least double what I'd had
before. But the police were quite decent, they put in a word
for me that time, said the boys had made things difficult for
me – which they had. Hardly left me in peace at all they
didn't, Sunday after Sunday they'd be round. Well to cut a
long story short I was back inside again, as I say, but this
time for twenty-one months in Wandsworth. And I knew
things were looking really black for me then all right, I didn't
know what the future could possibly hold.

I came out about the end of 1954. My mother seemed
much better then, in her health I mean, so we could start off

living together again in our own little place. When she was there it made all the difference, naturally: there was boys coming round still, but I kept them out in the garden helping me, and I hardly touched a drink for months on end. But it wasn't all that long before mother started going downhill again, and eventually they took her into hospital. It was then they told me what was wrong with her, and I must prepare myself for her not having long to live. They let her come back: she wanted to come home, you know, I think she must have known she was dying. They often do, don't they, when it gets to that stage? Of course I was glad to have her, I'd have done anything, cut off all my arms and legs, anything at all to save her. But it wasn't to be.

I'd got myself a bit of a job, part-time at one of the local garages, so as to be able to spend as much time with her as I could. For a while she seemed to rally, I even began to feel there might be some hope. But soon the pills and things they'd given her to stop the pain, she'd had so many the effect of them wore off, they lost their strength. In the end, for the last few weeks she was in agony, it was pitiful to see. I told you about it, didn't I – how she used to be crawling about in the bed trying to get out; she'd no idea what she was doing at all. I stopped off work altogether then, just so I could be with her whenever I might be wanted; I was scared even to go down to the shop for a packet of cigarettes even, in case she'd be calling for me while I was away.

It was no use and in the end she died. I suppose it was a blessed relief, really. But for days I just couldn't grasp it, you know; it didn't sink in what it meant. I kept thinking she'd be coming back somehow, she was only away at my sister's for a visit and any minute she'd walk in. Unbelievable to me, that's what it was – and when I finally did realize it, I didn't want to go on living myself at all. I kept everything in the house exactly as she'd left it, her slippers by the door in their usual place, all her clothes still in the wardrobe for her, the little ornaments she'd arranged exactly where she'd left them. Weeks it went on, months, and I was completely in a daze.

I tried a job or two, but they didn't last, there seemed no point in them, what was I working for? I'd get the idea of going out for a ride sometimes in the old Ford I had, on a day when the sun was shining. Then I'd say to myself, 'No, I couldn't bear it, I should be all the time wanting to talk to her as though she was sitting next to me.' And in the house I still did, I talked to her exactly as though she was there.

Then I really started drinking; I'd let days go by at a time without knowing where I was, what time it was, anything. And when I was drinking of course my mind started to turn again to this other thing. I knew it would, but I'd lost all wish even to try and fight it then. My own idea was to go down to the shop and buy two or three bottles of that cheap wine I told you about, and then sit in a chair and drink until they were gone. I used to see them on the sideboard, it felt like they were looking at me, beckoning me on. I had an idea I might even try and write a story about it once; I was going to call it 'The Blond Monkey'. That was what it was like; cheap white wine, well more a pale yellow colour really, and I'd be sitting there and watching it, and I'd know perfectly well what it was going to do to me, it was like an evil thing staring back at me. It was a monkey all right, a wicked one, very wicked: once it got inside you you were done for. If the shop was closed any time, I'd be washing the bottles out under the tap, can you believe it, trying to get out the last few drops? It was as bad as that.

I was notorious in the district by then; all the kids knew me, knew what they could get if they came. They'd be pushing notes under the door they would, if I was out. 'I'll be coming round to see you Sunday with my friend, will you take us to Brighton in your car?' All things like that, little devils they were; in fact they used to think I was funny, it made them laugh to see me carrying on. Some of them, even though they were so young, they knew all sorts of things, you know; they used to recite dirty limericks they'd picked up at school, or tell jokes – stupid silly jokes with rude words. I'd get really annoyed with them I would. I'd say, 'You mustn't use words like that, it's not nice. Now don't you ever let me hear you using words like that again!' I've never liked that sort of thing, particularly in children, I always wanted them to be proper, not loose with their tongues; I don't approve of it at all, I never have done.

That's how it was then: drinking, not working, staying

in the house on my own, and waiting for the boys to come round. Finding the notes pushed under my door, there's no getting away from it, as soon as I saw one I got a kind of a thrill because I knew it wouldn't be long before they were there. And that occasion, being perpetually drunk as I was, the police came in and actually found it going on, these boys running about half-dressed, and me sitting in the middle of it all in my chair. I can remember looking up and seeing the blue uniform and the brass buttons right there in front of my nose.

Well, it was impossible, wasn't it, it couldn't be allowed to pass any more? The judge was the same one I'd had in the previous case; he remembered me all right. He said, 'You're a menace, you are, I'm going to put a stop to your activities once and for all.' So he gave me seven years' preventive detention.

Seven years ... I really did, I thought I might as well be dead, I couldn't imagine ever coming out again. I used to sit in my cell and think, 'What's the use? This is the finish, this is the only place for me now, it's all over.' Knowing my mother had gone for good this time, and all I could do was be thankful she hadn't lived to see where I'd ended up, because that would have killed her if nothing else did. But after a while, you can't help it, I suppose, you start thinking and feeling again. You say, 'Well, time's getting on, it is passing, perhaps somehow it won't be too bad, there'll be an end to it one day. I'm over the worst now, I must have done a good time of it by now, mustn't I?' So you go and look at the calendar to see how much you've got left – and you see that all you've done so far in fact is perhaps three months.

I think what saved me was I got sent to Nottingham prison. I hadn't been there long before they gave me a job in the book-bindery. The man in charge, what they call the foreman instructor, he was a really good chap. He gave me a proper training in it, taught me how to do binding, sewing, guillotining, hand-stitching, gluing, collating, trimming – every single aspect of it that there was. It gave me a whole new interest; I think I was a good learner, and after a while I really started to enjoy myself and feel it was worth while. I've always liked working with my hands, es-

pecially something you can take your time over until you've
got it right. Tooling, blocking, lettering for the spines, it
was all very nice. The years went by, I won't say without
me noticing them, but at least with something for me to
occupy myself with; and when it came to the end of my
sentence the instructor said I was good enough to work at it
outside, so why didn't I write to one of the big printing
firms and ask them if there was any chance of a job. 'Go on,'
he said, 'you compose the letter and I'll help you with it.'
I wondered what they'd think, getting a letter like that from
someone on prison notepaper. But do you know, they wrote
straight away and said they'd take me on as soon as I came
out. It was marvellous of them, wasn't it? I'd got a skill at
last, hadn't I, something that would last me all my life;
even though I was over fifty then, this firm said it didn't
matter, they were still willing to give me a try even though
I'd had a big sentence like eight years.

I beg your pardon? Oh did I, I'm sorry, I made a mistake
then if I said seven; actually it was eight. It's like I was saying a few minutes ago, it's such a long time that you can't
always think of it exactly, a year more or less makes no
difference, you see.

After a long time in prison you forget other things too,
you know, about how you came to be there and so on.
Drinking – well, I'd gone without it all those years, so
obviously it wasn't going to be any problem for me to
keep on the same way. And the other business, that was all
over, I was getting on in years, I was sure it had all died
away. It'd taken a long time, but there it was: all I needed
to do was to keep on nice and steady just the way I'd been
in prison. I couldn't help but be all right now. That was the
way my mind worked.

And it was true, too, for what seemed like a very long
time. This would be 1962 now. The firm I went to work for
they were really excellent, they let me get into the work at
my own pace, they didn't expect too much from me at the
beginning. I went down to look at the bungalow, it was in
a dreadful state with no one living in it all those years, I
thought, 'Well this place is no good to me anymore, I might
as well leave it.' So I went into digs near the factory where I
worked – and I was very lucky again there too. A very

nice widowed lady, middle-aged, I'd say in her forties, something like that; with two little boys of her own, one aged about seven and the other one nine. Do you know, I never even thought anything about those two boys, not to do with sex I mean. I'd no more have dreamed of anything like that with them than I would fly. They were lovely kids, we all got on well together; and there was another lodger in the house, he had a Hillman Minx, the six of us used to go out in it for picnics together or visiting different places. Like one big happy family we all were. The boys called me 'Uncle Wilfred'. I was so fond of them I wouldn't have let anyone touch a hair on their heads. Now why should that be, do you think, that there was no trouble with them, not even a thought of it in my mind? Life's funny sometimes, isn't it?

Getting back do you think we should be now? Yes, we don't want to be late do we? That'd never do, they'd never let me come out with you again, they'd think I wasn't reliable. I wouldn't like to let them down, not after they've been so good and taken a chance with me. Oh yes if you could keep on coming I'd be delighted, I really would; I think it does me all the good in the world to have someone to talk to from outside.

*   *   *

On one of the roads back to the prison there was a public house called 'The George Borrow'.

—Now that's a funny name for a pub isn't it, I've never seen one with that sort of name before, have you? I wonder how on earth it came to be called that? He was a writer wasn't he, I read a book by him once, *Lavengro,* would it be, something like that? Gipsies, wasn't it, yes the gipsy people, he was very interested in them. Perhaps that's how it got its name; he stayed there once in the olden days, and he made a speech to the townspeople the next morning, standing out in front of it. What would he say? He'd tell them the gipsies were honest decent people, wouldn't he, just the same as they were only they preferred to wander about and not live in one place all the time. They had different ways, different habits, but they were good at heart and they ought to be allowed certain rights like any other human beings. He'd be a very good speaker too wouldn't he, a very passionate speaker, his eyes full of fire?

I expect it's something of that kind, don't you? There must be some story like that to it, mustn't there, to give it its name?

*   *   *

—I was thinking last time after you'd gone that it's only just under another year, you know, and then I'll be out. I don't know what I'll do, no: get a job, I suppose, try and make another start. I'll be sixty-one. I wonder if they'd have me back at that printing firm? There was nothing wrong with my work, they always said I was a satisfactory employee, good timekeeper, never took days off for sickness, nothing of that kind.

I did let them down, I can't argue about that. Two years I was with them, they must have thought I was all right; and then this offence occurred again. So no one could say I hadn't been given a chance, could they? It was nobody else's fault but my own. If only I'd had will-power. That nice woman I was staying with, the family outings and everything; I was well looked after, very comfortable. I don't know why I ever started, you know, going back to the bungalow again, I can't think what possessed me. Well no, that's not true; I can. It meant so much to me, it'd always been the home where I'd lived with my mother all those years. I couldn't keep away from it, I used to go there sometimes and stand inside looking at it, at the state it was in; I'd break down completely you know, and start to cry. I used to say to myself, 'Whatever would she say if she could see what it looks like now, whatever would she say?'

What I ought to have done was get rid of it – sell it, give it away, anything. But I just couldn't. I started to go there now and again, trying to do it up a bit, repair some of the holes in the roof, get it into a decent shape. Then after a while in the nicer weather I'd spend the whole of Saturday afternoon there; and before long Sundays as well. Of course I knew what was going to happen, I knew it perfectly well; in a way I sealed my own doom about it through what I did.

But I thought if only I could be left in peace to get on with the repairs it'd be all right. When some boys came round the first few times I told them to go away. Then there was a note through the door; and then another one after that. So I told one of the neighbours down the road that if she ever saw any boys in my garden while I was away, she was to phone the police and have them cleared out.

It was months afterwards, I'd forgotten all about it. She must have caught sight of them one afternoon when she was passing and that's what she did, just as I'd told her – and the police came down like a ton of bricks, they were everywhere, in through the front door, the back door, the windows, everything. And there we were, me and three boys: behaving indecently, we were, there couldn't be any argument about it. I thought with it not being an 'assault' charge it might go a bit better for me that time. Perhaps it did, perhaps that's why I only got five years and not another big sentence of preventive detention.

One of the boys was the younger brother of a boy who'd been involved the time before with me. It's not ... well the police did say it themselves in one of my earlier cases, that it wasn't just me on my own, sometimes these youngsters had egged me on. What I've done has been utterly wrong, there's no question of it; there's no excuse to find for it, after all they're only children and I'm a grown man. But it's never ever been a case of me deceiving them, trying to get them into the place under false pretences and then taking them by surprise.

I. ... I want you to know everything there is to know about it, both the best and very very worst. There's nothing I'm going to conceal from you or try to hide. It ... well I've got it here, I've brought it to show you; I've managed to keep it with me all these last years inside, just in case there ever came a time when there might possibly be someone I could talk to, and tell them the whole and absolute truth. This is just one of them; one of the notes that I've kept for if it was ever necessary to try and make this point. It's never been shown to anyone before, not to a soul in the world:

Dere Wil, I hop I can com to see you Sat. I hop you will be in at yor hous an you wil hav som mor sweetes for me. I

thogt abt you larst nite an it mad my dickey go orl hard.
With lov from Jimmy. XXX.

—The ancient Greeks used to indulge in it, didn't they?
Perhaps there'll always be people like that. Maybe it's something I got from my father do you think? He had a strong
sexual side to his nature, didn't he, only his consisted more
of the attraction for women.

Yes, my thoughts are if I'm going to be honest, that it's
true, it could, it could happen again. It seems to be something in your nature that you can't get rid of, it settles on
you, it won't ever let you out of its grasp. Some kind of illness almost that you're suffering from, it descends on you,
it's like a malady come upon you and you don't know what
to do. Even some of the gentry have this you know, nicely
educated people; you read about it, how it might happen
to a vicar or a teacher, someone like that.

But you couldn't expect other people to understand about
it, could you? They say, 'Well I don't feel like that, how can
he?' They think it's disgusting, it's horrible, they don't want
to know about it even, or consider it. And you'd never know
with someone, would you, if you wanted to talk to them,
just how they'd react? They all think it's something else, you
see; their mind springs on to something else. Because it says
it, doesn't it, when they read out the charge: 'Indecent
assault'? It's only natural for them, people think it means
more than it does. They think it must mean actually raping
a boy, or trying to, an actual sexual act of that kind, and
that you're dirty and horrible and cruel. But even the police
you know, they told my mother about it once; they said to
her, 'Your son's not one of these sex maniacs, don't think
that, it's just this weakness he's got for liking to fondle little
boys.' That was something at least; however awful it is,
that's something that could be said.

I can't help wondering though sometimes what they
would have given me each time if it had been that they
were charging me with: when you look at my record, I
mean, of what I've had so far for this.

April Is A Funny Month

Billy Atkinson

To a young woman walking late at night along a street on her own, or standing waiting at a lonely bus-stop, Billy Atkinson, five foot six in height and thirty-eight years old, must be a terrifying and incongruous apparition as he leaps suddenly out at her from a dark doorway, thrusting one hand up her under skirt and trying at the same time with the other to feel her breasts. He has dark greasy hair curtaining his long thin face, does not speak but grins fixedly all the time through his large horn-rimmed bifocals held together with adhesive tape, and breathes heavily with his mouth wide open, revealing the ragged gaps between his broken bad teeth. He wears an outfit that looks as though it might have been used once as a soldier's costume in the chorus of some third-rate musical comedy, made of thick sky-blue flannel with rows of brass buttons down the front. It is much too big for him, so he has to roll up the sleeves at the cuffs and the trousers round his ankles: on his bare feet are trodden-down laceless shoes splitting open at the welts and seams. His hands are red and rough, with fingernails like talons, half an inch long and encrusted with dirt.

If she screams with fright or shouts for help or hits him with her handbag – or rather, when she does, since naturally no one fails to react in some way – Billy at once stands motionless, nonplussed, worriedly shaking his head. If she tells him to go away he goes immediately: if someone has come to her assistance he waits placidly nearby on the pavement while they decide what to do with him.

When he isn't in prison or mental hospital, or living in the basements of abandoned warehouses or finding temporary sleeping-places for himself in falling-down shops or houses which have been condemned as unfit for occupation and will soon be demolished, Billy can sometimes be found staying for a few nights in the big reception centre for dere- licts and vagrants in south London. The staff are usually first aware that he is back again when he is noticed in the early hours of the morning rummaging through the enor- mous garbage containers outside the gates, looking for something not too decomposed to eat. Stale buns sodden with the drainings from tea-urns or overripe tomatoes squashed into yellowing cabbage-stalks come within this category. A few words and the offer of a mug of tea are usually sufficient to persuade him to come inside and register as a temporary resident.

The purpose of the Centre is not only to feed and shelter men but also to rehabilitate and place them eventually in some kind of employment. No progress has ever been re- corded over the last ten years in the reports of the inter- viewing officers which take up the bulk of Billy's file.

June 1958 'I regard him as virtually unemployable in any normal sense.'
Oct. 1959 'Retarded, almost totally inadequate, and very dirty in appearance. Doubtful if he is employable at all.'
Aug. 1960 'Any workshop or industrial training however simple is bound to prove useless.'
Feb. 1961 'A very dirty-looking and untidy man who seems to have nothing at all to offer any employer I can think of.'
Sept. 1962 'Since he left mental hospital I have discussed his case with the day centre. They confirm he can do no more than run an occasional errand.'
April 1964 'An utterly hopeless prospect. Needs constant supervision and should not be wandering about on his own.'
Sept. 1965 'No sense of personal hygiene whatsoever. As far as I can see he is not suitable for any kind of employment.'
Jan. 1967 'Filthy and penniless as usual. Has just come out of Wandsworth again. No satisfactory solution seems pos- sible.'

—No sir, of course not sir, I would have no objection at all to you looking at those papers sir. If you would like to look at them that will be perfectly all right sir, by all means. You will find in there, sir, pretty much what you might call everything about me, more or less. In my opinion I would say that if you were wanting to know everything about me, you would find it in there.

For instance things such as my name sir. It will very probably tell you, if you were to look inside it, that my name is William Atkinson. Not that it is Billy of course sir, you wouldn't expect it to have that in, but pretty well everything else. It would probably say that my name is William. It does say William? Well then in that case it's quite right – because that is my name sir. What you might call my full name, if you wished to, in a manner of speaking. I think you'll usually find that William is the full name of anyone called Billy, since Billy is short for William as a general rule. Not always of course – there have been people who were called William but not Billy. Quite a large number of people, now I come to think of it. Such as William the Conqueror, he's one who comes to mind almost immediately; or William Shakespeare; or King William, or William of Orange as I believe he was known. All those had the name of William but they were not known as Billy. At least so far as I'm aware myself they were not: I could be mistaken but I don't think I am. On the other hand there's people such as Billy Butlin or Billy Graham, I think very often you'll find that they are hardly ever known as William at all, at least not usually, or certainly only very rarely. I believe that would be correct sir, perhaps seven times out of ten, or even eight or nine times out of ten, on the whole it follows something along those lines; at least in my opinion it does although I could be wrong, but I don't think so. Therefore that would be perfectly correct if it says there that my name is William, even though I am known as Billy.

How would you be meaning sir, any other name such as what sir? Oh I see, no not so far as I can recall sir: I believe my parents just gave me the name of William and left it at that. Apart from Atkinson that is sir, that is my name as well. It goes with the name of William, the two go together you might say, and therefore you have the full name of William Atkinson. But there's no other name between, at least not so far as I'm aware of at all, no sir. There may be, I'm not saying it wouldn't be possible of course. I mean

there are other names which people have, such as John or
Edward or Henry and names of that kind. But I don't believe that's so in my case, not to my own knowledge of
the matter. Though of course I could be mistaken about
that, but I don't think I am.

I was born on April the 7th, 1930 – yes, that is quite
correct sir, how did you know that? Oh, it says there does
it? Well then in that case that is perfectly correct, because
that's when I was born, April the 7th, 1930. I think you'll
find on the whole sir that everything there in those papers is
more or less absolutely correct. You could take every word
of it as pretty reliable sir, at least in my opinion you could.
—It doesn't say very much else about you in fact, Mr.
Atkinson.
—Oh. No. I see sir. Yes thank you sir, that's very kind of
you, much obliged to you sir, I enjoy a cigarette now and
again when I can get one. Have you a light as well sir? Oh
thank you, ta.
—Would you mind if I called you Billy, would that be all
right?
—Oh yes sir, that would be perfectly all right sir. That is my
name sir, either Billy or William sir, strictly speaking either
of those would be correct.
—And I'd much sooner you didn't call me 'sir', I'd much
prefer it if—
—As I was just saying sir they're both what you might call
different forms of the same name. In some cases you have
William, such as in William the Conqueror; or William
Shakespeare; or King William—
—My name is—
—Or William of Orange as I believe he was known. And
with Billy Butlin or Billy Graham I believe I'm right in
saying that they've never been known as William, or at least
not for a very long time. Though I may be mistaken in that
sir, but I don't think I am.
—There isn't very much about you in here, only brief re-
ports for the periods you've actually been in residence.
—I think you'll find they're correct though sir, you could
take them as pretty reliable on the whole in my opinion.
—Where were you, for instance, before you came here?
—Oh nowhere sir, I wasn't anywhere.

—What I mean is, you came here again a week ago: where would you have been before that?

—Before I came here sir? Well I would have been in prison sir.

—Which prison?

—That would be Wandsworth I think sir. I may be mistaken, it could have been Pentonville, but I should think it was more likely Wandsworth sir, or possibly Brixton.

—What was it for?

—Two months sir: it might have been three, but I think it was two sir.

—No, I mean what offence?

—That would be assault sir; I could be mistaken but I should think it would be assault. Most of the time it's assault, sir, or sometimes it could be called attempted assault. But I should think most often, eight times out of ten perhaps even nine times out of ten, it would be assault.

—How many times have you done that?

—What, the assault sir do you mean, or the attempted assault?

—Both.

—Well it's usually the one or the other sir. I think you'll find I'm right in saying that if it's not assault then it's usually attempted assault, or what they call attempt to commit an assault I believe it is. It's very rarely you get them both together. It is possible of course, I have heard of it happening; but I should think in most cases it's very rarely that they'll be together. I'm not saying that it couldn't happen of course, but at least that's been my own experience when I've had anything to do with it. Oh no, that's quite all right sir, I'll smoke the rest of this later. Well that's very kind of you, I will have another as well then, I'm much obliged to you, ta. Do you have another light sir? Thank you, thank you very much.

—Let's try and sort this out. How many times have you been convicted of assault?

—I should say about six times sir, I believe it could be seven, but I may be wrong, or maybe eight.

—And of attempted assault?

—I think you'd find that was very much about the same, sir. It's very difficult to remember, but on the whole I think you could take them as more or less the same.

—What's the longest prison sentence you've done?

—Myself do you mean, sir? Well I should say it was twelve months, or possibly eighteen months, or twenty-one months, or possibly up to two years. A very great deal depends on the length of time that you're sentenced to of course, as to which is the longest. I should think if it was two years that would be the longest, because there's the one-third of your sentence that you're given back as your remission. Therefore if you were to think of two years which is twenty-four months I believe, and then to take eight from that which is one-third, you would be left with sixteen months wouldn't you? I could be wrong, but I don't think I am: twenty-four, twenty-two, twenty, eighteen, sixteen; yes I believe that's correct sir. Sixteen months doesn't sound as long as eighteen months, which it isn't of course, eighteen months is two months longer than sixteen months, but then you've got to take one-third from that you see, which would leave you something in the nature of twelve. At least that's my opinion, and I think if you go into it you'll find that I'm more or less correct.

—Billy, I'd like to come and talk with you for a little while every day while you're here and get you to tell me your life story, would you be agreeable to my doing that?

– Oh yes sir, that would be perfectly all right sir if you'd like to, that would be very agreeable to me sir. I should find it very interesting, I'd like it very much indeed sir, if you're sure it's no trouble to you.

*   *   *

It wasn't easy. Billy could spend, and often did, as long as ten minutes on one minute detail, making certain that he'd narrowed an occurrence down not only to its correct date but also to the particular day of the week, the precise hour and the exact minute, counting every part of it out with his talon-like fingers along the edge of the table. His mind frequently stuck like a needle in the worn groove of a gramophone record; he would recapitulate incidents endlessly, repeating the identical words and phrases every time, incapable of moving forward or back. Thoughts would evoke memories which led on not to other thoughts, but back to

the original memories again: descriptions which began as
though they were leading to some specific point would arrive
eventually after lengthy and tortuous convolutions at the
same subject they had departed from half an hour before.

He enjoyed talking; but I frequently had to abandon ordinary interviewing methods and interrupt him with a direct
question in an attempt to nudge the needle out of the
groove; sometimes he heard and answered it, and sometimes he did not.

This, in a shortened version and with most of the irrele-
vancies and repetitions omitted, in all the havoc of its ob-
scurity and desolation and implacably detailed logic – and
with its occasional moments of ludicrous comedy – is something of what he had to say.

—That is quite correct sir, I am thirty-eight years of age,
that's perfectly correct and I was born on April the 7th,
1930. In a house near Blackfriars Bridge it was, sir, an old
house, well more what you might call part of a house to be
truthful sir, the rooms up on the top floor. Big holes it had
in the roof sir, though it was quite a good roof otherwise: it
kept the rain out except in the places where there were holes
and when the rain came through we would put buckets on
the floor to catch it. Three buckets, or perhaps even four or
five. I could be wrong but I don't think I am, there could
have been five buckets or even six sometimes, but not more
than six.

No sir, I've no brothers or sisters, I never have had, I'm
what is called I believe the only one. My father, sir? Yes
well he worked on a barge, on the River Thames I believe
it was, he was what they call a lighterman, sir, and he did
that job all his life. No, I think he may well be alive at this
present time, it's possible, sir: in which case he would be
living somewhere else, since the old house we lived in was
pulled down. I was past that way myself a few years ago,
sir, and I looked to see if it was still there and it wasn't; I
believe there's an ice-cream factory or something of that
nature there now. I'm fairly sure it was an ice-cream
factory sir, though I could be wrong, but I don't think I
am.

I went to school in a street called Rupole Street I believe

it was called. There's two schools there, one called St. Edward's and one called St. John's, one of them would be for
Catholic children like, and the other for the Protestants.
I'm a Protestant myself sir, and so I went to the Protestant
one, but if I'd been a Catholic I'd have gone to the Catholic
one. I think I'm right in saying that, I think if you were to
go into it you'd find that was more or less correct. Yes I
quite liked school sir, we used to have a service once a week
and a bible reading from a big red Bible, and we also used to
have lessons – geography and history and things of that
kind, and arithmetic.

It would be what is called an elementary school I believe
sir; they taught you the elements of things, to give you a
kind of basis for the further knowledge which you would
pick up through your life. They also had writing and drawing; the teacher would put something on the blackboard, it
might be to do with geography – it could be history but it
was usually geography – and then you had to write something to do with that. Or for drawing, he would bring in an
apple perhaps or maybe a pear, and you would have a piece
of paper and a pencil and you had to try and imitate it, draw
it as exactly as you could, a picture of it on the paper. I
liked that.

My favourite subject would be history sir, which we had
on a Friday afternoon. I think it could have been a Thursday afternoon, but more often than not it was on a Friday,
say between two o'clock and a quarter to three, or it may
have been twenty to three; usually between twenty to three
and quarter to three, anyway. Yes, the school was near
where I lived, sir, not far from Blackfriars Bridge, in a house
that's now been pulled down and there's an ice-cream factory or something of that nature there now. It could be a
cake-factory, but my impression of it was that it was an
ice-cream factory; I don't think I'm wrong about that,
though of course I could be.

I left school in 1944, just after the doodle-bugs finished.
That would be in October 1944; no, September I think it
was, about mid-September, about the 14th or 15th of September, round about there, after the series of attacks on
London by the German doodle-bugs. They used to shoot
them across from Germany to England I understand; some

of them landed in the sea but some of them reached as far as London. I should think it would be about half of them reached London unless I'm mistaken. A lot of them were shot-down by anti-aircraft guns or our aeroplanes, so the Germans took to carrying them over in their own aeroplanes to make sure they got to London. Usually they would be in formations of five planes: it could be ten, but I think you'll find most often it was five, and then they fired them at London.

Of course before that there was what was called the blitz on London, that was bombs. I believe it would be in 1940, in about May 1940 that would be. May, June, July, August, September, October, November, December 1940; then January, February, March, April— I think the blitz finished in April 1941. No, my mistake, it was May, late May, round about the 20th or the 21st I should think. Once they dropped a landmine near where we lived; that would be very powerful and weighed about 1500 pounds. They dropped it at night; well actually I believe they started off with it in the daytime but it took them quite a long time to get it here and when they dropped it it would be early evening, or perhaps a little bit later than that, round about eight o'clock I would say, or quarter past. A land-mine was very powerful and could be compared to say a twelve- or fourteen-inch shell, probably more like fourteen I should say, and they dropped it on London and it came down near our house. It has a very powerful blast effect, I think it weighed about 1500 pounds which would be half a ton or even nearer to three-quarters of a ton I believe.

We didn't like that sir, it had rather what you might call a frightening effect, and my mother used to take me to a shelter with a view to calming me down as you might say. It was an underground shelter, actually it was underneath Blackfriars Bridge so it would be pretty strong, and we were down about thirty-five feet under the ground or possibly even thirty-six. We used to take what was called refuge there. That was during the early part of the bombing, the blitz, when the Germans were attacking London in May, June, July, August, September, October, November and part of December. Then they recontinued again in January, in mid or late January, the 21st or the 22nd I think it would be, and they went on then through February, March and April up to May.

We spent a long time in the shelter, up to three days at a time or once I believe even four or five days or six days or possibly a week. After that my parents decided to have me evacuated because the bombing showed signs of increasing again, and they had me sent to Boston in Lincolnshire, which is somewhere up near the north of England I believe. I didn't want to go to be truthful sir, but the roof had big holes in it and the house would shake when they dropped the bombs and the land-mines and so on, and there was a danger I believe of it falling down. It was a nice house of course, a very nicely built house. I should say from about 1923 or 1924, or possibly earlier than that, 1916; or it could have been earlier, 1910 or 1911 though I should have been surprised if that had been the case. As far as I could see the only serious thing it had wrong with it would be these holes in the roof and the fact that it was a bit shaky, which would be why they pulled it down eventually and put up I believe it is an ice-cream factory there now.

Oh yes sir, I lived there all the time, all my childhood during the war and the bombing and the blitz and the land-mine; I liked the house, I was very happy in it. Ourselves we had two rooms up at the top, one which we used for a dining-room and one for a bedroom. We ate our meals in the dining-room, and we slept in the bedroom. Of course we could have eaten our meals in the bedroom and slept in the dining-room, but we didn't, we kept the dining-room for eating in and the bedroom for sleeping in and in my opinion it was better like that. Though I could be wrong. There was a large bed in the bedroom where my mother and father slept, and a smaller bed for me. In the dining-room there was a table that we ate our meals at, it was about the size of this table or perhaps a little bit smaller, say from there to there, and we used it for eating our meals on, which would be egg and sausages and chips, or possibly egg and chips with no sausage; or sometimes sausage and chips but no egg. But not egg and sausage without chips, I don't ever remember that now I come to think of it.

I would say as a schoolboy I was about average, sir; not a great scholar or anything like that, but about average. I used

to play football in the playground, and also netball which is
something similar to football only you're allowed to hold
the ball in your hands which of course you're not allowed
to do in football. That would be on Thursdays that we
played football, and Tuesdays that we played netball. After
school I used to go to the pictures sometimes and things like
that, particularly on a Saturday. On Monday, Tuesday,
Wednesday, Thursday and Friday there would be school,
but not on Saturday and Sunday until Monday when you
would start school again right through until the following
Friday.

On Saturday I would go to the pictures, and we used to
have ration books that you could get sweets with, and my
mother would get the sweets on Friday for me to take to
the pictures on Saturday. Sometimes she would get them
on a Thursday, but in that case she would keep them until
Saturday for me. But most times she used to get them on
Friday. You used to have a certain amount of sweets allowed
for your ration, about four ounces of sweets and two bars
of chocolate; or you could have three bars of chocolate and
two ounces of sweets if you wished. Or now I come to think
of it, you could have all chocolate and no sweets; or alter-
natively all sweets and no chocolate, depending on what
you wanted. I think it would have been possible to have all
sweets and no chocolate: if you were to go into it I'd think
you'd find that was very likely correct, that you could if you
wanted to. And bread was rationed also, I believe it was
one loaf per person per week.

—Were you a happy child, would you say?

—That would be one loaf for my father on Monday and
Tuesday, one for my mother on Wednesday and Thursday,
and one for me on Friday and Saturday.

—A happy child, you would say?

—Yes, or you could have a certain amount of cake instead
of bread if you wished, depending on how you felt about it.
You could have one sultana cake and two loaves of bread,
or sometimes cherry cake. But very rarely marzipan. The
only time you could get cake with marzipan so far as I can
remember was August, September or October, and perhaps
in December or January. Then you generally got sultana
cake in February, March and April, and perhaps even in

May, but not very often in May, I don't think, though I
could be wrong.

—What was your mother like?

—Oh my mother was all right sir, yes. Her taste inclined
more towards the sultana cake I should say, whereas my
father he preferred the cherry cake, or even plain cake
sometimes.

—What was she like as a person?

—On the short side I should say sir, short to medium perhaps, about my own height, which would be more medium
in my opinion.

—As a person what was she like?

—Rather quiet, I would say, inclined to nervousness a little,
sir; she used to get rather nervous in the air-raids when we
went into the shelter for the bombing which used to start
most evenings round about seven-thirty or a quarter to eight.
But mostly seven-thirty, and then it would go on to eight
o'clock and from eight to nine and from nine to ten and
from ten to eleven; then on from there to twelve o'clock,
one, two, three, four, five, six, seven o'clock, more or less
like that. It didn't half used to make a noise sometimes,
bang bang bang it'd be like that; and then on other occasions
it was very very quiet.

  This was due to the Germans sir, they were our enemies
in the war. It was frightening in a way, but it could also be
quite exciting at times. On the wireless they would give the
news about how our army was faring abroad. It won quite
a number of different victories until the end of the war,
which was in 1945. Then it was announced that we had won
the war with a certain amount of help from the Russians
and Americans, and that Germany had lost.

—When you were evacuated up to Boston, how long did you
stay up there?

—In Boston in Lincolnshire, sir, that would be towards the
north of England I believe.

—Yes: how long were you there?

—I should think about two weeks, sir, or possibly one. If
you were to go into it I think you'd find that was more or
less correct. I came back sir because I didn't like it, it was
rather strange, I would sooner be at home; although there
were disadvantages of course such as that it had holes in the

roof and was very shaky. Eventually it was pulled down I believe sir, and I think it was an ice-cream factory was put in its place. I could be mistaken, it could have been a cake-factory, but in my opinion my own choice would be an ice-cream factory.

Oh thank you very much sir, that's very kind of you, I would like another cigarette, yes ta. By all means sir, yes I'll certainly be here tomorrow, as you say, we can continue then, there's no hurry, yes I'll look forward to that, sir. Oh begging your pardon sir, I hope you don't mind me asking you again, do you have a light?

*   *   *

—We were talking yesterday about your being evacuated to Boston in Lincolnshire.
—Yes that's correct sir, you've got it absolutely right, that's where I was evacuated to, to Boston in Lincolnshire which is towards the north of England I believe. I went to stay with a lady who had several children staying with her who'd been evacuated as well. A rather elderly lady in my opinion, but very kind, I believe her name was Mrs. Roberts. Her husband was called Mr. Roberts and he told me that he supported the Conservative Party. I should say myself that the Conservatives are inclined to lack support in London and get their help mostly from the outer parts of Britain such as Boston in Lincolnshire. After the war, and indeed during the war, they were inclined to frown on the Labour Party, were the Conservatives; but now of course the Labour Party is in power and they themselves frown on the Conservatives. The Labour Party on the whole supports the trades unions and they too frown on the Conservatives. But I think you'll find when they're in power the Conservatives frown on the trades unions, at least in my opinion they do. So then you've got the situation when the Labour Party is in power that they frown on the Conservatives and at the same time the trades unions frown on the Conservatives, so on the whole the Conservatives generally are pretty much frowned upon.

Yes sir I do, I find politics very interesting myself, and my own inclination is to support Labour and frown on the Conservatives. This would be from my father who supported the Labour Party himself and was a member of a trades union, which was the lightermen's union and is pretty much like any other union only it's for lightermen.

Oh he worked for the Government, sir, I remember he showed me a letter which had 'Government' written across the top. On his barge sir, he worked for them, taking shipments of coal it would be down to Rochester, or sometimes it was sand, but mostly it was coal and wood. Well not exactly wood, but more like drums of petrol and things of that kind. I forget the exact number but it would be thirty or perhaps thirty-five drums of petrol that were stacked in a row; or rather my mistake it was two rows and then they would put another two rows again on top. I should think it would be about eight barrels they had in a row and then another eight in the next row beside them, and then another two rows of eight on top. That would be one, two, three, four, five, six, seven, eight in one row, then nine, ten, eleven, twelve, thirteen, fourteen, fifteen, sixteen in the next. Then on top of that there would be seventeen, eighteen, nineteen, twenty, twenty-one, twenty-two, twenty-three, twenty-four; and next to them twenty-five, twenty-six twenty-seven, twenty-eight, twenty-nine, thirty, thirty-one, thirty-two. In that case it can only have been thirty-two barrels sir, not thirty-five as I said at first, I was mistaken there. Unless possibly it was nine barrels to the row, sir, in which case it would have been one, two, three, four—

—No it's all right Billy, it doesn't matter.

—Yes, I see sir, right-ho sir; but I could work it out for you if you liked, it won't take a moment for me.

—No never mind. Tell me about your father instead. What was he like?

—Oh he was all right sir, he tended to frown on the Conservatives quite a lot though, perhaps as much as I do myself, or even more so.

—What was he like as a person?

—Oh I would say about five foot eight sir, five foot nine or something like that, and very strong. He once picked up an anchor to show me how strong he was; it weighed I believe 112 pounds, and then he put it down and told me to have a try and I couldn't move it an inch. Inclined to be quiet, he never had a drink or anything of that kind. Also very kind sir, he gave me five shillings once to pay my fare on the bus

back home after he'd taken me for a trip down the river on
his barge, and he said I might either keep the change or
spend it on anything I liked. If I remember rightly I spent it
on sweets, that would be about two shillings all together, or
one and elevenpence, something like that. A very good man
I would say, sir, my father, very good and kind. He also let
me have a try at steering his barge once.

—Is he alive still?

—Oh yes sir, I would think he is, very likely; I could be
mistaken but I don't think I am. It would be a good few
years since I've seen him now, more or less not since my
mother died and I went in the Army, but I would think it
very possible he's alive, yes. Though he doesn't live in the
house any more, that was pulled down and they've put up
an ice-cream factory there I believe it is. I think he could
have gone to live in Rochester perhaps.

—How old were you when your mother died?

—Sixteen sir when my mother died, not long before I went
in the Army. No I don't know what she died of sir, just
what you might call an ordinary illness I believe. To be
truthful I was very surprised about it at the time sir, she
looked all right to me but they took her to hospital and
then she died. That would be on a Tuesday say, April
the 14th or 15th, I think it was the 15th, 1946. I think if
you were to go into it you would find that is very likely
correct.

After that sir I went into the Army and I was in the Army
for two years. They sent me a letter to go for my medical
report, and when I went they said had I had any afflictions
and I said no; and they asked me if there had ever been
any insanity in my family and I said no, not so far as I was
aware of, at least nothing serious.

A private I was sir, a private all the time; but I did know a
man who was in with me, he became a lance-corporal I believe it was, with a stripe here across the arm. He had done
very well, at least in my opinion he had. No I never went
anywhere with the Army, sir, only stopped in this country to
help the Army here. I was sent on a course to be a store-
man, sweeping the floors and that kind of thing which they
train you for, and I stayed mostly in the stores at Aldershot
to do my job. It's not the kind of thing you need to go

abroad for, I shouldn't imagine there's a great demand for that kind of work abroad.

—Were you ever in trouble in the Army?

—Yes I was sir, I was in what you might call trouble, yes. Only just the once though, so I suppose you could say that wasn't too bad, I don't think I caused them a lot of trouble except on this one occasion.

It was for what they called coming back late on leave sir, I believe it was twelve hours late or it may have been thirteen. I came up to London on a weekend leave sir, and when I caught the coach back it was on time but it wasn't on time in the right place, sir, if you understand what I mean. It wasn't late or anything like that, I would think it was more or less exactly on time, but that was in Brighton sir, rather than Aldershot which is where I should have been. So then I had to come back to London and start again and get another coach; and that was all right, that was on time, but the next morning you might say, rather than the evening before.

So I was taken before the commanding officer for that sir, and he asked me where I'd been and I told him what had happened. Actually he was a very nice man, well spoken he was, rather a tall man I should say, about six foot one or two, something like yourself sir, about your height.* I explained to him all about it, and he pointed out to me that I had broken one of the British Army's regulations and that therefore he would have to award me a punishment, which was that I must not go out of barracks again until the following day. 'Now do you understand that?' he said, and I said 'Oh yes sir, thank you sir, yes I do sir, I mustn't go out of the barracks again.' 'Until tomorrow,' he said, and I said 'Yes, I understand' and then I said 'Thank you sir, thank you very much sir, cheerio then sir, cheerio.'

He said to me 'Now go and tell the sergeant-major, will you, that you're not to go out of the barracks again until tomorrow?' and I said 'Oh yes sir, certainly I will sir, yes I'll go and tell him straight away.' So he said 'Yes, you go and tell the sergeant-major. Have you got it all quite straight, are you sure?' I said 'Yes sir, I have sir, thank you sir.' Then I went and told the sergeant-major I wasn't to be allowed to

* I am five foot six and a half.—T.P.

go out of the barracks until the next day. The sergeant-major said to me 'Well then,' he said, 'you'd better stop in the barracks, hadn't you, until tomorrow?' I said yes I thought it would be the best since that's what the commanding officer had said. So I stopped in the barracks until the next day. Then the sergeant-major came to me and he said 'It's all right now, you can go out of the barracks now if you want to' but I said 'No thank you, Sergeant-Major, I never go out of the barracks anyway' and he said 'No I know you don't but you could if you wanted to from now on.' So all that passed over and it was all right. But no trouble other than that one incident, sir.

Yes sir, I did like the Army, I was sorry to have to leave it in a way. When I came back home I had nowhere to go really because the house where I lived had big holes in the roof and had been pulled down. I believe it was an ice-cream factory they had put in its place. No sir, I didn't know where my father was then, I expect he had gone to Rochester, I think he must have done because I didn't see him again.

I started a job with a factory in Bermondsey, it was a very nice firm to work for and I was very happy there. What I was actually doing was sweeping the floor and keeping it clean. I think they were very pleased with me until I caught the blade on one of the machines with my brush and bent it: bent the blade that is, sir, the brush was all right. But the foreman was a very big man and he could be a bit abrupt sometimes, and he said it would be better if I went and worked somewhere else, I wasn't quite suitable for what they had in mind. I believe he was an amateur wrestler in his spare time. That would be about three days sir, I should think, two or three days I was with them before they said they felt I might do better elsewhere.

After that there was a job I had with a firm in Houndsditch I think it was; I could be mistaken but I think that's correct. That would be more or less the same sort of thing I believe, sweeping: a good job it was while I was there, which would be two or possibly three days sir. That's the length of time of most of my jobs I think you'll find if you go into it; I could be wrong but I don't think I am. There was also one I had another time in Islington. That was a very good job, going errands and making tea for the men. I was also in a job in a hospital, sweeping the floors there: a kind of mental hospital it was sir, I stayed there and helped them with keeping it clean until they said I could go. I've had some very good jobs of that kind in the different prisons too sir. More or less ten years I would think now sir, I may be wrong, it could be nine or eleven or even twelve, but I would think it was about ten years that I've lived on my own.

When I don't live in places like that sir? Oh I would say most often it would be in what might be called the basement of a warehouse, underneath it like, when it's empty and not in use by anyone for anything; or in an old building that's being pulled down, somewhere of that sort. Anywhere it's warm and not too damp sir; there's quite a number of places of that kind that are very nice on the whole I think. At least in my opinion they are, but I could be mistaken.

—These assaults you commit, Billy, why do you do them, what's going through your mind at the time?
—Well I should say it's mostly a matter of confidence sir, or self-confidence you might call it; I think so, at least in my opinion it is. Being a single man, you see, and not married, and not having an interest in sex or sport or any other hobby for that matter. On the whole I would say it was because I like it, I think it's quite a nice thing to do, especially in the case of a young woman: that would be about twenty-five to thirty, and then over thirty it would be what might be called a woman. I think you'll find that's right if you go into it, it's very rarely you'll find a young woman over the age of thirty.

I would call it largely a matter of confidence, perhaps over-eagerness on my part. Most young women and most women too for that matter sir, on the whole they don't seem to like it. Perhaps if one was not married she might, though I doubt it. I often think perhaps I ought to ask a woman before doing it, whether she is married and would have any objection. But that requires a great deal of confidence, I don't find it very easy to talk to women myself sir; and I think it's true to say that none of the women have liked it, at least so far as I've understood it they haven't.

Very often you'll find a young woman, or a woman for that matter, will probably scream or shout at you or hit you with her handbag, and then of course there's nothing you can do, you have to go away. There was one young woman, her husband was just over the road, I think he'd gone into a gentleman's convenience I believe it was, and when he came out he was very cross with me, he threatened violence to me as a matter of fact. I'd no idea this lady was his wife sir, and he told me to stay where I was until he got a policeman.

Sometimes you find people do that sort of thing, you have to stay there until they bring a policeman. It depends very much on the person, at least in my experience it does; or they may tell you to go away at once, something along those lines. A young woman could be very frightened by that sort of thing you see, couldn't she? The magistrate usually says to me, 'Have you done this sort of thing before?' and I say, 'Yes I have sir' and he says to me, 'Then you must go to prison until you stop', which could be three months, six months, twelve months or possibly two years.

Knocking them down, trying to take their handbag or anything of that kind, that would be very serious crime and you could get I should think three, five or even up to ten years' imprisonment for that. But in my opinion that sort of thing should be kept within limits, I wouldn't go in for anything like that myself. Similarly with rape, which would be the reason why I myself would never do it, I don't think you should let yourself get out of hand. Just feel under their skirts and for their breasts and so on, but I don't think it should be allowed to go any further on. Myself, I'd sooner have a job and a place to stay, I wouldn't think for a single person like myself it would be good to go too far with that sort of thing. I could be mistaken about that, but I don't think I am.

On the whole I should say it was a matter of luck perhaps more than confidence really, if you were to find somebody who liked it. In fact you'd have to be very very lucky indeed, I think, to find somebody who did. You can see a nice young woman on her own, or a woman for that matter, and take a chance in it: but so far, or at least this has

been my own experience, I don't think I've ever found anyone at all who cared for it, and so it has to be put a stop to
for three months, six months, twelve months, or two years
whatever the case may be. That's my opinion of it anyway,
I could be wrong but I don't think I am.

*   *   *

Hypomania is a mild manic-depressive psychosis, involving
acceleration and extension of thought, flight of ideas, pressure of talk and apparent inexhaustibility. Unprompted or
unchecked, Billy could speak for forty minutes without once
altering the quiet tone of his voice or the reasonableness of
his manner.

—I would say I like political books myself sir, something of
that nature. Herr Hitler's autobiography for instance, I
think that's a very good book for someone who takes an
interest in political things. It was written from what you
might call the patriotic German point of view, putting every
thing first for Germany. Then there is Mussolini's autobiography which is also a very good book, though in that case
it's from an Italian point of view. Hitler being a dark-
featured man, you might have thought he would have been
a friend of France; but that was not so, nor in Göring's case
either though he was more like Mussolini to look at. In fact
he could well have been Mussolini's brother, but I don't
think he was. And then there was Stalin who was a great
supporter of the trades unions, being a communist, although
Hitler himself I think would have claimed that what he
preached was a form of socialism though he called it 'national
socialism', being of a more moderate kind. To my way of
looking at it he could certainly be classed as moderately
socialist, and that would suit him as a dark-featured person
and would mean he could be born in October or December
and would take a belief in wood as a study. For instance
carpentry would appeal to him: he could take rubber, but
I rather doubt that because I think you'd find that Göring
was rubber and they would join forces so you'd have wood
and rubber together.

Mussolini was also dark-featured in a way, and he would
have an admiration for June and December and would tend

to favour the French who were also dark-featured although they favour May, June and July. On the whole dark-featured people prefer May, June, July, October and December, while fair-haired people favour January, February, August, September and November. The Chinese celebrate June and December and also the first of January, and would be inclined towards friendship with Italy, you see, because they would go to rubber first rather than to wood. That would make sense then because December is a wood month but January is rubber.

I think you'll find August is rubber but with some wood, and June is a wood month, well wood and grass; July would be grass the same as May because July is the son of May or June, whereas June in turn is the son of December. And April, well April is a funny month isn't it, because it's closer to summer than winter? You get January, February, March, which is mostly winter; and April can be inclined to cold but it's heading towards summer. I could be wrong but I think you'd find that April is rubber – because May would definitely be grass and June would be wood. January is rubber and February is wood and rubber, and March is rubber: then April is rubber but springing to wood, which is very funny. May goes to grass with a bit of wood and rubber, and June is wood and grass, followed by July which is all grass. You have say a field or a park in July, so that would be grass wouldn't it? And August, I'm only guessing, but I think it would take rubber, and then in September you'd have rubber leaning to wood. October is definitely wood, I doubt if you'd find it was rubber at all; then November is rubber and December is wood. Yes, that makes sense doesn't it, it definitely saves confusion you see, and apart from April which to my mind is a funny month you get it all sorted out and it gives you much more confidence; well in my case it does, and so I take a great interest in politics. Other people take religion as something to look forward to, or then again others take crime, such as dance-halls or slot-machines, where a good living can be made often only as a result of violence.

To me politics is knowledge really, and if you take a belief in something like that it helps you over your nervousness, or a couple of Aspros and a glass of milk can make you feel much more steady about it. In this sense nature is insoluble and so politics helps.

*   *   *

Like sightless fish in a black cavern, trapped in a sunless ravine uncharted beneath some deep and lonely distant sea, his thoughts flounder endlessly, churning through mud-choked eddies of swirling words. Once there was daylight, love and childhood, with his father strong, lifting an anchor and letting him have a try at steering his barge, and a mother who comforted him under a fearful sky. But that was a long time ago; now for this man there is only jumping from doorways in the dark, searching through garbage, wandering, prison, decrepitude and age.

A Boy Scout Whistles and Smiles

Graham Davis

—On Thursdays I always used to slip back to my digs for lunch. Barbara, my landlady, worked in a shop; Thursday was her day off so she'd prepare a meal for us and have it ready waiting on the table for when I arrived. As she was serving it out after I'd been upstairs and had a wash, she said, 'Oh by the way Graham, good news – there was a phone-call from the police down at Park Road this morning, somebody's found your wallet and handed it in. They said would you call and collect it.' There was about seven pounds in it, so naturally I was delighted. I said, 'Gosh, isn't it nice to know there are still some honest people around?' I knew I'd have just enough time before I was due back at work at two, because I passed the end of Park Road on my way to the bus-stop; so I rushed through my lunch and dashed out again.

I'd never been in a police station before: when I got there I said to the sergeant chap at the reception-desk, 'My name's Davis, I believe you've a wallet of mine handed in.'

'Yes, that's right sir,' he said. 'They've got it up in the C.I.D. room: first floor, third door on the right along the corridor.' I went upstairs, knocked on the door, and went in. There were two of them, one quite young and good-looking, and the other rather a big burly sort of middle-aged man. When I said what I'd come for, he said 'Oh, you're Graham Davis, are you? Would you sit down a minute please, there's a few questions we'd like to ask you.'

Honestly you know, I still didn't twig. I thought they just wanted to make sure it was actually mine or something like that. It was only when I saw he'd got the contents all spread out in front of him on his desk – the money, my club-membership card, the letters, my diary, the holiday photographs, my provisional driving-licence and everything – that I began for the first time to feel a bit uneasy.

He picked up a letter from Malcolm; there was nothing to it, it was mostly about things to do with the club and so on. 'Who's the person who wrote this?' he said. 'My priest where I used to live in London' I said, 'Father Riley. He runs the church youth club that I was a member of.' It had the name of the church printed across the top so there was no point in concealing it. Then he picked up a letter from Peter. 'And what about this?'

'Oh,' I said, 'That's nothing, just a silly letter from a friend – it's a joke letter, that's all.' I felt sick.

'How old are you?' he said.

'Eighteen and a half.'

'And how old's this friend, what's his name, Peter?'

I was trying desperately not to panic. But really what I wanted to do was jump up and rush out again, saying it was a mistake, I wasn't Graham Davis, I'd only been pretending, it had got nothing to do with me at all.

'Well go on,' he said, 'how old is he?'

I forget now what I said. I'm never a very good liar anyway, I think I just mumbled 'Oh he's about the same age as I am,' or something like that.

Then he opened the diary. 'And these names and addresses you've got here listed in the back of this – who are they?'

'They're just names and addresses of friends,' I said. 'Friends' names and addresses, that's all.'

I should think by then I was the colour of beetroot. I was trembling all over, I'm never very brave at the best of times, so he must have known he wasn't going to have a very difficult job breaking me down. As I told you, I'd never had any experience of the police in my whole life before, so when he said 'You can either make a full statement and tell us the whole truth, or we'll keep you here while we go and interview every single name on this list,' naturally I thought he meant that if I told him everything he wanted to know it would mean everyone else would be left alone.

So I did. The other chap, the young one, wrote it all out very slowly on a typewriter while I dictated it. Then they asked me to read it through to make sure it was correct, and sign it at the bottom. When I'd done that, the big one said 'All right, we're going to keep you in the cells now, you'll be put up in front of the magistrate in the morning.' They wouldn't let me phone my landlady, or try and contact my parents or anything.

The next morning I was taken into court. The police said it was a very serious charge, and they were opposing bail on the grounds that if I was let out it would hinder their inquiries. Then it dawned on me they'd tricked me. Even though I'd given them the statement telling them everything, they were still going to interview Peter and Malcolm.

I think there were two more remands in custody before I came up for trial at the Assizes. By that time I'd been allowed to write to my parents, and they had got legal representation for me. But it didn't make much difference. I pleaded guilty of course: I had to, after what I'd said in my statement. At least they didn't call anyone else to give evidence from the list of names they'd got: all they did was just put in statements from them.

The judge read them all through, and my own. Then he said 'It's quite obvious to me that you are the ring-leader of a very large circle, and have a most corrupting influence. In view of the gravity of the offence, I sentence you to three years' imprisonment.'

As I left the dock and was walking back down the stairs to the cells, I thought I must either have misheard him or he'd made a slip of the tongue. My solicitor had told me because I was so young and a first offender, he was fairly certain I'd get put on probation or at the most be given a very short sentence. 'Three months' I kept saying to myself, 'surely that's what he meant, it must be three months.'

There was a gaol-keeper at the bottom of the steps, and as I came down he said 'Well, what did you get?' 'Three years,' I said, – 'or at least, that's what it sounded like. But how could he, I can't believe it.' He laughed and gave me a pat on the shoulder. 'Oh you're all right then, lad' he said; 'he's done that deliberately to give you a good case on appeal, that's why he's done it.' Then my solicitor and my mother and father came down to the cells to see me. They were all talking the same way and saying the same thing.

In due course I came up before the Appeal Court of three

judges. There was no further evidence from the prosecution; just my own counsel, arguing this was an enormous sentence for someone who'd never been in any kind of trouble whatsoever before. Then they gave their judgment: it was short, they simply said they'd considered my counsel's plea but could see no reason for interfering. In their opinion the sentence of three years' imprisonment was justified.

I finished it a few months ago. The actual wording of the charge itself, do you mean? 'Buggery.'

*   *   *

The pressure of Manchester United's attacks in the first half was relentless, with wave after wave of the red-shirted players milling and swarming round Tottenham's goal. Best, the ball apparently fastened to his bootlaces, repeatedly threaded his way past one Spurs defender after another, delicately as a man tiptoeing through a field of tulips, before cutting in along the goal-line and then flicking the ball back towards Charlton, Kidd or Herd hovering menacingly near the centre of the penalty-box. Only a series of desperate tackles by Mullery and Kinnear and the determined blocking of shots by the granite-like MacKay kept United at bay.

Yet each time an attack was broken up the ball was cleared to the Tottenham wing for Beal or Gilzean to gather it in his stride and sweep down to the other end of the field before pushing a caliper-accurate pass through to the sprinting Chivers or Greaves. Panic, then, in the caught-out-of-position Manchester defence; Fitzpatrick hastily prodding the ball back to goalkeeper Stepney or Sadler making a last-minute flattening charge before a Tottenham player could shoot. On and on the struggle raged, the ball shuttling swiftly from this end to that, and as each goal in turn was threatened the crowd behind it gasped and roared and swayed. Perpetual bedlam of noise; shouts, boos, cheers, groans. The sparse turf of the pitch sparkling emerald-green in the floodlights, the ground packed to capacity, the cacophony of sound echoing and reverberating in the crisp night sky.

Among the 57,200 spectators Graham Davis in his suède sheepskin-collared overcoat struggled to keep his balance in the jammed mass of spectators on the terraces. Short and

stocky, with a curly brown beard framing his plump oval
face, he pushed and craned, twisting his head frantically to
try to get a clear view of the game through those packed all
round him. He had a large black-and-white Tottenham
rosette on his lapel; it kept falling off, and every few moments he disappeared from sight, burrowing down through
a forest of legs to retrieve it and put it back on his coat,
almost as though it was a lucky charm and while he wore it
nothing drastic could happen to his team. 'What happened,
what happened?' he kept asking anxiously each time he
re-surfaced.

George Best's speed and skill alternately delighted and
terrified him; as the Manchester player, his mop of black
hair flying and his arms windmilling, sped through the Tottenham defence he clapped and cheered with mounting excitement, calling 'Come on Georgie, come on Georgie!'
then suddenly covering his face with his hands and muttering
'No, no, for God's sake! What am I saying?'

Half-time brought a break in the play but no respite in the
tension. While they waited for the game to restart the crowd
kept up continuing cheers and counter-cheers as though it
was still in progress. Behind one goal a phalanx of red-
scarfed Manchester fanatics began to chant their anapaestic
chorus: 'Younigh-Ted! Younigh-Ted! Younigh-TED!' The
Spurs supporters at the other end of the ground caught
the rhythm and added their own extra syllable: 'Younigh-
Ted-Shit! Younigh-Ted-Shit!' 'Oh charming!' he said with a
giggle as he began to distinguish it, 'charming, I must say!'
Another section of the crowd began to parody a music-hall
song: 'Oh, oh, oh, oh, the bastard referee, bastard referee!
Oh, oh, oh, oh, the bas-tard ref-er-ee!' 'They ought to try it
themselves sometimes, by God!' he said.

The second half continued like the first, attack and coun-
ter-attack, the game running swiftly from end to end, and
as the tension increased the tackling became heavier and
more determined on both sides. A series of fouls in quick
succession fostered an explosive atmosphere: two players
fell to the ground together, exchanging punches, and the referee ordered them off. While the crowd was still simmer-
ing angrily, at a pause for a throw-in an apple hurtled from
the terraces and struck MacKay's boot. He picked it up,

took a bite out of it, munching with extravagant satisfaction and a casual wave of thanks towards where it had been thrown from. A cathartic gesture, dissolving the tense feeling. The game went on dourly and unremittingly, but with reliance once more on skill and stamina rather than deliberate roughness.

As it was a Cup-replay and neither side had scored at the end, there had to be half an hour's extra time. Graham held his head in mock agony, wiping his forehead with a spotless white handkerchief. 'I'll never stand it!' he said, 'I'll have a heart attack or something, I know I will!' When Spurs eventually scored their goal he yelled with joy, flailing his arms and thumping the shoulders of everyone round him in transports of ecstasy, disappearing and reappearing over and over again in the maelstrom of celebrants, green eyes shining and cheeks pink with exaltation. 'Glory Glory Alleluia!' he sang with all the other Tottenham fans, 'Glory Glory Alleluia, The Spurs Go Marching On!'

When the game was over and the crowd began to disintegrate and leave, the music from the Tannoy speakers was suddenly cut off for an announcement: the next night, at the Supporters' Club dance, the final choice would be made from the ladies present of 'The Tottenham Hotspur Beauty Queen!' In front of him a fifteen-stone bald man put up his hand to his head, primping imaginary waves and calling to nearby friends 'How about that then, do you think I ought to enter for it?' 'Go on, you great pouf!' they jeered back, and like everyone around him Graham laughed and cheered.

'Oh gosh!' he said, walking away from the ground, 'I've never seen anything like it. Two hours of pure football, wasn't it fabulous?'

—Oh, I've been a fanatic about football for six years or more now, ever since I started to take an interest in games when I got to my second grammar school. I think what started it was two other boys in my class who were ardent Arsenal supporters. One Saturday they had a spare ticket for the Arsenal–Spurs game at Highbury and asked me if I'd like to go with them. Up till then I'd never been the faintest bit interested, but I thought I might as well see what it was all about. It was a tremendous game, and Spurs won

3–2. The man who really knocked me out was the Spurs winger, Cliff Jones: at that time he was right at the top of his form, tremendously fast and accurate, and his swooping runs and crashing shots and flying headers left me spell-bound. He'd got terrific ball-control, speed, delicacy, grace, everything. I also admired the way he used his skill to avoid heavy tackles and keep himself out of trouble. Up till then it'd been the physical toughness required for games which had put me off them; but there was Cliff Jones demonstrating that you didn't have to play that way to be good. I don't doubt that he was physically fit and tough, of course to be a professional top-class footballer you must be, but he showed that other qualities were much more important.

So from then on I was a fanatical Spurs fan and went to watch them whenever I could. They were right at their peak at that time, they'd won both the Cup and the League Championship the season before, the first time anybody had done it for donkeys years, not since Preston in 1889 wasn't it? I collected all their programmes, photographs of the team, press-cuttings about their games; and on the few occasions when they did get beaten, as far as I was concerned it was nearly the end of the world.

I never had any schoolboy dreams about playing for them myself one day, I was realistic enough about my own lack of ability at games not to imagine that. But it did make me want at least to try and play, so I bought myself one of those plastic footballs and spent hours and hours practising on my own, kicking it into a bus-shelter and learning to trap it when it came flying back at awkward angles from the bench-seat inside. I didn't tell anyone at school I was doing it, and one day for the first time I casually joined in a kick-around in the playground. If I thought I was going to make an impression I was mistaken: schoolboys think everyone can play football automatically, no one made any comment at all.

I didn't ever get into the school first team, but I played for my class and house and so on. The main thing was that when I'd got at least the rudiments of it, I could enjoy it; and I did. After I left school it came in useful at the youth club too, I used to referee games for the younger kids, give them a bit of coaching and things like that. All in all I'd say

I've had more enjoyment and fun out of football, either
trying to play it or watching the big League sides like Spurs
or United, than I've ever had out of anything in life so far.
Only when it's skilled, though: I don't care for the bashing
sides like Liverpool or Leeds. Cricket? Oh no, that's a terrible game, old men's skittles, that's all that is: there's only
one game in the world so far as I'm concerned. If you wanted
me to, I could go on talking about it for days. Actually,
once you have got an interest in it, and a bit of knowledge
about it, you find it's a great subject for conversation everywhere you go: school, work, youth club, prison, everywhere.

I was born in 1948, and the first thing I remember is the
enormous rambling old house with a lot of stained-glass
windows, that we lived in on the edge of the Sussex downs.
To me as a child it seemed to have dozens of rooms: I kept
finding new ones I'd never seen before, all like stage-sets
complete with carpets, furniture, curtains, windows and
different views of the countryside outside. And the funny
thing was that each one seemed to have a different woman
permanently in it; it was her room, that was where she could
always be found. In one was my mother, in another there
was my elder sister Phyllis, and in another there was my
aunt Jose. Then up on the first floor there was my grandmother, an old lady with white hair and spectacles and a
high-waisted long black dress; further along from her my
auntie Annie who chain-smoked and spent all her time coughing; a bit further along still another old lady called Mrs.
Hargreaves who could do that cat's cradle thing with string.
And then away at the back of the house there was yet
another little room with my great-grandmother in it: for
some reason I could never work out she was always referred
to as 'Madam Ronald Tavistock'. This always used to puzzle
me as a kid because I knew 'Ronald' was a boy's name, and
I can remember wondering in the vague sort of way that
children do if she was really a man dressed up as a woman;
and if so, why? It didn't worry me, but I just felt it was one
of those odd totally inexplicable things about the adult
world which no one ever bothered to explain to you. I believe in fact that earlier in her life she'd been the wife of the

manager of a theatre somewhere in London in the early
part of this century, and had got her name, or her style of
address rather, from the days when she worked there in the
box-office.

Of course the one thing that *was* odd – that there wasn't
a man in the house, or apparently even one in existence
anywhere in my life – never struck me for a long time.
Naturally all these different women made a great fuss of me;
you don't notice something you've never had, so it was a
very long time before not having a father made me feel that
I might be missing something. In fact if I remember rightly
it was only after I started going to school at the age of five
or so, and heard the other children referring occasionally
to their 'daddy', that I thought it worth while finding out if
I'd got one myself and where he was.

When I asked my mother she said, 'Yes of course you've
got a daddy, darling. He came to see you once, don't you remember him, he was a soldier?' I said vaguely that I did remember, but I didn't. Later on when I started asking more
questions, she told me he was in the Army but he was away
in Germany and couldn't often come home. That was quite
true in fact: but what she didn't say was that their marriage
had broken down, and he had left her and married somebody else. But as I say, I was never really conscious of missing him.

As far as I can recall it, I would say my childhood was
quite a happy one apart from the fact that I hated school.
I'm a Roman Catholic and so the one I went to was the
local primary school run by nuns. I think I must have been
very stupid, or appeared to be to them, because my memories of it consist chiefly of being whacked on the bottom
with a slipper and made to stand in the corner for not getting my sums right. I can't remember any of the teachers
individually: they all wore black habits and white hoods,
and were likely to give me the slipper at any time for any
reason or for no reason, or at least that was how it seemed
to me.

I was always glad to get back home in the afternoon and
go and talk to Auntie Rose, or get Mrs. Hargreaves to do the
cat's cradle for me, or sit in the kitchen with my mother
and eat my tea. I was tremendously greedy as a child, I

ate and ate; my mother used to say proudly I had a marvellous appetite and would grow-up to be very tall and
strong. In fact I remained short and fat: really fat, all the
other children at school used to call me 'Fatso', 'Roly-
Poly', 'Big fat pig' and other charming things like that.

But at home there was peace and quiet and affection. My
mother was hardly ever cross with me, always gentle and
understanding. She was – in fact she still is – a very beautiful woman; I think her father had been an Indian, she's
got a marvellous olive complexion and grey-green eyes and
long dark hair. She was – and again still is – very religious,
and used to pray with me every night when I went to bed.
Her great ambition always was that I should become a
priest, and the final prayer every night was 'Dear Lord,
help me to work hard at school so that I may be a priest
when I grow up.' We always went to Mass and confession,
observed the Friday fast and so on.

Being such a devout Catholic herself, I know the subject
of divorce caused her great agony of mind. My father I believe wasn't a Catholic, but because he wanted to remarry
she let the divorce go through. Actually I think she's been
very brave in living with it because it's not something
a lot of Catholics will contemplate at all. In all my life I've
never heard her say a bad word about my father either,
even though he went off with someone else. He paid
her a small allowance I believe, for the upkeep of myself
and my sister; but she certainly can't have had a very easy
time.

Now you come to ask me, there's not a lot I can say
about my sister. She's called Phyllis, she's about four years
older than I am, and she's married and has two children. A
very quiet sort of person, rather artistic: I never had much
to do with her during childhood, and I know less about her
than I do about anyone else I can think of. We only meet
once in a blue moon, perhaps at Christmas or times like that.
She got married quite young, and went to live up in Yorkshire where her husband teaches at a technical college. As
long as I can remember Phyllis she's always been a rather
nebulous sort of person in my life. I have the feeling, though
it's only what you might call a hunch and is not really based
on anything, that she missed my father much more than I

did myself. Perhaps that's why she got married early and started a family of her own.

Of course I missed him too myself, I must have done, I suppose one could say his absence couldn't fail to have affected me in some way. But it's like if you lose a parent through death: you grow up without them there and you can't imagine how you might have turned out if they had ever been. No, I've never had the faintest desire to see him, to go and find out for myself what he's like, or even want to meet him. I don't feel deprived or bitter or anything: he's just a 'no-such-person', that's all. I think undoubtedly I was very lucky in getting so much care and affection from my mother; quite enough to make up for having no father, I'd say.

When I got to the age of about eight, it must have been increasingly obvious to her that I was so hopeless at school I wasn't going to have a cat in hell's chance of making the priesthood. Here again there must have been another conflict between her religious beliefs and her desire to do what was best – because there was another, non-Catholic primary school near where we lived; and that one had a much higher success-rate with getting children through the eleven-plus exam. Despite considerable evidence to the contrary, my mother persisted in believing that I had some brains, so after a lot of heart-burnings and discussion between her, my grandmother, my aunts, Mrs. Hargreaves, Madam Ronald Tavistock, Old Uncle Tom Cobbleigh and all, she took me away from the school with the nuns and put me into the other one instead.

The results of two years' teaching there must have seemed to her to fully justify the decision, because I passed my eleven-plus easily, high-up in the placings for the area. I could if we'd wanted have gone to the local 'posh' grammar school. But just at that same time my mother was offered a job as a travelling model for a firm making women's clothes, and she decided to take it. My sister and I were old enough to begin standing on our own feet a bit; obviously it was going to make quite a difference financially and in addition give her more of a life herself. So naturally she took it.

The firm she joined had their headquarters down on the

south coast. This meant we had to move to live down there, just the three of us, my mother and sister and I. She found a very nice flat, not actually overlooking the sea but near it, and we moved in. At first there was rather a problem about who should look after us when she was away, but this solved itself before long. The flat was really a bit too big and expensive, so she advertised for a lodger, and the man who came to live with us as a result was a very nice chap indeed. His name was Eric, he was a bachelor of about forty I should say, and he was the manager of a shoe-shop in the town. The wonderful thing about him was that because he'd always been used to looking after himself, he was good at housework, cooking and cleaning and all the rest of it, and he was perfectly happy to look after me and my sister when mother had to go away. Eric in fact became just like a father to us: he made us a meal when he got in at nights, took us out for picnics or to the fairground at weekends, and sat and played games with us in the evening. He was really terrific, and he got as fond of us as we were of him. A very gentle-natured man, kind, sensitive – there's nothing I'd want to criticize in him except for one – well, I suppose you'd call it one very minor fault, which I can see now was an unavoidable part of his make-up.

That was that just occasionally, when he got very depressed or upset about something, he would cry – and what was worse to my mind was the fact he'd do it in front of us, in front of me and my sister. I suppose it's ridiculous of me, but ever since I was tiny I've been brought-up to believe by my mother and aunts and other relatives that boys and men simply never cry – or if they do, it's only when they're on their own and no one can see or hear them. One of my earliest recollections is of my mother telling me, when I'd fallen down and scraped my knee or something and was making a bit of a fuss, 'Oh Graham, don't be a baby. Boys never never cry!' Even when I got spanked with the slipper at the convent primary school I took a great pride in recounting to her afterwards how this had happened, and it had hurt and I hadn't cried; and she always seemed to be much more pleased about that than annoyed with me for whatever it was I'd been in trouble for.

I think Eric had been with us six months or so when one evening I went into the kitchen in the flat and saw him sitting at the table with his head in his hands really sobbing – and honestly, it sounds ridiculous to say it but I was absolutely horrified: and even more so when he made no attempt to conceal it despite me being there. I don't know what was upsetting him – or at least I didn't then, but I could guess now – but at the time I was really shattered to see a grown-up in tears.

So as I say, much as I liked him – and I did like him, and look back on him still with great affection – I knew all the time in my own mind that he had this weakness in him. That's how I looked at it then: and to be honest, I can't help it, I still do. Maybe as I said a few minutes ago it was an unavoidable part of his character, and without it he couldn't have been the kind and gentle person he was. But to me – well the only word which expresses what I feel about it is that it's 'unmanly'; it's the sort of thing that men under any circumstances don't do.

I think that's probably what in a way too my mother found unsatisfactory about him – much as she liked him and was grateful to him, as we all were. There was this streak of weakness in him: and I'm quite convinced it was that which put her off. I don't think there was much doubt that he was in love with her, and would have married her if she'd given him the chance. I think he more or less worshipped her from afar, to coin a cliché; but for three years he certainly never proposed to her or anything like that. In fact the first and only time he ever did was the weekend she came back to the flat and told him and us she was going to get married to a man who worked up in London for the firm she was with.

That was the only occasion I ever knew Eric and her have a row. I could hear them shouting at each other in the kitchen, and my mother's words were as clear as though she were right outside my bedroom door: 'You don't own me, you know!' After that Eric was in tears nearly every evening, especially when he was on his own. I do feel sorry for him, because he'd devoted himself to us for nearly three years after all: but I think my mother was right in eventually marrying someone else, she couldn't have married him just out of a sense of obligation. Eric wouldn't have been right for her.

About a month or two afterwards Eric left, and mother remarried at a registry office up in London and then gave up work and came back to live at the flat with her new husband George. Although he's my stepfather I've never called him anything else but George; and I must say I've always got on very well with him, though Phyllis, my sister, didn't. She got engaged and married herself soon after that. George was a good deal older than Eric, also very quiet and undemonstrative and nice. He fitted into our life quite smoothly, but I never saw a great deal of him, first because he continued to work up in London and commuted there and back every day, so most evenings he wasn't in until late, and at weekends he and mother used to go out a lot; and then after only a few months he was transferred to another branch office of the firm, and we all went to live in a house he bought in north London. Then a short time after that he got promoted to area manager, so once again he was travelling about a great deal and only home at weekends.

This meant my transferring to another grammar school of course – and it was there that I first began to get keen on football. It was there too that I finally realized there was no point in wondering about myself any longer; I was a homosexual.

*   *   *

His short plump body in the white jacket and breeches was controlled and relaxed in the 'On Guard' position. His feet a stride apart, at right-angles to each other, right knee forward and over the instep, head erect, trunk square on; left arm up at shoulder height behind him in an arc, hand loose at the wrist; sword-arm firm, bent at the elbow, advancing to engage and the foil gently quivering, trying to feel the opponent's reaction on the blade. Going forward he made the first attack: a fast lunge and cut-over in Quarte, immediately scoring a hit. A few seconds later he took advantage of an attempted change of engagement to execute a counter and score again. Trying to parry on the lunge and return to guard he was not stable enough, and took a hit himself in Septime; and then two more in quick succession

in Sixte, while forcing his opponent down the piste. Behind
the mesh of his mask his eyes glistened with amusement at
his own impetuosity. But he continued to attack, and scored
again with a beat straight lunge. Two counter-disengage
stop-hits caught him off balance both times: one in Octave
and another in Sixte, and the match was over.

He laughed, out of breath, but pleased with his own
efforts. 'If I hadn't been so damn stupid' he said, taking off
his helmet, 'I might even have won.'

—I'm too aggressive, too keen to attack, that's my big fault
all the time. It's a great sport, though, fencing. The thing
I like about it is that your dexterity with your fingers and
the speed of your reactions are much more important than
physical strength. It's not really fighting at all, you know;
they call it 'a conversation of the blades'. I'm nothing like
quick enough for sabre yet: in that it's the footwork that's
important and I'm far too cumbersome. Still I'm only just
getting back to it again, it'll be months before I'm properly
fit. Prof says I never will be if I don't discipline myself a
bit more, work out a training programme and stick to it,
and stop eating sweets.

I took it up originally at the grammar school in London;
they had a master there who was very keen. There was a
boy I had a crush on, he did a lot of it too: to start with
I think I joined the fencing-class mainly to be with him, and
when that faded out I went on with it simply because I
enjoyed it. Altogether at that school I was much more interested in sports and games than I was in lessons. I never did
the homework I should have done, with the result I only got
three 'O' levels out of the six I went in for. Now I look back
on it I think I was stupid not to stay on at school for another year and try and get at least two more; but I was very
obstinate and independent-minded and I wanted to start
earning my own living.

George and my mother tried to talk me out of it but I
didn't listen. I had the idea that once I was working I'd probably continue studying at night school: that was my inten-
tion at least, but like so many other things it didn't work
out. Through a friend of my mother's I got a job in the
town down on the south coast where I'd spent most of my

life. I knew a lot of people there so I didn't mind going
back, in fact I liked it better than London. I got digs with
a very nice landlady called Barbara Bedford, who was a
young widow in her late twenties. She looked after me as
though she was my own mother, mended my socks, cooked
my meals and all the rest of it, and in no time at all we were
on Christian-name terms.

The job was nothing special, it was as a clerk with a
wholesale stationers; the hours weren't long though, and it
gave me plenty of spare time – which I could have used,
and would have used if I'd followed my original good intentions, for study. But I was far too interested in the social
side of life: the local church youth club was particularly
good so I joined and helped the priest to run it. Because I
was a sports enthusiast, he left nearly all that side of it to
me – football, fencing, canoeing, badminton, volleyball.
There were about a dozen different groups, so naturally I
was involved in something or other nearly every night of
the week.

I suppose that was what the judge was referring to when
he said that I was the ring-leader of a circle and had a most
corrupting influence. I expect in his eyes, because homosexual activities sometimes took place between members, it
meant that that was the sole, or at least the main, purpose
of the club: and because I was the club leader, therefore
I initiated the other boys into it.

That wasn't so: I shouldn't think there was more sexual
involvement between members than there is in an average
amateur dramatic society. Well perhaps that's a bit of an
over-statement, because it's true most of the boys were a
few years younger than me. But homosexuality wasn't
something I introduced to the club: it was going on before
I got there and I expect it continued after I left.

It's difficult for me to talk about the subject with much
detachment or insight because I've no other form of feeling
or experience to compare or contrast it with. As I told you,
I've been a confirmed homosexual ever since I first became
aware of sex itself as a schoolboy. Strange how people
always use that expression isn't it, 'confirmed' – as though
it was something like a religious belief, or an intellectual
decision you took? To me there was never a conscious

making-up of my mind at all: boys attracted me physically, girls didn't, and it was as natural as having brown hair or two legs.

It's not that I dislike girls or find them repulsive or anything of that kind: I enjoy their company very much and get on well with most of them, like my landlady for instance. But how anyone could ever want to make love to them was, is and I think always will be as ununderstandable to me as I suppose homosexuality is to a heterosexual.

In every boys' school there's always an element of homosexuality, an undercurrent of it – well it's more than that, it's often quite open in the changing-rooms after games and so on. To some boys, perhaps to most of them, it's only a phase and after a time they grow out of it. If that suggests I think those who don't remain immature, that's not true: some grow out of it because they're heterosexual basically, that's all. But I'm not and I never was: my liking for boys increased, and once I'd recognized it as something unalterable in myself it didn't make me unhappy. I knew it was supposed to be wrong and unlawful and all the rest of it: but so is sex generally, when you're at school; you're given the impression the whole thing shouldn't be talked about anyway.

The first person I ever met who understood it was another boy at school, two classes lower than me. He was a sweet kid, only about eleven or twelve, a lovely looking boy with fair hair and blue eyes, always cheerful and bright. Did you ever see the film *Smiley*? He was just like the boy in that; in fact in my own mind that's what I always called this kid. I say he understood, and I know he did; though I never knew him well enough even to discuss the subject, and there was nothing between us. But I could tell, just from a look he gave me now and again, that he knew what I felt for him – and he probably reciprocated. This was at the first grammar school, and I moved away before we got a chance to know each other better.

Then as I say, at the school I went to in London, the whole subject was much more out in the open. There was the usual experimenting between boys, some of it serious and some of it not. I certainly didn't feel out of place, alienated from my companions as they say or anything like that. It

was all light-hearted and easy-going, no one got terribly
emotionally involved.

Coming into a new area we joined the local church of
course; and the priest was this man I told you about, Malcolm Riley. I liked him as soon as I met him, he seemed
to have a great sympathy for youngsters, he could talk to
them easily and naturally; he was always interested in what
you were doing at school and how you were getting on. He
ran the youth club attached to the church – games, debates,
social evenings and all the rest of it, and I joined. We used
to spend hours talking in his room after the others had
gone home, and on one occasion I took the bull by the horns
and asked him straight out, I said I was a homosexual and
was this very wrong and sinful? He made nothing special
of it at all; he merely went on talking in an ordinary reasonable voice and said that although it was against the law and
therefore wrong in the eyes of society, he didn't feel that
something as natural as that could ever be wrong in God's
eyes for people like us. Up till then he'd never mentioned
being a homosexual himself. He introduced it casually, just
like that, and then passed on to talking about other things in
the same unemotional way.

I got very fond of him, and he did of me. Later
there was sexual activity between us, as there was between
him and several of the other older boys in the club. It was
understood he had no special favourites, and as far as I
know he never attempted things with boys who weren't that
way inclined themselves. But homosexuality definitely was
one of the features of the club, even though it never appeared as part of the printed programme, you might say.

After I was charged Malcolm was interviewed several
times by the police, but they never accused him of anything, and his bishop sent him away somewhere, Ireland I
think. To my mind this was a pity, because there was no
doubt he really was very good in youth club work, as a lot
of homosexuals are. They have this affinity with boys which
isn't just a sexual thing at all, at least it's far more than that.
You get it in teachers too sometimes, and social workers.
Homosexuality may be their basic motive, the thing that
takes them into the work; but it can be an asset, it isn't
always necessarily a bad thing.

As Malcolm was the first person with whom I had the full experience of the physical act of sex, some people would consider that he seduced me, since he was thirty-two and I was sixteen. But to my mind a statement like that would be ridiculous: the fact that he was the first was purely coincidental. It could be said too I suppose that in the same way I seduced Peter since he was fourteen and I was eighteen. Yet I knew him for over six months before the subject of sex even arose, and by then we were so in love with each other that what took place was no more than a logical progression of what already existed. A lot of people can't understand that homosexual love is really no different from any other kind. Nor that an older person can love someone much younger: they think it can never be anything else but sexual lust.

Well, I've not seen Peter now for nearly three years: his parents forbade him to have any more to do with me. But if he was to come in through that door now, I know what effect it would have on me; I'd go just like a jelly inside. Knowing it, that's why I've stayed in London since I came out of prison. If I were to go back there, I couldn't very well help running into him before long and then we'd be back where we started. He's seventeen and I'm still under twenty-one, so the change in the law about homosexual behaviour in private between consenting adults wouldn't cover us.

It's lonely though: I live in digs because I don't want to lose my independence by going back to my mother and George. I look at other boys, and I'm aware that they're attractive – but they're not Peter. All I've got's a collection of photos I took of him at school sports-days and on camping outings. And this silver ring I wear, which he gave me when – well, it was to celebrate a special occasion. Perhaps I'll get over it in time; people do get over love affairs, so I'm told.

When I was in prison, the psychologist said that as far as he could see I'd always be homosexual but I must try and 're-orientate' my attitude about it. He never told me how, or to what – so I suppose I'm still disorientated. I try not to think about it too much: it's all past now. I'm working again, I've joined a fencing club, I go to watch Spurs, try and keep bright and cheerful – what else can I do?

It's like what they tell Scouts – no matter what the adversity stay cheerful: in all circumstances, however difficult, a Boy Scout whistles and smiles.

All Irishmen Drink

Nat Burke

A cheerful breezy sort of chap, Nat Burke, you might say; gregarious, good company, always ready for a game of cricket in the garden with the kids, a family picnic in the woods or a quiet walk across the park. Not much more than five feet tall, with a large square head on a small body, but making up for lack of height with an expansive friendly personality and plenty of charm. Full of the irrepressible gab of the Irish of course: loquacious, genial, sentimental, even garrulous at times. Enjoying gossip and banter and a bit of a wag too, usually at his own expense: a man never entirely serious with himself, especially in front of the ladies. There is an air about him of being at forty-five not quite the mischievous character he was once perhaps; but the hair greying at the temples looks as though it gives him maturity now, and in his deep brown eyes an apparent glitter of amusement at life changes swiftly into sympathy or compassion if the conversation demands. A soft and modulated Dublin voice, equally fluent for serious discussion or frivolity, and a store of jokes for the evening's late hours.

'Was it you who told me the one about the nun who dropped the plate? Well there was this nun you see, she was serving the dinner to the others in the convent and she dropped a plate right by the Mother Superior. "Oh blast!" she says, "it fell out of me hand." And then, "Damn!" she says, "I said 'Blast'." Then "Hell!" she says, "I said 'Damn'." Then "Oh Christ!" she says, "I said 'Hell'. Oh Jesus God, now I've said 'Christ'. Ah well," she says with a sigh, "I never wanted to be a bloody nun anyway!" '

Fastidious about his personal appearance, smooth-shaven, hair short and neatly trimmed; unobtrusively

dressed in a dark blue lounge-suit, a soft-collared white shirt
and dull red tie. Working as a dispatch-clerk in a department store, living in digs, smoking too much and eating too
little, poorly paid but saving a bit of money when he can.
Most nights staying in, listening to the radio, now and again
having a break at weekends and coming out to stay for a
couple of days with friends.

But in the long night hours of talking then about himself
there is no charm left, no humour needed, no wit to defend:
only the voice frail and faltering frequently, often clear and
agonized, torn with tears, sometimes lashing out at himself
in a verbal rage, swearing his protest at the tumult of his
soul. Haunted by sex and religion, tormented by the in-
dignities which each inflicts on him relentlessly in turn;
stumbling through the ruins in the wasteland of his past,
and finding no signs. To himself repulsive and unclean, with
no glories or achievements to look back on, lost on a meaningless itinerary on a wretched path which had and has no
end.

In the inside pocket of his jacket he keeps a slip of paper;
most nights he takes it out and looks at it when he's getting undressed for bed. Someone wrote out two words for
him once and gave it to him: it says 'Via Dolorosa'.

—If you were to ask me how it was just at the moment, I'd
say it was O.K. Just about O.K. Life's busy, it's interesting,
I'm working, my digs are good, I'm paying my way. I have
a friend or two, I get enjoyment from reading books or
taking myself out to the cinema once in a while. That's it,
that's all: a quiet ordinary life, like anyone else. That's
something, I suppose: I try to accept what comes and be
thankful for it, to keep on reminding myself how much
worse off I could be. It's been a year now since I was last in
trouble: and I've lived every day of it, every minute of it,
one step at a time. Yesterday's gone, I got through that;
and today's finished now too. Tomorrow's still to come, but
perhaps at the end of it I'll be able to mark it up as another one that I somehow got through. But it's not easy,
Jesus it's not easy, no by Christ it's not that.

*   *   *

At quarter past two in the morning he leaned back in the armchair and took a clean white handkerchief out of the breast pocket of his jacket, unfolded it carefully and buried his face in it and wept.

Nat Burke: age 45, single. Occupation: clerk.
Age 26, 3 months' imprisonment for larceny
Age 29, 6 months' imprisonment for indecent assault
Age 31, 3 months' imprisonment for larceny
Age 32, 4 months' imprisonment for importuning
Age 34, 3 years' imprisonment for importuning
Age 41, 6 months' imprisonment for importuning
Age 44, Conditional discharge for importuning

—The story of a lifetime, but not of a life. Who'd want to know that person, to listen to what he'd say? A dirty little Irish pouf, a nasty mixed-up Catholic queer, feeling so sorry for himself he can hardly speak for crying. I'm sorry I can't help it, it comes over me; there's this great big baby inside of me and I have to let it squawk for a while before I tell it to lie down and belt up, and all the other things you say to kids to make them keep quiet. But how can I explain it to you, that it's not really sorrow at all? Nor self-pity, but in a way I don't understand myself I'm crying because I'm happy at being alive and for the good there is in the world and the bit of it still left in me. When you're born, they slap you don't they to make you cry, that's the only way you learn to breathe? All right Nat Burke, your infant's made its little demonstration, now put it down and let it sleep. I'll make another cup of tea, eh, and let's have another fag.

I'm sorry about that: and yet I'm not sorry, it's only right that you should see. All I've got for you is words, the curse of the Irish, talkativeness that they use for speaking when they're covering-up what they don't want to say. But it's not that I don't want to say, it's not that anymore. I do: only it's the same old bloody volubility that gets in the way. I'm going to try though, I want to try; for my own sake I want to try. Two years ago I'd have talked your head off, I'd have made you laugh and maybe once in a while I'd have made you want to cry. But all the time I'd have been thinking somewhere inside of me what effect it was having on you; some part of me would have been detached and looking at that aspect of it all the while. The years I've talked and talked, and said nothing to anyone, least of all to myself; the years I've spent screaming to anyone who'd listen to me, 'What am I, tell me what I am, am I a Catholic or am I not, am I a heterosexual or am I a hundred per cent queer?' It was always other people I wanted to tell me what I was; and whatever they said I'd start to argue the opposite straight off. Nights I'd lie in bed, in the nick perhaps, and carry it on with myself; and whatever one part of me said, the other would jump up straight away with all the arguments on the other side. 'You can't be a Catholic, you don't accept the teachings of the Church. But you were born a Catholic weren't you? You know really that's the true Faith, you'll have to come back to it before you die. But you can't be a homosexual because you do like women and you hate men. Yet you must be because your body only responds to men. Physically women leave you cold. All right, so you're queer: accept it. I can't accept it, I don't want to be queer. Well you're a Catholic, it only takes faith: I haven't got the Faith, I don't want to believe in God.'

Forty-five years of debate, of kidding myself that eventually out of it all I'd arrive somehow at the truth. And as I see it now, it was all for nothing. The truth's not in the answer to either of these questions, they're both of them irrelevant to what I really am. What I am is a defeated man. But not by those things, no.

Perhaps it's only when you come to recognize what it really is that's beaten you that you can ever begin to start learning how to fight. Don't ask me with what, I don't know, to be honest I think I've no weapons at all; for an educated man it might be easier. All I can say is this, that for once I want to try. If I tell you the whole story, maybe even while I'm telling it I might learn a bit more about myself; I might somehow come to believe in that thing I've been short of up to now. An unknown feeling, which goes by the name of hope, I suppose you'd say.

To start at the beginning, to try and keep it in order for you, I was born in Dublin and my father had a cycle shop. I was the youngest of his four children. He'd be about thirty-one when I was born, and my m-m-mother she was roughly the same age. And you'll notice that's the only word I can't pronounce; I don't normally have a stammer or a speech impediment, except on that one single word. It's very rarely indeed I can ever say it without stuttering, and the harder I try the worse it is.

We'll try and get this over before I go any further; if I don't come out with it now it'll be hanging about in my mind all the time I'm talking to you, waiting to be said. So here it is to begin with, one of the most important things I want to say. M-m-Mother was the only woman I've ever really loved in all my life, I worshipped her, and that feeling, that love for her, will stay in me all the rest of my life until I die. And I've got to tell you this straight away at the beginning, and you won't understand anything if you don't understand it. But in a way I killed her; that's the thought I've had ever since I can remember.

All my life she was never anything but a sick woman, and when people talked of her they always used to say 'When she was well,' and there was the implication with it of 'which was before you were born'. Whether she had a bad time having me or what I don't know – but there was three before me and then me and then she had no more. Being a good Catholic woman and only in her thirties there should have been; so I can only presume that when I came something went wrong. We lived too for a time in my early childhood in a little flat above our doctor's surgery, and this also gives me the idea that it was because there was always the need to have him close at hand.

She herself? No she never indicated it, there was no suggestion from her of that; only from myself, an idea, a vague feeling that I grew up with. I suppose the truth of the matter is that when I got old enough to ask, by then I was too scared, I didn't want to know whether it was my fault or not. And now I still don't: a nag, that's all it is, and reasoning about it tells me it's got no foundation. But you don't reason about things like that, you keep them close to yourself because they're so much part of your life.

My sisters were Sheelagh and Maureen, when I was born one was six and the other was four: then before me there was my brother Jimmy. He was always called Jake: a bad lad he was, a wild boy, always getting into scrapes and causing no end of trouble around the district, but it made no difference to my parents. In fact my father used to laugh and say to him 'Ah Jake you're a terror and that's for sure', but with great pride in his voice as though it was something to his credit. I could never understand this, I thought that if I was good and well-behaved this would increase my standing in my father's eyes; but it never worked out that way at all. Jake was the one he took with him to Croke Park to watch the All-Ireland final every year, Jake was the one he said would do well at school. Maybe – you see it comes back into my mind without me thinking hardly – but if I were to put it down to anything, it'd be to the same, that perhaps my father held it against me that me being born had spoiled the health of his wife.

There was something with my sisters too, I think it was because she wasn't strong they were sent away to live with one of my aunties down in Cork. It may have been because we didn't have the money or what, I don't know; but again I always seemed to think that in some way it was connected with me. I was a sickly child myself, and I was kept because of that, and Jake was kept because my father liked him: but Sheelagh and Maureen, they were all right and they grew up to be fine women both of them, married and had families I believe. Though I've never seen either of them since I was a child. It's all so confused in my mind you see, there's so much about my childhood I've never inquired about from anyone because I've not wanted to go into it too deeply. My mother loved me the best, that I do know, that's why she kept me. And that ought to make me feel, it ought to have made me feel then, that I couldn't be entirely bad. But the feeling I had was I was a kind of punishment on her, I was the cross she had to bear.

When I was little I used to mess myself at school and run home to her because I was so ashamed; and she'd keep me near her for a few days, send a note to the teacher to say I wasn't well and tell me I could stop at home for a bit with her. I was a delicate child she said, and I needed understanding: and sometimes I'd hear her and my father rowing about it because he said I ought to be back at school and learning to stand up for myself, I shouldn't be m-m-mollycoddled, that was the word he used.

I didn't like the school, it was the nuns that ran it, and one of them I remember always was making a great fuss of me, putting her arms round me and kissing me, and I hated the feel of her clothes, the stiff black poplin of her habit, I can recall it still. She frightened me, tall and gaunt she was, and I could never see her face properly because it was half-hidden by the hood. She was trying I suppose to do what she thought best, but I hated her for it because all the other kids as a result always called me 'teacher's pet'.

Most afternoons round about tea-time my m-mother would take me with her to our church which was just a few minutes away round the corner. 'Come on now, Nat,' she'd say, 'let's go for our prayer.' That was the time I liked best, being with the two people I loved best, my mother and God. The smell of the incense, the flickering light of the candles, usually only the two of us alone in the church. I prayed a lot and I prayed very hard, and my prayer was always the same: 'Please God forgive me and make my mother well.'

It was strange, although she was a very religious woman, a very good Catholic, my mother believed in fortune-telling and there was a gipsy woman she used to take me to see once a week for to have our fortunes told. She lived in a little house down by the Liffey near the docks, her name was Millie. About twenty-six she'd be I suppose, very dark and swarthy and a beautiful face with big gold ear-rings; and the most peculiar thing about her was she had no legs at all, only two short stumps covered in stockinette that stuck out from under her skirt. She had a high wooden stool she sat on, and she moved herself around on this by holding the sides of it with her hands and rocking it side to side or forwards and backwards, whichever way she wanted to go. You'd think as a child I'd be frightened of that, but I wasn't; I really loved the visits to her, and we'd stay and talk for hours. She always told my mother she was going to live to a great old age, and me she said I would grow up to be big and strong. A great wide smile she had and strong white teeth, I can see her now.

When I was ten I went on to another school, one that was run by the Christian Brothers. At first I hated it because I was the smallest boy there and all the others would pick on

me and knock me about. But then one day, I don't know
how it happened properly, but I fell in the river and was
nearly drowned: and for some reason this made me very
popular at school, some of the older boys treated me almost
as though I was a mascot and made a great fuss of me. I
was happy then.

When I was twelve it happened that I started getting involved with some of the other boys in the school in homosexual games, we'd go out down to the river swimming and
play about with each other afterwards. What frightened
me about it was how much I liked it and looked forward
to it even, and then afterwards I used to feel terribly
ashamed. At this time there was a girl lived near us, I think
she'd be about fourteen, and she had the reputation round
our school of being a bit of a tart. Some of the boys would
talk about her and boast about what she'd let them do, and
there was one had a photograph of her, a snapshot he'd
taken with her agreement of her lying on a rock somewhere,
pulling her skirt up and no knickers on underneath. So one
day I sent her a note to say I'd like to meet her after school
and I said in it what I'd like to do to her. A silly stupid
note, coarse like only a schoolboy can be; I gave this note to
a girl-friend of hers and asked her to give it to this girl for
me. But she didn't, she gave it to her teacher instead. There
was a terrible fuss, her teacher told my teacher, and I was
given the strap and told I was a dirty little boy. So after that
it seemed safer to confine myself to boys. Though I don't
want to suggest this was against my inclinations because it
wasn't, only that from then on I never even tried again to
interest myself in girls.

It was a great sin of course, homosexuality, I knew that.
The only person I could tell about it was God and I could
never bring myself to say it in confession to the priest, he
seemed a barrier between God and me. That was a heresy,
to think like that, and never to make what they called 'a
good confession'. Round about then we moved to live in a
different part of Dublin, a poorer part because my father's
business had failed and instead of having his own shop he
had to work as an assistant in someone else's. In my own
mind as a child I used to tell myself that one day I would
confess my sin to the new priest, only not until I got to know

him better. Meantime it was something that I kept between myself and God.

We had a period of great poverty then; I can remember I was always being told off by my father to go down to the hostel run by the St. Vincent de Paul, and ask them for a voucher for us to get clothing or food. I felt bitterly ashamed of it, and of the other things I had to do like going to see another member of the family to ask for the loan of ten bob or a pound. All in all I was very mixed up and unhappy about everything, and suddenly it came to me one day that the best thing to do would be to run away.

I went to one of my aunties I think it was, and said my mother had sent me to ask for the loan of a pound. When I got it, I went straight to the railway station and bought myself a ticket and jumped on the train for Belfast. This was after school in the afternoon, so it was dark in the evening when I got there: not knowing the place at all or where to go or what to do, and it was raining. I just wandered the streets on my own, and then I started to cry and I was sheltering in a shop doorway when a policeman came up to me and asked me what was the matter.

When I told him he took me down to the police station and gave me a cup of tea. They kept me there for the night, and in the morning they took me back to the station and put me on the train for Dublin. I think they must have phoned through to the police there to tell my parents where I was and that I was coming home again. When I got off the train in Dublin, my father was waiting for me; and he was so kind, I'd never imagined he could ever be like that. He took me back to my mother, and she was crying and she kissed me, and they both made a great fuss of me, and never an angry word from either of them.

My father made a joke of it; not long after he said I was growing up and learning to be a man, so it was time I left school and went to work. He got a job for me the next year as a store-boy in a brewery: a good job for those days, I think it was about a pound a week wages, free lunches, a new suit every year, and special night-classes you were sent to to improve your education; and when you'd passed certain exams there you automatically got promoted up in the firm.

I felt really happy then, fourteen and away from school and being treated by everyone like I was no longer a child. There was a man in the stores, he said since I was working there I ought to know what it was they were selling, and he opened a bottle for me for my first drink. By the time I was fifteen, I was helping myself to it at every opportunity, and it got to where seven or eight pints a day of it would be quite normal. There was another lad there, a boy of seventeen who drove a wagon and horses for the deliveries: he was my friend, he was my mate, and I used to wangle myself the job whenever I could of going out with him to help with the deliveries. A tall strong good-looking chap, he was very attractive to me. I liked to be with him: drink and homosexuality, those were our two main activities.

That was the year my mother died, when I was sixteen. She was taken to hospital, and she was in there for several weeks but I'd never go and see her, I didn't want to: once I got as far as the door to the ward and then I ran away, I couldn't bring myself to go in. When she died I cried; and thinking of it, I've been crying still inside me ever since, it's something I've never got over, the loss of her.

After that, I drank more. What I could get at work for free as a member of the staff wasn't enough, I had to have it after work too. My money wasn't sufficient to pay for it, so I took to helping myself from the petty cash. My father and Jake were closer than ever after she'd gone, they did nothing hardly but drink and go gambling at the horse-races together; my father became very depressed too, one night he said when he was drunk that without my mother life had no meaning, he took up a knife from the kitchen table and said he was going to cut his wrists. He didn't though, he cried instead, and Jake cried and I cried: and that was the way we lived, from scene to scene, emotional demonstration to emotional demonstration, and there was nothing any of us had for a home except this lonely place in which lived three drunken men.

When I was eighteen the brewery gave me the sack: for everything, bad time-keeping, being drunk at work, not going as I should have done to the evening-classes for the exams. I got a job then in the stores of another firm, a wholesale drapers; and it was just the same. My friend there was a man of thirty who was married; like myself he enjoyed drinking and homosexual activity and we had a very close relationship. I began to get the idea that my trouble was really religion, it was this which made me unhappy, and if I could escape from it life would be better. I had a lot of friends that I drank with who were soldiers, and one night one of them said to me 'Why don't you come into the Army Nat, that'd be the best life for you?'

So I ran away to Belfast again, only this time I knew what I was doing. I went up there and volunteered for the British Army and at the same time I went to see a Protestant priest and said I wanted to be received into the Church of Ireland, and he took me in. My father was furious when I went back and told him; and from that day to this I've never set eyes on him or my brother again.

With the Army I was sent over to England, to a big supply depot in the Midlands. There was a unit of Canadians next to our camp, and I got very friendly with some of them, one in particular a corporal called Mike and he and I became big buddies. Buddies that is for the homosexuality and drinking: one night we got pissed and were looking for somewhere to do it, and we went into a doorway of the local R.C. Church. To me that seemed the end of it then, the end of the hold of the Catholic Church over me I mean; it was almost a deliberate symbolic desecration of it, and I can remember thinking that I must have broken its hold over me for ever.

Not long after that, it'd be at the end of the war now, I was sent over to Germany with my unit, to the Rhineland. The fighting was over and it was our job to help try and tidy up the mess. For a few months, six months perhaps, the drinking seemed to decrease while I was there, perhaps because I was working hard and there was always plenty to do, and I was making myself useful in the office of one of the administrative officers answering the phone, doing clerical work and so on. In view of the responsibility I had, he upgraded me to sergeant and I really thought I was getting on, getting to be useful and able to take responsibility for a change.

But then the old drinking habits started to return. It got so bad that for days I never knew whether I was pissed or

sober: and with it came another great uprush of homosexual activity too. Anyone, anywhere, anytime; I didn't
care. I took to prowling round the dormitories at night,
watching out for the soldiers who came in drunk and then
getting into their bunks with them. Some of them were too
tight to notice, some of them kicked me out, and a few let
me stay. But one night I picked on a wrong one, and he
suddenly threw me out on to the floor and started to give
me a real beating up with his fists, shouting and screaming at
me that I was a fucking dirty little pouf and he was going
to kill me. All the lights came on, he was dragged off me
by the others and they sent for the guard. Of course I was
nowhere near where I should have been in my own quarters,
and there had to be an inquiry. Other men said I'd been
hanging round their dormitories too, and the upshot of it
was that I was reduced to corporal and sent to see a psychiatrist, who gave me some pills and recommended me for
early demobilization, and I was sent back to England.

When I came out of the Army I got myself a job in a
hostel in Yorkshire for refugees, as a sort of general super-
visor, looking after the accounts and all that. I stayed there
about six months, drinking a lot and having a series of
homosexual affairs with some of the men not far away at a
naval barracks on the coast. I was pilfering a bit, and then
one night it seemed as if the whole thing was going to blow
up in my face: there was going to be an audit of the hostel
accounts and I knew I was going to be in trouble. I waited
till everyone else had gone home and stayed on to lock up
the offices for the night. In the safe there was about three
hundred quid in notes, so I stuffed it all in my pockets and
walked out. I went on a real blinder then: Birmingham,
Newcastle, Hull, and I ended up stopping the night in a
lodging-house for seamen in Grimsby with a young seaman
I'd picked up. I gave my raincoat to the landlady for safe-
keeping, there was still about £180 in the pockets; and she
found it and straight away rang up the police. They came
round for me and arrested me in bed with this boy: of
course the hostel had reported the loss and my disappear-
ance, so they already had a pretty good idea who I was.

For that I got three months and was sent to Birmingham·
gaol. Because I was in for stealing and the place was

crowded, I wasn't kept separate as I would have been if the offence had been a sex-charge. Instead I was put three in a cell, and this suited me fine because both the other two there were by no means disinclined that way themselves. In fact I learned then what I've always known since, that prison is the ideal place for the homosexual.

When I came out I didn't know what I wanted to do, except that it must be something in all-male company; and by telling a lie or two about myself, I got back into the Army again. This was at the time of the Korean war, I don't think they were too bothered about checking up, and I was sent out there on a troopship with a unit of Canadians as a kind of liaison clerk. The first place we got to was Singapore and I wrangled myself a job as a permanent assistant in an Army reception centre, where I stopped for about a year.

I got into trouble after another incident at a mess party, importuning some of the Australians round the back of a shed in the grounds. Too drunk to know what I was doing, to be at all selective, or even careful; I used to wait round there for anybody who came out for a piss and then try and lay hands on them. So what it was finally was a charge of indecent assault because some of them complained, and I was sentenced to six months in prison in Singapore to be followed by ignominious discharge, and when I'd served my time I was sent home. Once again I didn't mind prison a bit; to be in a place where there was only men suited me fine and there were lots of opportunities for sex.

Back in England once more, thirty years old and never staying sober for longer than I could help, I got another job with a firm of wholesale caterers, and was living in a working-men's hostel down in Wimbledon. I hadn't been there long before I saw the warden's office door had been left open one night, and I walked in and helped myself to £14 and took off for Portsmouth where I wanted to try and find some sailor friends I'd known in Singapore. I don't quite remember the details of it now, but I know I suddenly came to my senses in the early hours of the morning on the sea-front at Southsea. I looked at the sea and thought that what I ought to do was just go down and walk out into it until I drowned; but instead I went back into the town and

walked into the first police station I saw. Another three
months, in Winchester this time; and once again I didn't
mind.

After coming out from that I got a job in Hull at a seaman's hostel, where I had everything I wanted – somewhere
to live, work with an all-male community, and plenty of
opportunity in the evening for drinking in the club bar with
the boys. The only trouble was that when the place was
closed for the night I'd be hanging around outside trying to
find one or other of them who'd come back to my place with
me for the night, and eventually someone complained. This
time it was four months for importuning.

As soon as I'd done that, it was back to exactly the same
sort of life, hanging round pubs looking for drink and men,
staying with anyone who'd have me for a night. Until one
man I approached in a gent's lavatory took his card out of
his pocket and said 'All right you, come on, you've tried
the wrong feller this time, I'm C.I.D.' Sometimes men'll say
that to you and you never know whether they are or not:
they'll walk you out and along the pavement and then
they'll suddenly burst out laughing and tell you they were
pulling your leg or trying to scare you off. But this man
wasn't, he was C.I.D. all right, and he took me into the
local station and booked me. In view of my previous record
I got a long sentence: three years.

I didn't mind at all you know: I'd been inside three times
before for short ones, and the way I looked on it was that
I was only going back to where I was happy; before I'd
been you might say only temporarily there, but now I was
going back on the permanent staff. When the judge gave
me the sentence he thought it was a punishment: but I said
'Thank you, sir'. After all he was doing me a favour. I
hadn't been long inside before I wangled myself a job
assisting one of the screws who was the same way as I was;
we made a happy pair in our work, which was supervising
the baths.

—In that three years my problems seemed to be sorting
themselves out a bit. I could get no booze, so that took
care of that one; I was in a place where the company was
congenial, all male, and where homosexuality was not only

possible but within a certain group was actually welcomed. So all that was left me to think about was religion. Although I'd given up the Roman Church, there's something about being a Catholic that never leaves you; I began to feel the pull of it again calling me back. For a while I took up painting in prison: I'd never painted before and I wasn't very good at it. But more and more I found myself trying to do representations of the Crucifixion, the Agony in the Garden and so on, and in a way this seemed to be helping me to sort things out in my own mind.

There was a priest used to come into the prison; we had long talks, and I started to get something approaching peace of mind, accepting myself for what I was – a homosexual, but believing that if I could only make my peace with God about religion as well, I would be all right. When I came out I went to live in a hostel for ex-prisoners, and the people who ran it encouraged me to go and try treatment as an out-patient at a psychiatric clinic. Because my previous experience of psychiatry had been in the army, being given pills to subdue my sexual instincts, I wasn't very hopeful of treatment, but all the same I decided I would give it another try.

The clinic's approach was that you went for talking sessions twice a week, and they tried to help you understand your own problems by discussing them. The two that seemed to be the major ones were homosexuality and religion. I hated the treatment in fact, because at that stage in my life I didn't really want to discuss things with anyone: after every session I used to go straight into the first pub and have a few drinks to wash the taste of queerdom and Catholicism out of my mouth.

After a few months the therapist said that he thought homosexuality was something I would have to try to reconcile myself to. I'd probably never change, but I might learn to live with it and find a way of leading my life that wouldn't inevitably lead to me getting into trouble for it. As for the religious side, he said he felt this could be better dealt with by a Catholic theologian, so after a time he passed me on to a Jesuit psychologist who ran a psychiatric clinic attached to a church in south London.

I went to this man feeling I'd made a bit of progress.

But if I had, he very soon disabused me of that idea. He said the most important thing of all was for me to become a true practising Catholic again, this was my only hope of salvation – and that it could never happen so long as I went on being a homosexual. 'All you are really,' he said, 'is not a homosexual at all, but just a dirty little boy.' Every time I saw him he hammered away at this theme, telling me to repent and give up my 'unnatural' practices and come back into the Roman Church, otherwise I'd suffer eternal damnation.

He so upset me and put me off that I ran away, I literally ran away from his church one night after seeing him, and instead of going back to the ex-prisoner's hostel I hitchhiked a lift off a lorry driver and went up to the Midlands, where I lived rough for a few days. All I could think of was that I wasn't ever going anywhere near the Catholic church again, and it seemed to me that I was never ever going to be able to sort my life out at all. I'd thought while I was in prison that this time when I came out I was going to be able to find shelter in the Church; and all I got when I turned to it was the promise of hell-fire.

I got myself a job in a club as a barman, found digs, and decided that from then on I was going to settle down and lead my own life without turning to anyone, priest or psychiatrist, for help. What friends and acquaintances I had were mostly down in the south, so I just cut myself off from them and made up my mind that I was going to lead a completely new life and become a new person.

I didn't, of course: I was the same person leading the same life, and only the surroundings were different. It's hard for me to recall many details of that fourteen-month period at all. Looking back on it now it just seems to have been one continuous orgy of drinking and importuning, and the fact that I wasn't arrested and sent back to prison sooner than I was can only be put down to the luck of the Irish. I had no idea who I was importuning and I didn't care when it was or where: gent's lavatories, pub bars, railway stations, even out on the streets, I was quite compulsive about it.

I used to finish work in the club about ten-thirty when the bar closed, and by then I'd always filled myself up with whisky or beer, entirely at other people's expense, because everyone asks the barman what he'll have. My only thought was to get my coat on and go out and find someone to spend the night with. I wasn't a prostitute in the sense that I was doing it for money, that never came into it at all. What I wanted was sexual contact with another man, but at the same time I was completely promiscuous, it had to be a different man every night. The excitement of it was in doing it with a stranger; and the next morning it was over, I'd no desire to continue an association with that same person at all. In the mornings I hated and despised myself in fact, and the feeling never wore off until the afternoon when I was back at work in the club and had slipped a few drinks inside of me, when once again I would be back to what I called 'normal' – half or three-quarters pissed, and on the look-out for the next attractive man.

Fourteen months as I say; and almost any night during that time I could have got myself arrested for all I knew or cared. When it did come, I was picked up by two coppers who'd been keeping watch outside a gent's lavatory and said they'd seen me going in and out of there for half an hour, approaching every man who came in. This time it was only six months, though I'd been expecting at least another three years. As soon as I came out I went straight back immediately to the same way of life. Another job in another club, different digs, but otherwise exactly the same.

To say I was hardly sober whenever I was out of prison wouldn't be far from the truth. And I could go further than that and say another thing: I didn't know or care what I was doing or where I was half the time. One Saturday morning I woke up in a hospital bed, I'd been brought in late the night before with bruises and cuts, unconscious – and I didn't know, and neither did they, what had happened to me. Was it a road accident, they said; or had somebody attacked me; or had I fallen somewhere? All they could tell me was that I'd been found in the early hours of the morning lying in the street. I've still no recollection of it myself at all, I couldn't tell you whether someone had beaten me up or what. I remember the face of the ward sister, the look she gave me when she came to my bed half-way through the morning and said, 'The X-rays show there's no bones broken so if you don't mind we'd be glad if you'd get up and go home now because we need your bed.'

They have lots like me of course, in the big general hospitals with busy casualty departments – bums, drunks, drifters, picked up from the street and brought in – and they don't like them. I just swore at her, and said it was all right, I was going anyway; and if she was part of the human race, I was glad I wasn't a member of it. Which I wasn't, true enough by then.

As soon as I'd dressed and left, it was back to my digs, and just in time to go out again for a drink before the pubs closed. It was Saturday, and the next day I spent it all in bed, then back to work as usual on the Monday morning. One of the things which I used to pride myself on was that no matter what happened to me or where I went, I could stick at my job in the day and do it well enough to keep myself going until the night. Even after an occurrence like that, I was proud of myself at being able to turn up for work again afterwards as though nothing had happened.

The other thing I was proud of was that I could arrange my day's drinking so that it didn't interfere with my work: in other words I knew exactly how much I needed to keep myself going, but I never overstepped the mark to the point where I was incapable. I had it all worked out: one drink every so often, to keep myself up to a certain pitch of unconcern; but never more than that, else it would show and I'd lose the job. Around nine or nine-thirty in the evening I'd start increasing the intake, knowing that by the time it began to take effect I'd be knocking off work and have the courage in me to go out on my nightly prowl until I found a man. A strange word, isn't it, to use for that, 'courage'? But that's what it took – courage to quell the old sense of sin in me, and to go out and offer myself up as a kind of sacrificial victim to a stranger who I didn't know whether he'd beat me or kill me or turn me in to the police or what. The rougher they were the better I liked them, and the more they attracted me. Big men, tough men, virile men; I've never been able to stand the effeminate types at all. Living dangerously, that's what I thought I was doing; and the danger of it was one of the essential parts of it, one of the parts I most enjoyed. To be bashed about, to be degraded.

to be abused: I didn't protest, I didn't try to escape them. These were the things which I sought.

And when it came to arrest or imprisonment, I really honestly didn't mind. There was nothing anyone could do to me – not man or God or judge or anyone – that I didn't in my heart feel that I deserved. It was only when somebody for the first time didn't punish me that I stopped to think; and I realized that up till that time, no punishment anyone had ever inflicted on me, whether it had been physical violence or contempt or a term in prison, had ever come anywhere near the punishment all my life I had been inflicting on myself.

I don't know how or why, suddenly at the age of forty-four, I should decide that I'd had enough. It would be nice if I could say to you that I met someone who changed my outlook, or heard a piece of music, or read a book. But life isn't like that, at least it isn't for me. To this day I still don't know why it was that when I came up in court and the magistrate asked me if I'd anything to say, instead of saying 'No' and adding under my breath 'Get on with it you old bastard, and put me back in the nick', I thought for a moment and then said 'Please sir, I'd like to be given a chance.' I know even less why on that particular morning of that particular day, that particular man should have looked straight back at me and said 'All right, I'll remand you in custody for a week for a report.'

But that's what he did; and a probation officer came down to the cells to see me and asked me what exactly I meant by being 'given a chance'. Was I hoping for probation? No I said, I wasn't. Well, what did I mean? I was hoping, I said, that I might be able to have some kind of treatment; and when he asked me what it was I wanted treatment for, I started to say 'homosexuality' and then suddenly I changed my mind.

Only then did it dawn on me: all my life, all those years, the two things that had troubled me most of all had been sex and religion, and I'd not been able to solve either of them. Now there was only one thing left to face and perhaps this after all was the one that really mattered, though it had taken me so long to realize it. 'What I really need treatment for,' I said to him, 'is for drink. I think I'm an alcoholic.'

This was the first time in my life that I'd ever said it to anyone, including myself. And as soon as I'd said it, I regretted it. I wanted to take it back with a laugh and say 'No, I'm only kidding you, really my trouble is that I'm queer. Send me to a place where they'll cure me of that.'

Because the mind of an alcoholic is a conniving one, he'll attempt to deceive people not so much because he wants to mislead them particularly, but much more because he wants to mislead himself. And if he's an Irishman, he starts off with a very bad handicap in the way he uses words. He uses them by the hundred under the guise of talking, when all the time what he's doing is just saying them and not really telling people anything at all. He's not using them to express his own thoughts, only to cover them up: so long as he's talking and making noises he's safe as a man hiding behind a water-fall.

He'll even talk endlessly about alcoholism when he has to, trying to kid everyone that so long as he can talk about it freely it must be all right, and fundamentally he's got it beat. But because he's talking so much about it, what he's really still only saying is that it's the subject which is uppermost in his mind. He'll rant and rage about it, he'll weep and cry – so that you and he can see what a struggle he's putting up against it, and how it's tearing him in half; then at the end of it inside him a voice says 'By God, that was exhausting but you got through it, and what you really need now to pull yourself together is just a little drink.' You fight it not just yesterday and today and tomorrow, but for the rest of your life; you know you're going to feel like this always, there's no release.

All my life I've been three people – Catholic Nat, homosexual Nat, and drinking Nat. The real one's been the third, and he's spent his time hiding behind the other two, letting them out to fight between them in order to see which one wins. What are you, Nat, Catholic or Protestant: what are you, Nat, heterosexual or queer? Solve those, Nat, and you'll find an answer for yourself for life. Stand up now bravely, and say what you are: that's the way he puts it, the treacherous sod.

A drinking Irishman, you see, well that's normal isn't it, everyone knows that all Irishmen drink? That's what the

man said to me at the brewery when I went there to work:
'You might as well know what it is you're selling.' And a
Catholic Irishman, that's normal too, everyone expects that.
So the abnormal one was the queer; and if the Church
wouldn't accept that, then change the Church, become a
Protestant. But that in its turn to the born Catholic who
can't get away from his birthright is sin. Being queer is a
sin, denying the faith is a sin. The only thing that isn't sinful
is drinking: that's not sinful, it's manly, all true Irishmen
do it.

Being small all my life, the drink helped there too, it made
me feel bigger and stronger. That's the theme they always
plug in the adverts on the telly, don't they, that drink's
something for men? And all my life I've doubted if I was a
man, I've doubted if I was a Catholic: the only thing I've
never doubted was that the solution lay in forgetting it all
in a good drink. And it worked, over and over I proved
that it did: it made me stop caring, it made me feel brave.
I'm drunk, you see, even as I talk to you now, I talk as
though I was drunk don't I, rambling about from one subject to another, spinning it all out in this never-stopping
flow of words. But now I realize this: that I don't have to
drink to be drunk, that I act and think like a drunk person
without ever touching a drop. Alcoholism is a permanent
state of suffering from an incurable disease.

*   *   *

Weeping and gasping, endlessly talking and grasping for
words to explain, chain-smoking and gulping cup after cup
of tea, Nat Burke with his collar awry and his clenched
hands trembling like shot-down birds in his lap, tried to
make sense of the appalling meaningless agony he'd had for
a life, and to find in it something worth saying. Out of himself he tried; to dredge statements that came not as reactions to what someone else had said, but only after long
silences, self-inflicted, hard as hammer-blows.

—I accept now that I'm homosexual; but I don't go out
trying to prove or disprove it any more. I live with a chap
and we're beginning to have a relationship that's not just
only a sexual one. I don't know whether it'll last or not;

but this is the first time I've ever been prepared to consider staying with one person. I accept too that I'm probably a Catholic for life, and will remain so even if I'm not a very good one. These are things I don't argue with myself about any more, or expect someone else to decide for me.

Always, you see, before this I've had to be told; and I've been content to leave it like that, to put myself in someone's charge. When I was a kid, my mother said I was sickly but she would look after me and I never questioned that. The time I ran away, the police took care of me in Belfast and sent me home; Millie the fortune-teller told me that what I tried to do didn't really matter, everything had already been decided by Fate. When I was sent to prison, that was the same thing again; and when I picked up a man, what I was doing was letting him decide what should be done with me.

Right up to that last time, when the magistrate said the probation officer had made arrangements for me to go to an alcoholic unit, still there was somebody else in charge. And when I got there, the first question I asked them was 'What are you going to do with me?' And the answer, which I didn't believe when I first heard it, was 'Nothing: if anyone's going to do anything for you, it's going to be yourself.'

And to be faced with the prospect of trying to do something for yourself, when the only quality you've got in any way developed is cowardice – that's the most terrible thing of all. You're put in with a group of others and you live together day and night, and all there is to do is talk. And at first it's bloody infuriating, because no one'll listen to you; as soon as you start about yourself, they say 'Oh fuck that mate, I've got problems of my own' – and they want you to listen to them. So everybody hates each other, everybody thinks everyone else is a thoroughly selfish bastard who's so wrapped up in his own problems that he can't think about anyone else but himself at all.

And that's when it strikes you, when you see how self-centred they all are, how preoccupied they are with their own miseries and unable to think about anyone else: that's when it strikes you for the first time that you're exactly the same. You're not different, you're one of them; and you see at last what being an alcoholic means. Bank managers, architects, bus-drivers, layabouts, you: you're all the same. This thing has got you all beaten: where you've been, where you've come from, what you've done – it doesn't matter any more. You're here for one reason and one reason only: the drink has got you beat.

When I was there I wasn't different from everyone because I was queer or Catholic or anything else; that didn't matter. I wasn't different because I'd had less education than that man, or unlike the other man I could work if I wanted to and get myself a living. I wasn't different because I was forty-four or five feet tall or had brown eyes or was in love with my mother. I was one of a group of people who however different they were in their stories or their outward appearances were fundamentally all the same.

I stayed there six months nearly, and all that time no one ever told me I shouldn't drink, in fact like everyone else I was free to go out and have a drink whenever I wanted. But somehow you got into the habit of instead of going out for a drink when you were depressed or worried or uneasy, you talked to somebody else about it instead. And maybe that particular night the idea wasn't troubling him too much and he'd listen to you while you talked; and on you'd go until you'd said all there was to say and you'd tired yourself out with it and all you wanted to do then was go to bed because you couldn't be bothered to do anything else. A night or two later, and it'd be your own turn to listen to somebody else.

Of course there were slips, what we call 'skids': someone would actually do it, instead of talking about it they'd slip out and go and get themselves drunk. When they came back they'd be cursing and blinding, blaming everyone for not stopping them or for not coming to fetch them back out of the pub, for not caring, for not looking after them, for anything they could think of: all alcoholics are the same, they'll blame everyone but themselves when they fall.

While I was there, I was one of the lucky ones; somehow or other on the nights when it was bad for me, there was always someone around to talk to. After four months I started going out to work, and just going back to the unit

to sleep at night; another two months after that and I felt
well enough to ask to be discharged.

Cured? No, I could never say that: I'm not cured and I
never will be, and perhaps one day before long I'll have
to face up to the fact that I ought to go back. I know I'll
never win; I've had four skids myself since I left. I have to
try and accept that progress was last Tuesday when I got
through a bad day; last Saturday when I got through another; and sitting here now waiting for the next, and saying
to myself will I get through that one when it comes. Day
by day you live with it, and night by night, and no one
who's not been on the journey could ever really understand.
But you don't ask them to, you don't have to make them,
it isn't so important any more. Only the alcoholic knows.

There was an old man there on the unit the same time as
I was. I don't know his name or what he'd been; all I know
is that he used to be a Catholic much the same as me, and
we'd talk for hours about it and what it meant. When I was
leaving he said he'd got a present for me; and he took out a
piece of paper and pressed it in my hand. Just these two
words on it, 'Via Dolorosa'; and I've kept it with me ever
since.

And that's all I can say; that life's painful, it's bloody
awful, and mine certainly so far has had no dignity or sense.
But it's mine, and I have to look at it as it has been: I lived it
and I'm still living it, and it's all I've got to live. Maybe you'll
find it in you to look at it with contempt or with compassion; perhaps I've got to learn to look at it with one of
those two myself. But I'm not asking you this, I'm asking
myself – which?

Marriage Brings Problems

Harry Mills

Each summer evening twice a week he timed his arrival to coincide precisely with the striking of the clock on St. Hilda's Church as it was chiming eight away over on the opposite side of the deserted square. He would come in from the street and stride purposefully up the stairs, rap firmly on the door, and then push it open tentatively and enter with a hesitant smile and a hand extended in greeting, shyly proud of the small triumph of this exactitude.

—Hear that, well I've managed to make it right on the dot again haven't I? I like to be prompt for appointments whenever I possibly can, I think it's most essential people should be reliable over matters like that you know. Another lovely evening isn't it, and how are things with you? Good, oh yes I'm fine myself thanks, fine. Still a bit tired I must confess, it always takes me a little while to get used to the night shift: somehow I don't seem able to get off to sleep in the mornings properly you know, when I get back to my room. But my goodness when it comes round to six o'clock in the evening and I ought to be getting up, it's the exact opposite then, I feel I could go on sleeping for hours! I think it's only a question of practice though don't you, finding the rhythm of it again? After all I've been a night worker most of my life haven't I, most of my life, it's not as though I've not experienced it before. Shall I sit in my usual chair then here? Well yes now let me see: how far did we get exactly, last time?

*   *   *

His raincoat folded neatly and laid carefully over the back of another chair, he twitched-up the knees of his trousers to

preserve their creases; folded his hands in his lap and
blinked his eyes behind his horn-rimmed glasses, crossing
one leg over the other and raising his foot, tilting his head
slowly from side to side as he stared concentratedly at the
toe-caps of his meticulously shined brown shoes. A tall,
handsome man with neatly parted curly black hair, a long
thin face and a pointed chin; straight backed in a smart
green tweed sports-jacket and grey flannels. His voice was
quiet, restrained, firm; the dignity and deliberation of his
speech never varied, however faraway the pained and puz-
zled look that came often into his eyes.

And every evening when he had finished talking and it
was time for him to get off to the bakery where he worked,
shaking hands again Harry Mills always said, politely and
calmly, the same thing.

—If I'm not here on the dot anytime, you mustn't bother
waiting for me will you? You'll guess what's happened, and
where I shall most likely be; and if that's so, I'll drop you a
line as soon as I possibly can.

	Age			Charges
1942	20	Conditional discharge	(2)	Sent to mental hospital
1943	21	1 month's imprisonment	(3)	
1944	22	3 month's imprisonment	(4)	
1945	23	6 month's imprisonment	(7)	Broken engagement
1946	24	6 month's imprisonment	(4)	Attempted suicide
1947	25	3 years' imprisonment	(10)	
1948	26	—		
1949	27	—		
1950	28	Fined	(4)	
1951	29	Conditional discharge	(6)	Sent to mental hospital
1952	30	—		
1953	31	18 month's imprisonment	(11)	Broken engagement
1954	32	7 days' imprisonment	(1)	
1955	33	1 months' imprisonment	(2)	
1956	34	12 month's imprisonment	(3)	Attempted suicide
1957	35	Conditional discharge	(6)	Sent to mental hospital
1958	36	—		
1959	37	Fined	(1)	

1960	38	12 months' imprisonment	(16)	Broken engagement
1961	39	3 months' imprisonment	(2)	
1962	40	4 month's imprisonment	(4)	
1963	41	Fined	(3)	Attempted suicide
1964	42	Conditional discharge	(5)	Sent to mental hospital
1965	43	—		
1966	44	6 months' imprisonment	(11)	
1967	45	3 months' imprisonment	(7)	
		(Total: 9 years, 3 months)	(Total: 112 charges)	

—She used to gad about with a lot of men, my mother did, a great lot of men. When she was young she must have been very pretty you know, very striking looking, always rather tall she was, and with long dark hair and brown eyes. Most of her life when she worked it was as a domestic servant in hotels, a chambermaid, that sort of thing. There was something in her of a wandering disposition, though; she never stayed for very long in the same place. Her mother and father, my grandparents, they were not like that at all: a respectable working-class couple they were, and they lived near Salisbury. I think he was a carpenter or something of that kind, and I lived most of the time with them after I was born: my mother didn't want me, I didn't fit in with the sort of life she wanted to lead.

Though there were times I was with her, there must have been because I can remember some of them. Exactly where or when or for how long I don't know. The only recollection I do have clearly is of her once taking me out shopping and keeping on telling me to hurry up, because I wouldn't keep pace with her. I was all the time stopping to look at things in shop windows you know, until eventually she said she wasn't going to wait any longer and off she went and walked on round the corner. When I got there I couldn't see her, there was only this street full of people; and I remember I kept running up and down it, crying because I was lost.

Somebody took me to a police station and they were all asking me who I was and where I lived and of course I didn't know. All I could tell them was that my name was Harry, but nothing else apart from that. They must have got me back to her eventually, but I don't remember the details of how; only the feeling of being lost and frightened in the street, I've never forgotten that. Then the next thing I remember is being in hospital; again I don't remember what for or how long I'd been there. When I left a lady came for me in a car and I didn't want to go with her because I liked being at the hospital, all the nurses were very kind and made a fuss of me, and I kept saying 'I don't want to go home, I want to stay here, please don't make me go home.'

The lady in the car was what would be called a Child Care Officer nowadays I suppose: anyway, she explained to me that I was going to be looked after by someone else who was going to take full responsibility for me and I needn't go back to my mother any more. Being put into care that would be called, wouldn't it? I was too young then to realize what it all meant of course, but from little bits I've been able to discover about it since my mother had never bothered to have much to do with me and she'd more or less left me to my grandparents to look after. They were quite elderly people; apparently there'd been lots of rows between them and her and she'd taken me from time to time to live in different places with her for a while but had got fed up with me, until eventually the whole thing came to a head and the local authority took over.

I did hear once some years ago my mother was living as a sort of housekeeper with quite a well-known politician, but I don't know whether that's true or not. I've not seen much of her since I was small: a few times when I was fifteen, once in my twenties, and the last occasion would be about six or seven years ago. I don't love her at all and I don't think she can ever have loved me: whatever way of life she chose to follow, having a child certainly didn't fit in with it. She always wanted her independence, she's never been married for instance although I understand she's lived with several men.

For a very long time I'd no idea at all who my father was, but fortunately just at the period when it might have started to worry me I was taken by the lady Child Care Officer to live in this big children's home in Hertfordshire. There were about a hundred and twenty other boys there all like myself who came from broken-up homes: everyone would be more or less in the same boat as far as not having one or other parent was concerned. So I didn't think myself very much different to anyone else; and the other boys didn't question you about your own background or where you came from, because they were in the same sort of situation as you.

I stayed there from when I was six until when I was nearly sixteen. It was a private foundation run along Church of England lines, and fees were paid I suppose by grants from the local authority. I understand the only qualification to get into it was need, and there was always a pretty long waiting list so I gather my own situation must have been considered quite a needy one in order for me to be given a place.

Nearly all my childhood recollections consist of there. I can remember the first sight of the house when we got to it, like a great big country mansion with an enormous gravelled drive curving across the front, and at the side there were low stone railings looking out over a sort of sunken rose-garden with old walls round it and a big pond with water-lilies in the middle. The sun was shining, there seemed to be mile after mile of lawns and trees, and inside there were polished wooden floors and staircases, big rooms with french-windows, and lots of sofas and chairs with bright cushions and covers on. I was quite sure it must be some kind of palace: I couldn't really believe I was going to be allowed to live there.

As well as being such a lovely place, it was also one of the best-run children's homes in the country in those days. The staff were chosen not only for their ability as teachers but also for their skill at dealing with the problems of young boys from deprived backgrounds. There was very great and constant friendship between the children and the staff. Everybody was on Christian name terms, and they took a real interest in you and tried to help you in every way they could, not only in lessons but at all other times too. They made a feature of discussions and debates about all sorts of subjects – sports, politics, religion, everything you can think of – and the emphasis all the time was on getting you to think things out for yourself and do them not because you were told to, but because you could see for yourself they were right.

Naturally a place like that had to have a very remarkable headmaster; and it did have one nearly all the time I was there. I think it was about a year or so after I went there that he came, and he was still headmaster when I left, though I should think he's certainly retired by now. His name was, well we all called him by his Christian name which was Tom: nobody ever called the staff 'Sir' or 'Mr.' or anything like that because you looked upon them as your friends, which is what they were.

Such a thing as crime, even petty crime like stealing or not telling the truth, well it never existed in that place. I don't think it ever crossed our minds there was any other way to behave than the right one. For instance once at morning assembly after prayers Tom said there'd been a window broken in one of the back kitchens the night before, and he said 'Nobody's been to tell the cook yet that they did it. Would the boy responsible please hold up his hand?' And straightaway, you know, the boy stepped forward and put his hand up.

Another time I got into trouble myself once, for some very trivial thing like talking after lights out in the dormitory, and doing it about three or four nights in succession until eventually one of the monitors reported me to the Head. Tom took me into his study and said I knew very well we weren't supposed to talk after lights-out, and if I went on doing it the only punishment he could give me was the cane. And he said he wouldn't like to have to do that, it would embarrass him very much, so he'd be very grateful if I'd do as I was told from then on. Which of course I did.

I suppose you could almost make that a criticism of the place; it didn't properly prepare you for what the outside world was going to be like, and when you left you found things could be very different from what you'd been brought up to. People did want to hurt you if they could for instance, and they'd be looking for an excuse to do it rather than for one not to. The other thing that was wrong with it as I see it now, was that it was for boys only, and I think it would have been better to have girls there as well. Certainly in my own case I've had great difficulty in getting on with them and felt shy of them for years, which I think perhaps I wouldn't have been if I'd had more contact with them when I was young.

But I don't want to criticize the place really, because I'm sure no one could ever have had a better upbringing in any other children's home, and there were all sorts of advantages I got from it which have remained with me all my life. Liking music, to give one example: we had a master there called Nick, who was very fond of playing the piano; about once a week on Saturday or Sunday evenings he'd give a recital in the hall that anyone could go and sit listening to if they felt like it. Bach, Brahms, Mozart, Beethoven, it was always good music of that kind; I got a great deal of pleasure out of it then, and I still do even though I've never been able to play a note myself.

Though I won't pretend it was a perfect life there; obviously it wasn't, because whatever they did for you and however hard they tried to make up for what you didn't have, it still couldn't be the same as a normal home background, could it? Every so often you were bound to feel lonely, and conscious of the fact that you were different from most other children. As I got older I became more and more aware of it; that I had no proper home, no parents to come and visit me, I didn't seem to belong in the world. It was then that I first got into my habit of going out for long walks on my own, all round the countryside, walking and walking, and feeling restless and unsure of who I was or where I fitted in.

One night, I suppose it couldn't have been long before I reached the age when I was going to leave, Matron was doing her nightly round of the dormitories and I remember she found me kneeling up at the end of my bed, looking out of the window into the dark. She asked me what I was doing, and I told her I was trying to imagine what life was going to be like outside, and looking at the stars in the sky and trying to puzzle out what life was all about. A few mornings later Tom brought this subject up at the end of morning assembly; he said Matron had told him she'd found one of the older boys looking out of the window at night and wondering what life was all about. Of course he didn't mention my name or give any clue as to who it was, but he said he thought it was a question everyone there ought to think about for themselves. He said 'I'm going to think about it too, I'm over fifty myself and I must admit I still don't know the answer to it either.'

Well when I was almost sixteen, I had to leave the home. I was put to live in a hostel up in London and found a job in a hotel, a sort of bell-boy and general porter. I think it was chosen because it was a sort of living-in job so it settled the problem of both work and accommodation at one go. I might have been all right there, I think, if I hadn't been so – I think the word's institutionalized – by living so long in the home. But I was, I found myself not able to make friends or even talk to anyone very much; it was a very lonely life for a boy so young.

After about a year there I got into trouble; I was taken to court for stealing a radio set. It was quite true that I had stolen it, three or fours months before, out of one of the guest's bedrooms in the hotel. I knew it was wrong to steal, so I've no excuse to make really. Only it hadn't been to sell, I'd no intentions of that sort, I'd taken it more or less for company in my own room at night; but one time when the manager came in to tell me about something, he spotted it and remembered the complaint there'd been. I believe the guest it belonged to insisted on it being reported to the police; anyway as I say I was taken to court. The circumstances were explained, who I was and where I'd been brought up and so on, and the court took a lenient view. I think I was bound over to be of good behaviour for twelve months or so.

The much worse part of it was when they read out the details about me in court. I knew I was illegitimate of course, I'd been aware of that since I was little; it'd gradually dawned on me while I was at the home that like a lot of the other boys there I had a mother who wasn't married, and I didn't have a father. What I hadn't realized though, until that day when I heard it said in court, was that my father had been my mother's brother: I wasn't just a bastard, I was the result of an incestuous union too.

—Not long after all that court business I left the job in the hotel and went to live with my grandparents again in Salisbury, and I got a job in a local hotel working in the kitchen. But living with them wasn't very satisfactory, they'd only a very small house and after a few weeks I moved out into digs on my own. Still a very solitary sort of character I was, but I did manage to get myself a friend who I went out with a few times. One of the chambermaids in the hotel, a few years older than me and from what I remember of her quite a nice girl. There was nothing serious between us though of course at that age, it was more for companionship than anything.

After a time I heard that my mother had come down to my grandparents' for a holiday, so I went to see her. What I wanted to do was ask her about my birth, if what had been said about me in court was correct. When I tried she was very abrupt, she said of course it wasn't true and wouldn't talk about it. Though later on after she'd gone out of the house for a while, when I asked my grandma about it she didn't contradict it at all; and she just started crying and said it'd be better if we didn't discuss it. So I've always taken it since as being true.

A few days after I'd tried to have the talk with my mother I took my friend along to my grandparents' house to introduce her to them. My mother was still there, and she and this girl didn't hit it off together. There was a bit of an argument, though I can't remember what it was about now. Anyway it meant I couldn't take her there again, and not long after she got another job somewhere else so I didn't see her any more. I felt very lonely after that, and I got in touch with the home who'd brought me up to ask them if they could help me find work in London again. They arranged for me to go and live at a Church Army hostel and be trained as a baker. I liked that, I liked that very much; I think it's a good way of making a living for a young boy to learn, and certainly the training they gave me was good. Altogether I should think it was just over three years I was there learning; and in fact when I was called up in 1941 I was taken into the Catering Corps in the same trade.

After the six weeks or whatever it was everybody had to go through of square-bashing to start off with, I was sent up to Yorkshire and worked in the camp bakery there. It was all right, but the big disadvantage from my point of view was that the work was divided into three shifts and I was put on the early one; I think it was from six in the morning until two in the afternoon and it meant that I had a great lot of time on my hands during the day after I'd finished work.

It was there that I first started my walking about round the town and so on, and getting into trouble. It all came to a head when there was a complaint from the wife of one of the captains in my own unit, and the result was I was put in front of the local magistrates court on two charges. They gave me a discharge on condition I went to an Army mental hospital in Birmingham.

When I got there the doctors said there was no reason why I shouldn't go on working, I wasn't physically unfit or anything like that, so they gave me a job in the bakery while they treated me. Unfortunately the hours I worked were exactly the same as I'd been doing at the camp in Yorkshire, so I still found myself with a lot of time on my hands for walking around and I was constantly getting into trouble even while I was a patient at the hospital. The treatment they gave me consisted mainly of different kinds of pills: they'd try one sort for a fortnight, then try another sort and so on; but none of them seemed to make much difference.

In the end however they said I was all right, though I could have told them myself that I wasn't. I was re-posted to another unit over in Northern Ireland, and there I was put in charge of the catering for the officers' mess. The work was hard and the hours were very long, so I spent most of my time on the camp either working or sleeping, and I kept out of trouble completely for about at least six months.

Then I was transferred again, to another unit down in Dorset, from where I was supposed to be going overseas, I think it was to the Middle East. Most of the time there seemed to be spent waiting and hanging about with nothing much to do, and before long I was in trouble again through my usual walking about, and this time I got a month's imprisonment for it. After that I was considered not suitable for sending abroad, and I was shuttled around between various camps and units for the next twelve months at a loose end until I ended up in prison again, this time for three months.

It wasn't until towards the end of the war in 1945 that I got much chance of settling down anywhere for very long. Then I got a fairly permanent billet at a camp in Sussex, on the coast near an anti-aircraft battery where there was a unit of A.T.S. girls. We used to mix quite a lot in the canteens and soldiers' clubs and so on, and I fell rather heavily for one of these girls who came from Scotland and was called Jeannie. We went out a bit together, and we seemed to get on very well; she was a quiet sort of person like myself and after a time I asked her if she'd like to get married when the war was over and she said yes she would, so we got engaged. Then almost immediately she was posted somewhere else; that sort of thing often happened in those days of course, but it upset me because she was more or less the only friend I had. Anyway, there it was: she went off to the East Coast right up into Northumberland, and for several months we got no opportunity of seeing each other at all.

So of course I got into my usual trouble again, and this time it was six months' imprisonment. I felt it was no use pretending to Jeannie, I'd better tell her all about myself. I wrote her a letter telling her everything, that this was the third time I'd been in prison and what for and all the rest of it – and I thought she might as well know the full story, so I told her about my birth too, who my parents were, everything. I got a letter back to say she was sorry but she didn't feel that she could possibly marry me. At the time I took it very hard indeed, because I did have the faint hope that she might just possibly react differently. Anyway, she didn't; she said she thought a marriage would be nothing without children, and obviously we'd never be able to have any, so she didn't see any point in going on with it.

When I came out of prison I was still in the Army, and I was sent then to a unit in Gloucester, but this time not as a baker. Instead I was put on a kind of toughening-up course, cross-country running, climbing up and down barricades, crossing rivers on ropes and that sort of thing, almost like a commando-training it was. I was very physically fit, I'd be twenty-three or twenty-four then I should think, but I never

really felt I'd make a very good commando, I'd much
sooner be making cakes; and before long I got off that and
back into my own trade again. Then I was demobilized,
and once more I went to live in Salisbury. My first job
there was in a shop, a kind of café and pastry-cooks combined; but once again there was the same old trouble with
shift work, starting first thing in the morning and finishing
early in the afternoon, and then having nothing else to do
for the rest of the day but walk about. My grandparents
were getting on in age and I couldn't go and see them too
often, and I was living my usual lonely sort of life in digs.
Eventually I was arrested again of course, and by that stage
I was getting pretty desperate about myself. While I was on
remand it suddenly came over me that the best thing to do
would be to put an end to it all, so that night in my cell I
tied one end of my tie to the window bars, stood on a chair
and knotted the other end round my throat as tight as I
could, and then jumped off.

I don't know what happened, I think when you try and
strangle yourself you make a lot of noise while you're chok-
ing: anyway somebody came in and cut me down, so it
didn't work; instead I got another six months' sentence. I
served that one I think it was in Winchester; and almost as
soon as I came out I started my walking about, it was only
a week or two before I was arrested again. This time it was
quite serious because there was an assault charge in it as
well: a lady hit me on the head with her umbrella, and she
kept on hitting me and hitting me in a corner, until eventually I hit back and in fact I knocked her down.

The police took a very serious view of that indeed; I was
charged with more or less everything they could think of,
and the outcome of it all was that I got a really stiff sentence
of three years. In a way, perhaps this is hard for you to
believe, but I felt a certain kind of relief, you know: I was
going to be in prison for two years even with remission, and
I knew that meant two years of peace and quiet with no
possibility of trouble at all. Once you make your mind up,
that there's no alternative to it, in a way you do feel relieved; you know that for a certain time at least your
worries have been taken off your shoulders for you. And
while you're serving the sentence you get the feeling too

sometimes, that if you can live nice and quietly in there and not be any trouble to anyone, then surely you can do the same when you get out, and everything seems very simple to you.

When I came out I thought I'd be all right to try London again, so I came and lived up in the East End and worked once more in a bakery, this time for quite a big firm. The first few months passed off quite well, I thought perhaps being in prison for so long had quietened me down. But it was not to be, my trouble started again and I was as bad as ever over the next couple of years, though I did manage to stick in my job. In 1951, well obviously it couldn't go on and when I was next charged they decided they'd have another go at trying treatment for me. I was discharged on condition that I went as a voluntary patient into a mental hospital in Buckinghamshire. I stayed there a year, it must have been at least a year. I was given what they call 'aversion therapy', electric shocks and all the rest of it. It seemed to work, on the whole I think you could say it was a success, and I was discharged as cured towards the end of 1952.

Then I went to live for a while in Oxfordshire, round that part of the world; I got a job at one of the motor-car factories as cook in the canteen, and all went fairly well again. In my spare time I joined a club connected with old people's welfare, doing a bit of catering for them. It was while I was there that I eventually got engaged for the second time, to a girl called Joyce who I met there at the old people's club. She was rather like me, in some ways our backgrounds had been the same because she'd been brought up in an orphanage too. I had hopes that if I could really settle down and get a bit of money behind me we might make a go of things together. But that didn't work out either; after a few months she said her feelings had changed and she wanted to break it off. I rather got the impression there was someone else in the picture; however, there it was, whatever the reason she didn't want to go ahead.

I stopped going to the old people's club and I did what I've done before, came up to London and looked for another job. I think at that time I had quite a series of jobs of one kind or another, mostly connected with bakery work. In between times I was getting into a lot of trouble, a great deal of trouble through walking about round different places. I went back to prison two or three times and everything seemed to be falling to pieces again, until it reached the stage in 1956 when I had another try at finishing it all. I'd been to the doctor for some pills to help me sleep, and one weekend I took a Green Line bus right out into the country, and went into a wood and sat down in a clearing and took the whole lot. I said a few simple prayers first and I can remember feeling very calm and peaceful about the whole business, not a bit frightened but in a way rather happy and relieved. I was right in the middle of this wood on my own, it was a beautiful sunny day, and I know I was thinking as I got drowsier and drowsier that this was the perfect way to die.

I was really very surprised when I woke up in hospital and discovered I wasn't dead after all. Apparently there'd been a man taking his dog out for a walk through the woods; this dog had found me and the man had sent for assistance, an ambulance and all the rest of it. One of the doctors who came round to see me in the hospital asked me if I believed in God: when I said yes I did, he told me the way to look at it was that God must have decided He didn't want me to die yet because there were still things for me to do. When it's put to you like that, it seems a reasonable sort of argument, I think. A few months later when I was in my usual trouble again, I asked the court if I could have another try myself at being treated for it.

This time it was a big hospital in Surrey that I was sent to. Their method was to give you drugs and medicine to keep you calm, and encourage you to join in group discussions and that sort of thing. They also gave you Pentathol quite a lot, that's an injection to help you talk about yourself to a psychiatrist. It was a very nice hospital, you were given a lot of freedom so long as you behaved yourself and co-operated with them. I'm afraid I didn't behave as well as I might have done, though; I used to go out walking about from there while I was still having treatment, with the result that for a period I was put in a maximum security ward where you're locked in and get no privileges at all. I had to stay there for about two months, to be taught a lesson I suppose would be the idea of it, and then I was let back on to the open ward.

When I was discharged from the hospital I tried living and working up in London again: I got a room in Cricklewood and had a fairly good job in another bakery. I met a nice girl and went out a lot with her, pictures and so on, and once more I felt things might be looking up if only I could get myself settled. Her name was Peggy, she came from a nice family, I really thought the world of her I did, you know. I told her about being illegitimate and she didn't seem to mind that; and then I took my courage in both hands and told her about who my father and mother were as well – and she seemed to take that in her stride too. When I asked her if she'd consider marrying me despite all that, she said she would, and the week after that we bought an engagement ring.

There was only one thing left to get over then; so one night I invited her back to my room and made a little meal for her, and after it I said 'There's still something else I've got to tell you, which is that I've been to prison nine or ten times.' I told her about the mental hospitals too and all the rest; and she said of course it made the whole thing different. Most of all she said what she resented was the fact that I'd been deceiving her, I ought to have told her long before we decided on being engaged. In the end she got really angry, she pulled off her engagement ring there and then and put it on the table and walked out.

This would be about 1960 now; and from then on things seemed to go steadily from bad to worse over the next four years. I was in a lot of trouble all over the place, in and out of prison, a whole succession of different jobs: it ended up with me taking another overdose of pills and being found unconscious in my room by the landlord who'd come round to see why I hadn't paid the rent. So it was into hospital again, out for a bit, and then after that back to the mental hospital, altogether for about twelve or fifteen months.

Since then I'm afraid the pattern's gone on pretty much the same. If you look back on it over my record, for the last twenty-five years or so I never seem able to have kept out of trouble for very long. Every single year, almost, there's been something. Now I'm forty-six and that's getting on isn't it? I suppose the only way in which you could say things have changed is that six months ago I got married.

Whether it'll work or not, I don't know: for someone like me it's bound to happen that marriage brings problems, really quite big ones.

—No one knows what to do with me; I have to accept that as a fact. I suppose it's a matter really of keep hoping, isn't it, try this and that and then perhaps one day something'll work, it'll die down, there'll be no more trouble. People say it's up to you to make an effort, and I think that's true, I do, there's a lot in that. But I don't think people know how much effort I have made, over the years; time after time, and for each occasion when I've failed, there's been perhaps half a dozen or more times when I've succeeded and stopped myself. They don't know about those of course, they only know about the failures there's been.

Up to now I think I've had every possible treatment that there is: imprisonment, drugs, aversion therapy, group therapy, psycho-therapy – whatever you can think of, you name it and I've had it. And they all work for a time. Imprisonment's a success, it puts me out of harm's way for a while; but apart from that aspect of it I can't see it does much good really. It certainly doesn't alter my character or disposition in any way, and if there's anything in the idea of deterrence, I should think that's long lost any relevance it might possibly have had. I don't even consider it now; I don't think 'Oh I might go to prison' or worry about being caught. It never comes into it, when I'm walking about such thoughts no longer even enter my head.

The mental hospitals are good, they work too, they do a lot for me. But it's only while I'm there; and then as soon as I come out the effect wears off. This one I've been to the last two times, it's a very good place, they do everything they possibly can to get you to concentrate on what you might call the positive side of life: art classes, pottery, socials, dances. They have all those things, as well as the therapy sessions they give you either in a group or on your own, where you're encouraged to talk about yourself and your problems. I've had it all explained to me dozens of times; how it's something to do with my feelings about my birth and my upbringing, my sense of inferiority, my resent-

ment towards my mother and all the rest of it. I think
there's a lot in that, it's very probably all true. But understanding it and learning what it's all about still doesn't seem
to make a blind bit of difference you know, when I get outside.

I think on the whole, the people who've been the most
helpful of all to me I should say have been the police. One
particular station, the one at Bone Lane, they know me very
well, they've had to take me in dozens of times. The Inspector in charge there, he's a very nice man indeed. Last
year there was an occasion when two of his constables arrested me in the street, and I must admit I lost my temper a bit.
We had quite a fight really, because I didn't want to have to
go with them. Well this Inspector, he came down to see me
in the charge-room; and he gave me a really good talking
to. He could have made a lot of trouble for me, you know,
if he'd wanted to with my past record, especially because I'd
resisted arrest. But instead of that he gave me a cigarette
and told me to sit there until I'd calmed down; then he went
away for a bit and when he came back he really laid into
me.

He said to me 'Now look here Harry' he said, 'I know you
and you know me, and I'm getting fed up with all the bother
you're causing us. Don't you think we've got enough to do
catching criminals and all the rest of it? We're very busy
indeed, without you making a nuisance of yourself as well.
And what's more' he said, 'we get lots of fellows in here
who've been stealing and breaking into places, because they'd
sooner do that sort of thing rather than work for their living; they're too downright lazy and dishonest to work. But
that's not your case now is it? You can work and you do
work; you're working now and you're making a living – but
if I were to charge you, what'd happen to you? You'd go to
prison again, that's what; you'd lose your job, you'd be
right back at the beginning with nothing behind you at all.
And that would be a complete waste of time and effort all
round now, wouldn't it? So you go off home will you Harry,
and let's forget all about it. And just bear this in mind for
the future: you've not to fight any more of my policemen.
If they pick you up you've to behave yourself and keep
quiet and go along with them when they say.'

I've been in that police station quite a few times since you know, when I've been walking about at a loose end round that area. I've gone in and I've said to them 'Look, I've not done anything but I feel as though I'm going to; can I sit here for a little until I feel better?' And they'll let me do that, they give me a cup of tea and a cigarette, and then one of them will walk me to the bus-stop and see me on the right bus for home.

But of course they're not all like that, not all like that by any means. In fact that's the only one I know of where you can actually go in and talk to them and they won't pinch you for it. In some of them they'd be only too ready to stick every charge on you that they could, including any spare ones they've got waiting until there's someone comes along that they'll fit. I think perhaps there's more the police could do if they were allowed to, a lot of them; but they're under whoever's in charge aren't they, they have to follow the lines he lays down for his particular area.

My wife, she says we ought to go and live next door to Bone Lane and then I'd be all right. She says it half as a joke you know, but of course I have to explain to her it's not as simple as that. When I do go walking around I never know where I'm going to end up, quite often I haven't the faintest idea where I am at all. And anyway I seem to be all right more or less, wherever I am with her.

—She and I, we say that poem to each other sometimes, that one of Robert Browning's, 'Rabbi Ben Ezra'.

> Grow old along with me!
> The best is yet to be,
> The last of life, for which the first was made:
> Our times are in His hand
> Who saith 'A whole I planned,
> Youth shows but half; trust God: see all, nor be afraid!'

Oh I learnt it at school I should think, originally. It's a long poem but between us we can just about manage to get through it together, all the way from beginning to end. She's the only person I've come across who likes it as much as I do; in fact that was how we first came to speak to each other. I was walking through the lounge and I saw her sitting over by the window with her back to me, looking out over the lawns. I didn't know who she was or what she might be thinking, it was just something about the look of her. I don't know what made me say it; but I went up and stood behind her and I said 'The best is yet to be.' And she said the first line of it straight off and then went on for about the next twenty or thirty lines, she knew it all.

Mary's her name. She'd been a patient there herself for six years by then, and very ill, she'd never been allowed out at all. She's what they call a schizophrenic, has to take pills every day of her life; they've told her she'll never be able to manage without them ever. We've known each other about three years now; after I was discharged I went back to see her regularly once a week, to take her out for a walk or to go to the pictures, whatever she felt like: or only sit in the lounge if she preferred.

Right at the outset we agreed we'd take each other just as we were, and what had happened to us before wouldn't come into it. I don't mean we hid anything from each other, because we didn't: she knows nearly everything there is to know about me, and I know the same about her. That ten years ago she was a prostitute on the streets for example, and a few other things besides. Neither of us is perfect and the other knows it: but what's done's done and we love each other for what we are now, which is all that matters.

The big test to me really was whether she'd stand by me when I got into trouble again. I'd not pretended to her that I thought I wouldn't, but all the same it had proved too much for the others in the past. Mary's proved herself different: I've been in prison a couple of times since I've known her, and she just shrugs it off, she says perhaps one day when we can be together it might be all right. She's had one or two relapses herself with her own trouble, had to be confined to the ward for weeks at a time, hearing voices and all the rest of it. She always quotes that at me, she says 'We've both of us got excuses for giving the other one up if we want to, we've just got to take each other completely as we are.'

It was a risk getting married of course, but six months

ago we decided we'd do it, we'd take the plunge. And even in that short time there's been a bit of progress; just a bit. She can come out nearly every weekend now, from Friday night till Sunday night, so that means we have two days and two nights together completely on our own. Sometimes perhaps on a Saturday afternoon we'll go out for tea or something like that, but most times we don't go very far away from our room since the time we've got together is so short. Mary doesn't like it much, going out, she always feels people are staring at her; she's very self-conscious because she's still a mental hospital patient.

Well I know what that's like, don't I, that feeling; I should do, I've had it often enough myself coming out of prison. That's just one of the many ways we understand each other. She understands my feelings about being a failure and an outcast, she feels exactly the same, and we can talk to each other about these things.

Only a couple of months ago she said she could never live anywhere except an asylum, that was the only place for her. And I told her it wasn't true, which it isn't; most weekends she gets through two whole days outside with me. Then I think it was only a week or two after that and the positions were reversed; she was cheering me up through one of my depressions when I said I couldn't ever see myself being cured, I'd end up one day for good in a prison cell. But Mary said I wouldn't, I'd end up happy with her in a house of our own, perhaps even a bakery of our own, where I'd have to work for ever and ever to earn enough money to buy her all the things she wanted. 'That's what you'll be sentenced to, Harry' she said, 'a life sentence of working for me!' She was laughing, you know; that's what we do, we laugh at each other for feeling so sorry for ourselves, and we can make each other cheer up like that in turn. But not when it's really serious; then we don't laugh, we talk to each other and try and help. I try and encourage her to feel that one day she'll be all right, and she does the same for me. So long as we talk to each other and can tell each other how we feel, then we think there's still a chance; and so long as we've got each other, that's the main thing.

Though I don't know how many men have got a wife like her who, when they tell her they've been out walking around all day in the street would put her arms round them and kiss them and say 'It's all right, I love you and I'll always love you; hold me in your arms Harry, so long as we stay together sooner or later we'll both be all right.'

The two of us are throw-outs from society, rejects, failures; and we know it. But together at least with each other we do sometimes seem to make a little kind of success.

* * *

Always the same posture, upright and neat in the chair; always the same level tone of voice, dispassionate and grave. Composed and calm he talked each night on into the fading light until often all that remained visible of him was the thin mask of his face, hanging disembodied like a long pale lantern in the darkening shadows of the sad and suffering air. Harry Mills, twenty times convicted in twenty-five years for over a hundred offences; with more than double that number of offences committed in addition, for which he had never been charged.

An indecent exposer. To some a distasteful figure to be looked on with anger or contempt; to others a sick person who ought to respond to treatment of some kind; and to some people perhaps someone to be regarded as a joke, almost with derision and as a figure of fun.

But not to himself; never, none of those things. To Harry Mills it was something he alone in desperation had to try and live with; a compulsion like an all-pervading blight, eventually and inevitably laying waste every effort, hope or dream he'd ever had through the other greater agony of all his burdened guilty life.

—You can tell you're illegitimate; it's not a very nice thing to have to say, but on the whole it's something you can get over probably, it's not all that unusual. But the other thing, that your father and mother were ... well you do have a terrible feeling, you see, that no matter what happens you couldn't ever really be normal, having been born like that. It's a feeling somehow of shame, that there's something different about you and there's no way round it, you are what you are and nothing's ever going to change it. It has been explained to me it's in no way my fault, that there's nothing in it for me to feel guilty about myself. But I can't help it, I do. I've never for instance in my whole life considered that it would be safe for me ever to have children myself in case I were to pass this, well, this hereditary taint on to them. I do not believe I could ever be the father of a normal child, and I know this feeling will always remain in my mind whatever anyone says. It's the only thing so far that I still haven't been able to bring myself to tell my wife.

You can't be as good as other people, you simply can't: not when you've been born like that. And I think that's been proved, because certainly I'm not normal, I'm not normal myself, and I don't think I ever will be. It's such a terrible, revolting thing to do. Oh yes, I think that too: not only other people, you know: I'm disgusted at it myself as well. I think it's right what they say in the charge, the wording of it, 'insulting behaviour'. That's what they usually describe it as; and it is, I don't think there's any doubt about that. I am insulting people, that is what I do.

Middle-aged women, smartly dressed, no one else. Someone who reminds me of my mother, a doctor said once, he pointed that out to me, and I think that might be right, that I'm still trying to insult her. No, it's not a prelude to a sexual assault, there's never anything like that in my mind. Just to shock. If a woman looks disgusted and turns away, then I'm satisfied. A woman smiled at me once, and came towards me instead; I ran away from her as hard as I could. I'm very frightened if someone makes an advance towards me like she did; all you want to do then is get right away.

I can't tell you why I do it; when it's happening I'm not conscious of anything except this feeling of being contemptuous towards women and wanting to try and give one a shock. I know when it's coming on usually; first there's this feeling of great restlessness and wanting to go out for a walk. In a way I walk to try and calm myself down, to tire myself out, and sometimes I get back to my room and I think 'Well that was all right this time, all I did was walk.' Then later it comes back to me, the memories come back, the incidents here and there, and I realize it wasn't all right, that wasn't only what I did at all.

Usually it's in the afternoon when I've got nothing to do

except wander around. That's why I always try to get myself work on the night-shift because with that I'm so tired
I stop most of the day in bed. The morning shift is the worst,
six till two; after that I don't go home and go to bed like I
ought to, I go walking around. So if I possibly can I avoid
that shift and try to keep on nights.

You know you can never be cured, all you can do is try
to come to terms with it somehow because you know you'll
always have it. You've got to try and cope with it to the
greatest amount that you can, and then you've got to live
with the rest. It comes in spasms mostly, you'll have quite a
few months when it never happens at all, you can't remember any more what it was all about. You think you must have
faced up to it finally and fought against it and won; then
suddenly it starts again.

There's been days when I've been out for hours and hours
on end and never stopped, walking up and down, round and
round, street after street, woman after woman I've seen and
done it to every one. Over a hundred complaints in a
month the police told me they'd had at one time; and of
course not everyone even goes to the trouble to go to the
police and complain. One woman was a magistrate, and I
did it three times to her; she insisted the police catch me in
this park where I happened to be each afternoon as she was
walking home. They sent two women police in plain-clothes
in to walk through it and that was it, I did it straight away
to them. That was one of the times I got six months I
think.

You see with a list of convictions like mine, you're always
bound to get a prison sentence or sent to hospital, they've
got to try and do something with you, haven't they? A very
sick man, I've been told; but I can't understand that, because
I can work and I do work, very hard, the full time that I'm
supposed to, every single shift. I never pinch a day off or
even an hour off or anything like that, I'm proud of my
work and of being reliable. And a sick man, anyway what
does that mean? First they tell me I'm that, and then when
I've been in the hospital for a while they tell me I can go
because I'm cured. But I never have been, after a few months
it all starts again.

You sit in your room sometimes wherever you happen to

be living at the time, usually with me it's a furnished bed-sitter somewhere, and you think: 'What am I going to do, what's the point of it all, will I never be able to conquer this thing and stop?' Or must I accept that all my life I'm going to be in and out of prisons and hospitals for always doing the same? Am I always going to be a useless rotten man? This business, it's so futile, so meaningless, such a terrible waste of time.

I think all you can do is persuade yourself that life here isn't all, there must be an end to it eventually and something better to come perhaps in the next. I know Beethoven felt that, didn't he, when he found out he was going deaf? He wrote to his brothers about it, I read his letter once in a book. He was going deaf and he knew that as time went on he'd only be able to hear his music in his mind. Then he wrote his Third Symphony, the 'Eroica' they call it, don't they? When you listen to that, you know what he felt, that this world isn't everything, there are other things much greater and better beyond. Those who can't achieve worldly happiness can always listen to that music and learn from it; that man knew there was more to the world than what he was suffering then.

You never know, do you, when the end is going to be? You think everything's over but you can't tell, it might only just be the beginning for you after all. The last twenty-five years, they've been terrible. Perhaps the next will be better, but even if they're not, even if I go on exactly the same as I have done, perhaps just before I'm dying it'll all eventually come right and the last few minutes of life will have some meaning. If they do, those minutes to me will be worth far more than everything else all added up that's gone before.

I think that's the only way there is to look at these things myself, I can't see any other way. I'm a religious person and I believe in God, even though I don't go to church. I believe He's got a purpose and a way for you to follow, even though it might be one that you yourself will never understand. I think He had a purpose in bringing Mary and me together, I think it was for something: between the two of us we've got to try and work out what it was. He's set us problems to solve and put difficulties in our way, just like

He does for everyone else; but I can't help feeling that He knows what He's doing and somehow, in some way, perhaps after a lot more things to go through yet for both of us, it will eventually come right in the end.

A Very Shy Sort Of Person

Charlie Cox

—There's only one thing I still feel I could never do, and that's poncing. To me it's the worst thing of the lot, I'd never stoop to it – or at least I hope I wouldn't.

Maybe I'm old fashioned, or sentimental about women or something – but I just can't stomach the idea of poncing at all. I've nothing but contempt, real, deep contempt for ponces.

—There's no other limit you'd set yourself?
—No.

(*The Courage Of His Convictions*. Tony Parker & Robert Allerton. Hutchinson, 1962)

—Yeah I remember that, I read it myself, I think it was while I was in Wandsworth one time; if I remember right they had it in the library there. He'd done the lot hadn't he, that Robert Allerton – blagging, wage snatches, robbery with violence, smash-and-grab, blowing safes, carrying fire-arms, assault on the police, grievous bodily harm? They all talk like him when it comes to the subject of living on immoral earnings, all the villains say that sort of thing. No matter what else they might have done, as far as that one's concerned the reaction's always the same. 'Poncing, ugh, that's horrible, you can't get any further down. A ponce is the very last one on the ladder, he's the bottom of all the lot, the absolute lowest of the low.'

They don't like any kind of sex case at all, mind you, but they will sometimes grant you the point that if it's little girls or little boys that a bloke's in for, it's not absolutely out of the question there could somehow just possibly be something the matter with the man's mind. But not with ponces, oh no, never; there's no reasons anyone would even begin to listen to for people like them.

There was one brought into the Scrubs when I was there on one of my early sentences once, doing a two-years I think it was for shop-breaking. Six or seven of the chaps on the landing I was on set up a little reception committee for him the first night he arrived. Did him all over with salt-pots in socks, bashed half his teeth in, kneed him in the bollocks and kicked him down the stairs. Nobody lifted a finger to help him, they wouldn't dream of it; that's the law of the nick – any time there's a ponce in, anyone who wants to can give him a kick or a cuff whenever they feel like it. He doesn't need to have done anything to them for it; it's quite sufficient him just being what he is. I used to think exactly the same way about it myself when I was there: I must admit I've given one or two chinnings to ponces on my own account now and again while I've been inside.

Why does everybody feel like that? Well when you come to think about it I should say it's resentment and envy mostly; perhaps because there's such a lot of money to be earned at it and in such an easy way. After all it's much simpler and more profitable than thieving: and it's a lot less dangerous too all round. I mean, you're not hurting people are you, not hitting them over the head and robbing them or anything like that? It doesn't need much planning, and it's not so dangerous for you yourself either; so long as you use your loaf about it there's far less prospect of you getting caught. There's no property missing, you don't get the Law coming round all the time after you breathing down your ear, asking you where you were last Tuesday and who with and all that sort of thing.

Anyway in my opinion I think most of those villains who carry on so strong about it, they would, they'd do it themselves for all they say about it, if they ever really got a proper chance to. It stands to reason: anyone who takes the trouble to think about it and go into it carefully can see for themselves the money's very good indeed, and it's just waiting there asking to be taken. All in all, myself I think there's no question of it, it's one of the safest and easiest ways of making a living that there is: there's not a shadow of doubt about that at all.

Of course a lot of them, those villains who talk like that, the plain truth of the matter is that they're married to right old slags themselves, so they don't really have the opportunity. You can't do it properly or hope to make any kind of success out of it, unless you've got a really nice attractive wife like I have.

*   *   *

A small, sinewy, athletically-built Cockney of thirty-seven, he moved delicately and precisely as a cat, almost as soundlessly round the room, putting one foot rapidly in front of the other, his shoulders hunched and his body tilting forward, his heels hardly touching the ground; always as though he was ready instantly to dart off out of sight at any unexpected incident or sound.

'Very nervous, a very shy sort of person' was Charlie Cox's first description of himself, and it was correct. To remain for any length of time in one place was a nervous strain, and talking about himself was not something he'd ever done much of; by nature he preferred to be out and about whenever he could, constantly on the move. Often at the beginning he would glide silently to and fro round the room, frowning anxiously at the walls or up at the ceiling, restless and perturbed. When he did eventually stop moving and sit, it was always to poise on the edge of a chair or settee, with his hands thrust deeply down into the pockets of his leather-shouldered navy-blue donkey-jacket as though he was afraid of losing them; the collar of it turned up and his legs pressed back under him so that his toes just touched the floor, his body as rigidly coiled as a tightly-wound spring.

His short black hair was cut in a shaggy fringe across his forehead, his eyes gleamed like pebbles of anthracite from under thick black overhanging eyebrows. His expression was brooding, puckered, savage, dark. Bronchitic, sudden metallically grating explosions of coughing left him periodically breathless; in between, his rapid voice was never louder than a rasping whisper, with an occasional disconcerting noiseless laugh, hissed out staccato like short power-bursts from a mechanically driven compressor. Only the tightening of lips and a faint creasing at the corners of his mouth revealed he thought something amusing. He talked to the floor.

What he said about himself was neither boastful nor penitent. He was what he was, he did what he did, he thought what he thought. Life had always been wintry, bitter and hard; whatever was got from it had to be taken; at no time had much ever been given to him. But his recollections were touched more with asperity at the inadequacy of what life offered than with resentment, disappointment or self-pity.

Successes were few, and any he had achieved had never been much more than small triumphs over a continuing and inescapable restriction by impersonal authority. For him, to have failed completely as a child and a youth on probation, or under both approved school and borstal systems, was the summit of achievement; he spoke of it with a burning determination to emphasize it. Failure to comply with regulations, or take advantage of what others described as 'chances', was the only way he had ever known of asserting or preserving his own character. Persistently unamenable to any attempt to apply discipline and aggressively recalcitrant, he had never been for any period longer than twelve months out of the hands of one authoritarian system or another between the ages of ten and thirty-five. What he had retained of his personality and individuality might not be widely sociably acceptable in many places, but at least he could look upon it as his own.

He talked of but did not apologize for it. Narrative was easier than introspection, though often he would suddenly produce an unexpected and sharp extrapolation. With his chin tucked down into his chest, in a voice so quiet that it could often scarcely be heard, he flicked through words as though they were the hard wooden black beads of a rosary.

—My old man was a rough sort of chap, a bit of a dodgy character in a way; very quick-tempered, ready to have a go at anyone who was outside the family. 'Get this bleeding old bike out of here!' I used to hear him shout at night downstairs in the hallway when he came home. It was one of the other tenants' in the ground-floor front room, he kept it there because there was nowhere else to put it. I can't have been more than about four or five, I tripped over it one day and fell against it and cut my face. My old man came down to see what I was yelling about; he had a new white pullover on that his old lady had bought him, when he picked me up he got blood all down its front. He yanked open the door of the room where this bloke was, he said 'Come on you, outside in the street!' They had a bout of fisticuffs which my old man won; then he marched inside, picked up the bike and chucked it out on top of the other feller just as he was getting up; he said if it was left there again he'd wrap it round his neck for him. Then he took me back upstairs and started shouting blue murders at me for the mess I'd made on his pullover.

A nice man though; I did, I liked him a lot. Dead straight, never in any kind of trouble in his life; he ended up a guard on the gate at a factory. A great fighter, he'd take a swing at anyone any time, it didn't matter if they were twice his size. When I was a kid one of the first things he did was taught me to box. He said so long as you could take care of yourself in a scrap you'd be all right; a good little 'un who knew what he was doing and was quick on his feet never need be scared of anyone.

Those days, before the war, he worked as a docker mostly. We lived in Canning Town: him and two or three of his brothers and sisters and their husbands and wives, all near one another in these houses round a square near the railway. Old tenement houses, some with rooms empty because the floors were rotten and damp all down the walls, others with perhaps three or four lots of people using each room for eating and sleeping in altogether. Very poor properties, low rents and far more people in them than was ever intended. Cramped conditions, but in those days there wasn't all the rehousing schemes that there are now; you were lucky to have one room any family could call its own. There wasn't a lot of work in the docks; this would be the 1930's, it was all the casual labour system, you went down to the gates each morning to see what you could get. I reckon my father did as well as most, he was usually working, though there were long periods when things were not easy. He used to talk about packing-up the docks trying something else, perhaps moving away and making a fresh start. He never did though, I think he was too fond of his family and relatives; that area was his own and where he belonged.

A hard-working man when there was work to be had. He didn't gamble or smoke or drink hardly at all, except at Christmas time when all the families used to get together in one another's houses to celebrate. Everybody's kids were collected up and put in one room with their cakes and sweets and lemonade, and then down below the grown-ups had their own party. It could last nearly all day and all night, the kids were supposed to keep right away. We didn't though: we used to creep downstairs and watch them through the railings. We thought it was dead funny to see them with their paper-hats on, some of them so drunk they could hardly stand up, singing and dancing and carrying-on. Next day they'd all be sobered up, back again to how they usually were, quiet and respectable. I can remember seeing my old gran once, dancing about with a funny hat on and a bottle in her hand; I couldn't hardly believe she was the same person as the little grey-haired old lady who hardly ever spoke to you or laughed at anything during the rest of the year.

I had a sister called Wendy, she'd be about a year older than me. I didn't have a lot to do with her; there were always so many kids around, some of them related to you and some not, you had your own particular friends. You looked on yourselves as all being in the same family anyway, which more or less you were. There was one boy called Jimmy for instance, I couldn't tell you to this day whether he was my cousin, my half-cousin, the boy belonging to the woman next door, or what. As far as I was concerned he could have been my brother for all I knew. The only thing I remember particularly about Wendy is one day I had a new outfit on, red corduroy, a sort of a siren-suit thing with one of those pixie-hoods; I'd been told not to play out in it, but I went down to show it off to the other kids. Wendy gave me a push for something or other, I fell on the ground and it got all dirty. It was me that got told off for it, I had to stay inside then for the rest of the day and wasn't allowed out to play.

It'd been bought for me by my mother. She was a great one for always trying to keep me clean and tidy, she was for ever coming out looking for me to see what I was doing and where I was playing and who with; and then taking me back home again because I'd got dirty scrambling about round the railway arches or in the old houses where we liked to go. Her idea of getting you to do something was to tell you once, then if you didn't do it straight away, wallop, she'd give you a whack on the ear.

I don't know what it was with her, I never remember her being affectionate or anything like that. She always gave you the impression kids were a bloody nuisance and she hadn't a lot of time for them. I think she was quite a bit younger than my father, eighteen or nineteen perhaps when I was born, while he'd be nearly in his thirties. Very fair hair she had, and blue eyes; I look nothing like her, I'm much more after my father's type, thin and dark.

I didn't go much on schooling; I went to one of those very big old-fashioned gloomy sort of buildings that must have been built at the beginning of the century, I should think. In the middle of a street, high walls all round it, just a little concrete playground for you to run about in, only a few yards of space between the school and the building next door. Those who weren't any good at lessons got shoved to the back of the class while the teacher did his best at the front with a few of the bright ones. Now and again he shouted out to the rest of us to get on with reading or with doing something to keep quiet. Only elementary subjects; reading, writing, arithmetic, that was about as much as they could manage to get into you. Myself, I liked English best; I was always trying to write stories about cowboys and Indians and that sort of thing, but my handwriting was so bad no one could ever read them: not even me when I looked at them afterwards.

I didn't like school at all, I was only waiting for the bell when I could get out and go off playing in the streets with my mates; football, chasing about, climbing in and out of places we weren't supposed to go like empty shops or old houses, throwing stones at people, fighting. There wasn't much else to do really in your spare time. The noisier and naughtier you were, the more friends you had: it was no good being quiet or sensible, no one wanted to know those who were. I was always little for my age, I had to create twice as much mischief as anyone else in order to keep up with the rest. As far as that's concerned, I haven't changed a lot either since I was a kid.

When the war started I'd be about nine or ten. Like most of the other kids I was evacuated in the very early days; the whole school was shifted to a town down in Somerset. I can't say I was very happy about it, I don't think most of the rest of us were either; we were stuck right out in the country, living scattered about in different houses all over the place. I was put in with about six other kids who I didn't know even though we all came from the same school, with two old schoolmistresses who had a big house in the middle of miles of fields.

A bus came to fetch you in the mornings to take you all to school, then it took you back again in the afternoon, and that was it. There was nothing to do, nowhere to go, and you were too far away from your own friends to be able to go and play with them. The only form of entertainment was going out for walks. For a kid coming from the area like I did it was so boring I thought I'd go potty. I've no idea where my sister was, I suppose she'd be somewhere else in the district. Nobody thought of putting us in the same house together, there'd have been no point to it any-way even if they had, I'd much sooner have been with my own friends.

I'd been there a few months I should think, and then one day I got a big surprise, my mother turned up. She said she'd come to live in that part of the world so she could be near me and Wendy, while my Dad had gone off and joined the Army. Even though her story was she'd come down to be near us, we didn't see much of her: she'd call in at the house where I was living from time to time with a bag of sweets or something like that, but then it was always 'I can't stop now, I'll try and come next week and take you into the town and we'll go to the pictures.' I couldn't make out what she was doing there at all.

Not long after I got an even bigger surprise. There was a knock at the front door, one of the old schoolmistresses opened it, and there was a soldier in uniform, it was my

Dad. He came in and had a talk with me, he asked me how would I like to go back to London with him there and then. 'Course I jumped at it didn't I? The sooner the better as far as I was concerned. I said what about Mum, she was coming too; but he said, 'Oh never mind about her, she can stop where she is for a while.'

And off we went to London. He took me back to the house, I think my gran was there and one or two of my aunties and uncles; I was right pleased about it, it was where I'd wanted to be, back at home. My old man explained to me he was in the Army so he couldn't stop for long, but he said he'd be coming back again to see me soon. A few more days and then the next thing is my mother turns up once more. 'Come on,' she says, 'your father's in the Army, he can't look after you, you're coming back with me.' So off we go again, back to Somerset. I didn't like the idea, but there's not much you can do about things is there, when you're only a kid. If I had any thoughts she was going to take me to live with her though, I was soon put right on that: I was in with the old schoolmistresses again, and told to stay there till she got somewhere to live herself, and then she'd have me on her own.

But anyhow, on her own wasn't quite what she meant. A few days later she came to the house and said she'd got a place for us, a flat over some shops down in the town. When I arrived I found there was someone else there already; a feller she said was my Uncle Jack. He was a new one on me, he was just some bloke she'd picked up and was living with; though naturally at the time I took it he was really an uncle of mine. You believe everything grown-ups tell you, don't you, when you're a kid.

I can't say I liked him much, he seemed a right miserable kind of a bastard to me. I don't know who he was, I think he must have been a chap who wasn't medically fit for the Army or something. While I was there he never seemed to do any work or have a job, nothing like that; I don't know what they were living on. Then Wendy started to come into the picture a bit. She was brought to the flat a few times and Mum kept saying 'When your Uncle Jack gets some business attended to, then we can all live together here, won't that be nice?' I wasn't very enthusiastic about the idea myself, I don't think the feller can have been either from what I could tell from the expression on his face.

Next thing though, a few days later I'm in the flat on my own one afternoon when I'd come back from school, the door bell rings and there he is again, my old man. 'Right son' he says, 'come on, I'm taking you back where you belong'; ten minutes later we were down the station and on the train once more for London again. I reckon what was going on was some kind of court business about who should have me and where I ought to be. Anyway, I know in the finish I finally ended up with the one I didn't want, my mother, back in this flat with her and the feller in Somerset. I don't know what happened to Wendy, she didn't move in, I didn't see her any more.

I was really fed up with everything, all this being taken up and down from Somerset to London and back again; being told one week by my old man I was going to stop with him, then the next week my mother fetching me and saying that I'd got to stay with her. Course, nobody asked me what I felt; if they had I'd have said that I didn't want it to be either/or, I'd sooner us all be back together in our home with the different members of the family all round in London, like before the war.

It mightn't have been too bad if I'd seen a bit of my Mum while I was supposed to be living with her: but I don't know what she was doing, I think perhaps she'd had to get herself a job. There was hardly ever anyone in at the flat when I got home from school, and most nights she and this bloke seemed to go out too. About the only consolation as far as I was concerned was living in the middle of the town meant I could see more of some of my mates at school, quite a lot of them were billeted round about. My Mum didn't seem to mind where I went or what I was up to, so long as I was home by the time she and her feller got in at night. That was never much before midnight so there was plenty of scope. There was a gang of us, about three or four kids, right little villains we were, pinching stuff out of the Woolworth's in the town, roaming about at night getting into empty houses to see what we could find. Loose change to buy sweets or cigarettes, cigarette lighters, comic books, all the usual stuff for kids, we'd take anything.

Down one end of the town there was an Army storage place, a lot of those tin huts, Nissen huts I think they were called. We were always climbing over the fence into there, having a look round to see what we could find. One night we couldn't see anything we wanted, so we just decided to mess the place up. All there was in the hut where we were was a lot of tin cans with screw tops on them; we ran up and down opening them all, letting the stuff inside pour out every-where. Course it was petrol, wasn't it; and when we were leaving, one of the lads lit a cigarette and then chucked it in through one of the windows.

They must have thought the Jerries had come, the whole place went up like a light. Talk about riots, everyone was going mad, soldiers rushing about, alarm bells going off, fire-engines, police, the lot. We all thought it was a great joke didn't we, we were standing in a field the other side of the fence watching it, splitting ourselves with laughing. We were so busy enjoying it we never saw the Law coming, before we could turn round a police-car came tearing into the field and pulled up beside us and all these coppers came down on us.

It was serious, I don't know how much the damage was but it must have been a few thousand pounds I should think; on top of that it was only a matter of luck really that no one had been hurt. There couldn't be any question of it, we'd have to go away, so the four of us were sent to different places as far from each other as they could find. I was given a three-year probation, with the condition of residence in a probation hostel in Bristol. 1941 or 1942 that was; anyhow I know it was a few weeks after my tenth birthday.

—It was some place, that probation hostel I was telling you about last time. Off and on I've been in some kind of nick or another most of my life since, but I've still not come across one as tough as that. It had the lot; bars over all the windows, broken glass along the tops of the walls, wire-netting covering up any little spot you might think of trying to get a foothold on, chains and padlocks and double-locks on the doors. Talk about security, it could have given the special wing at Durham a head start. Inside it was green and cream walls, stone corridors, long tables and benches

all bare wood, frosted glass you couldn't see out of, and upstairs the dormitory was one big room with iron beds and
horsehair mattresses in two rows down each side.

You had a little cupboard that high by the side of your
bed, that was the only place you could call your own: you
had to keep all your clothes in it, your soap and towel,
everything. Those cupboards were the only things in the
whole place that didn't have locks on; they were inspected
every day while you were out. If anything was missing, or
anything in there that shouldn't have been, you automatically lost privileges; like you weren't allowed in the recreation room for three nights, or for a week you couldn't have
your mug of cocoa before you went to bed. There wasn't a
lot you did have, so they had to think really hard when it
came to finding something they could take away. The recreation room, not being allowed in there was a big laugh;
all it had in it was an old radio set and a table-tennis table
without any bats or balls, and a lot of plain wooden kitchen
chairs to sit on as a change from the benches everywhere else.

There'd be about sixteen boys there I should think. For
work you all did the same thing; you were taken out every
morning, half-past five in winter, half-past four in summer,
in an open truck to go and work on a farm about ten or
eleven miles away. You weren't given any choice what to
do when you got there: digging, potato-picking, cabbage-
cutting, whatever it was they said wanted doing you did it.
About eight o'clock you'd knock off for half an hour for
your breakfast, which had been brought in the truck with
you; a milk-churn of porridge which of course was
stone cold, and a mug of tea. Midday you had your dinner
in a shed they called the 'canteen'; that was because people
used it for eating in. Just a long wooden table and benches
again, and usually you got some kind of stew and suet stuff,
and then some suet pudding.

At the end of the day, which was often quite late in the
summer, back you went in the truck to the hostel again for
your evening meal. More often than not that would be stew
again, and bread and potatoes. Then you had an hour in
the recreation room before you went to bed. That was five
days a week, Saturdays you did cleaning in the hostel and
games, and on Sundays a parson came in and gave us a

service, him and another one on the piano. Sunday afternoons if you were one of the good boys you got taken out
into the park for football: if you weren't, you stayed in and
sat around in the recreation room.

I don't expect they had much time for places like that
with the war on: the staff seemed mostly throw-outs from
the services, middle-aged men who didn't have much interest in anything except a quiet life. They ran the place
strictly according to the book. There was a system of mark-
ing for everything; work, behaviour, progress, washing your
ears, anything else you could think of. When you got to a
certain number of marks and had been there a certain
length of time, you were allowed out for an hour on your
own to spend your week's pocket money, which was about
sixpence. Nearly every time I went out I came back with
something I'd nicked, a packet of fags or a few bars of
chocolate; then I was kept in the following week of course
as a result.

Eventually towards the end of my time I was let go and
spend a few days with my mother, to make arrangements
for what I was going to do when I was discharged. She was
still living with that bloke, and I didn't fancy going there
for good. I hadn't been with her more than a day when I
broke open the gas-meter while she was out, lifted about
thirty bob in silver that was in it, took off down to the station and got the train to London and went back home. When
I got there, one of my aunties told me my old man wasn't
there, he was working at an Army depot in south London
and had moved into a flat near. She gave me the address and
I got myself over there to see him. Then there was another
shock for me: he'd found himself another woman and he
was living with her. I don't think she was any too pleased to
have me turning up on her doorstep.

I didn't tell the old man I'd scarpered from the hostel, I
let him think I'd finished my time and was free. He said I
could stop with them a few days while I decided what I was
going to do, he let me sleep on the sofa in the living-room.
Course it wasn't long before two of the Law turned up to
take me back to the probation hostel and charge me with
the gas-meter breaking my Mum had reported. One of the
coppers was a right narky sort of a bastard; he kept saying

to my old man 'I expect you know more about this than you're letting on.' He was all the time suggesting to the other one they ought to get a warrant and come back and have a proper look round. I really thought my old man would put one on his chin, I think this woman was afraid he would too; she told them to clear off and take me with them, the quicker we were gone the better as far as she was concerned.

That was it, back to Bristol then, up to court for absconding and doing the meter, and sent off straight away to approved school. Right over the other side of the country that one was. I'd be thirteen. It looked to me as though I was never going to get back with either of my parents, let alone with both of them together.

I suppose because it's got the name school in it, a lot of people would think an 'approved school' was a place where they tried to give you some education. Maybe at some of them they do, but the one I was at wasn't much different from the probation hostel, except that it had its own farm. You worked right there in the grounds instead of having to be taken out in a truck. Otherwise it was more or less the same sort of thing. No, I tell a lie, there were a few other things you could do: brick-laying, plastering, working in the sewing-shop, making overalls, but nothing else I can remember. There were lessons for a couple of hours twice a week, Tuesdays and Fridays; sums and spelling, but on the whole you'd been put there to work rather than improve your education.

All the same, you did improve your education; even though it wasn't in the way they intended you to. Any method of thieving you didn't know about, or what the chances were of earning at it, all the facilities were there for learning it from the others who were in with you. Between them there wasn't much someone or other hadn't done; they had some right hard cases too, big lads who'd already got quite a bit of form for violence. While I was in there that bit of knowledge I'd got from my old man about boxing came in useful. Being only a little 'un I could have got plenty of aggravation for myself if I'd let anyone think they could mess me about. You've got to show them you're not frightened, especially if you're small; so I was always ready to have a go at anyone.

Course naturally this doesn't make you very popular with the staff. But you can't take that into account: in those sort of places it's everyone for himself, the weak ones go to the wall. You've got to let it be known you'll fight anyone who tries to have a go at you. Either you're one of the lads or you're not; and if you're not then everyone's on your back and your life's a misery. By the time you've reached sixteen you've usually made up your mind whether you're going to be a villain or not; if you haven't, approved school is a good place for helping you decide. As far as I was concerned, by then I was; I don't think there's been a day in my life since when I've ever given any thought at all to the idea of going straight.

When I was due for being let out, they told me they'd written off to my mother and father and they'd said they didn't want me back with them. When I asked who it was exactly they'd written to, it turned out it was my mother and the bloke she was living with, not my own father at all. By then it was too late for them to get in touch with him, they just had to discharge me to the address I gave them, which was where my home had been in Canning Town. I knew my old man wasn't there but I told them he was, so they gave me a travel warrant for London.

Off I went to the address he'd been before; this time when I got there him and this other woman were married and had got a kid of their own. The war was about over, my old man was out of the Army then, but he didn't fancy going back into the docks again. He wasn't sure what he was going to do or where he was going to live. I stopped with them a few days, but me and this woman couldn't hit it off. I didn't like her face, I didn't like her cooking, I didn't like anything about her: and I think she felt more or less the same about me. My old man said I ought to try and get work and settle down, but by then I'd made up my mind anyway that whatever else I did, I definitely wasn't going to work for my living.

I went down to Somerset to my mother's again for a bit, but that was no good; all she could suggest was that I got work selling newspapers, or labouring. Obviously she wasn't too keen on having me around, she said I couldn't live with her; I suppose she was worried about her gas-meter.

Anyhow, a few days more and I decided there was nothing to keep me in that part of the world, I'd best get back to the smoke. That was the last I've seen of her since.

One thing about approved school is you get to know a lot of people there who'll help you when you're out. I hadn't been back in London long before I teamed up with two or three of the lads who'd gone out before I had, they were working shops and warehouses in the East End. Those days everything was in short supply: clothing, dried-egg powder, tea, petrol-coupons, it didn't matter where you broke into you couldn't help get something someone would give you a good price for. I was supposed to be still on my licence from approved school and reporting to the after-care people; I never bothered, there wouldn't have been much point, I couldn't have convinced them I was making a straight living. For a while, a few months, things were going quite good. I was living it up a bit, making myself some money. But I was getting rid of it as fast as I had it, spending it on having a good time round the clubs drinking and gambling.

It was in one of those places I first met Betty, she was what they call a 'mystery', that's a girl no one seems to know who she is or where she comes from, but she's always hanging around. An attractive girl she was, red hair and blue eyes, she looked Irish but she wasn't; after a while we shacked up together in a little room off the Bayswater Road. She was only a kid herself, about sixteen I suppose she'd be; I'd be seventeen or just under.

Course it couldn't last could it, I got done for a store-breaking down the Mile End Road. Somebody must have grassed us I think, I know I dropped over this wall at the back coming out and my toes never touched the ground, there was a bunch of coppers there holding out their arms for me and lifted me straight into the police car.

The next thing on the list they could give me then was Borstal. The first one they put me in was an open one down on the South Coast. An open one, I ask you: obviously I did as soon as I got there, I had it away I think it was more or less the very first night. Then they tried me at another open one; that was on the coast too but miles away from anywhere, a sort of an island with a narrow strip of land they could easily seal off at a bridge between it and the main road. This one was another of those farming places, only their speciality was fruit trees. Rows and rows of them as far as you could see, that all had to be sprayed and disinfected and have their branches cut off and dug-up and replanted again and arranged in a different order; it was incredible all the different things they could think of for you to do with them.

It wasn't my line at all, as soon as I got there I started thinking up ways and means of getting away. The first time I tried, I was picked up only a few miles along the main road thumbing a lift, and sent back and put in the punishment block for a couple of weeks. All you do there is spend the whole day keeping the place clean, scrubbing and mopping the floors, all by numbers. 'One two three' splosh splosh splosh with the mop. 'One two three four five six' with the scrubbing-brush. 'One two three four' with your drying-off cloth. They keep you at it like that for hours, you end up just like a machine.

What it does for you I don't know, except convince you next time you're on your toes they won't get you back again so easy. There was another feller on punishment with me, Scotch Johnny they called him, a real hard nut; I said to him 'I'm going the first chance I get as soon as I'm off this lot, how about you?' He said yes he was game, so as soon as we were out we fixed it we were working on the same patch of fruit trees together, to give us a chance to talk and think something up. We decided it was no good going for the main road, you could never get far enough along it before they'd discovered you'd gone. It'd be better to let them think we'd got over the bridge and gone that way, but stay hiding on the island instead until after the hunt had died down.

That was what we did a few weeks later, we slipped off one afternoon after the roll-call at tea-break, and went down to the shore where we hid under some bushes near a stream. We'd stuffed as many cakes and buns as we could in our pockets, we lay low two days and nights, then we worked our way round back towards the bridge. We didn't risk going over it in case they were still keeping a look-out, instead we crawled along underneath it and eventually we got on to the mainland. We'd worked out they would be

expecting us to go east along the road towards London, so
instead we went west. Course we were pretty well starving,
the first thing we had to do was break into a house at night
to get some food; naturally that meant the Law would soon
hear whereabouts we were, but we couldn't see any way
round that. During the next day we stayed holed-up near
some beach huts; it was getting on to late spring, so there
were quite a few holidaymakers about. In the finish we were
spotted; two coppers came down on the beach after us.
Scotch Johnny slipped on the pebbles, they soon caught up
with him; one of them held on to him while the other one
chased me. I dived in under one of the beach huts, under the
sort of raised foundation it had. There was an old iron bar
lying there, I started thrashing about with it whenever he
tried to get at me. A crowd came up, how long it would
have gone on I don't know, I was really wild; I wasn't going
to let that copper get hold of me even if it meant flattening
him. After a bit one of the holidaymakers, a middle-aged
bloke in swimming trunks came up by the side of the hut, he
said 'Come on son, stop being so silly, eh? Where do you
come from then, where's your home?' When I told him he
said, 'Oh yeah, I know that part of London myself, I used to
live quite near there.' He went on chatting away to me
like that, till at the finish he got me calmed down and persuaded me to come out and give myself up.

Well then, so it was back to the punishment block and the
old 'One two three' for another fortnight. I was still determined I wasn't going to give up though, I spent most of my
time trying to work out another scheme for getting away. I
waited a month or two until they weren't watching me as
carefully as they had been, then off I went again, only this
time on my own. I knew I'd have to be quick; and I was, I
got over the bridge before they even noticed I was missing.
Just for luck this time I thought I'd go north, across the
main road. I didn't stop running till I got right in the middle
of some woods, and then I just flaked out. When I woke up
it was pitch dark raining, so I thought I might as well stay
where I was until morning.

Course they don't bother really, they don't have to do
they: they know you won't get far. Even if you do, it can
only be a matter of time before they've got you again,

you're bound to show up somewhere. You might think
yourself the great fugitive, the escaper on the run and all
that, but to them you're just another Borstal absconder
who's bound to be caught sooner or later. What was it that
time with me, oh yes I know, something really stupid: the
old village bobby on his bike, he comes pedalling up behind
me while I'm walking along a lane next morning. 'Hello,
sonny' he says 'Out for a walk then? All right, come on.'
He snaps one end of the cuffs on me and the other on his
handlebars, and off we go, him walking and me pushing his
bike. You could push him over, try and jump on the bike or
something like that, but you think well what's the use,
where am I going anyway, I've got nowhere to go. I might
as well give up and get back to the scrubbing in the punishment block.

After I'd had it away three times, they decided it was no
use bothering any more with me in these open places, so
they transferred me to a closed one. Actually a closed Borstal is nothing different from a prison; in fact the one they
sent me to was the wing of a prison in London. Funnily
enough, by then I was so fed up with trying to run away
from that open one I'd probably have stopped the rest of
my time there if they'd left me. But as soon as they put me
in the closed place, that started me thinking again about
new ways to get out. After a few months I got given a job
in the welding shop; in a fortnight I was working on my own
up at the end of it, cutting up old iron bars for salvage with
an oxy-acetylene burner. Every now and again I was having
a go with it at a metal panel in the wall under the bench;
by the end of the week it only needed one kick and I was
through it and outside. Where was I, the chief screw's back
garden, and his old woman taking the washing in off her
line. I went right past her and up over the wall, dropped
down into the street and away. Lucky for me there was a
market the other side, crowds of people milling about, it
was easy to nick a pair of overalls off of a stall and get
them on over my Borstal gear round the back out of sight.

I did better that time, I think I managed to stay out at
least a week; I was living by thieving, sleeping rough in
parks or deserted buildings. I'd plenty of mates I could have
gone to, but no one's too keen on having you when you're

on the trot: they don't want the risk of having the Law round looking for you every time afterwards when you're missing, so at times like that you do them a favour and keep away.

About a week and then the inevitable, I get my collar felt while I'm pulling another job. I think that was a shop-breaking, anyhow it's back to Borstal again, with a bit more added on to my sentence, and I'm on special watch all the time. Next time I got a chance for going it was a straight absconding; I was due for release in a couple of weeks, they'd sent me out shopping with one of the screws, I just ran for it in the street. Two days wandering about, I'm picked up once more, and that's another extra bit of time to be done. In the finish I did the full three years' Borstal, every day of it; I'd lost all my remission, everything. Course they didn't like that, having to write somebody down as one of the total failures, but they had no alternative with me. What's more I did a Borstal recall as well; that's like an extension of it they can give you if you offend while you're still on licence, so they had me back for that after about only a month.

It taught me one thing, though; there's no point in doing your sentences the hard way. After that, whenever I went back inside I always did it easy and kept quiet; they had no alternative, they had to give me my full remission every time.

—From when I came out of Borstal till two years ago when when I was thirty-five, I've been in prison another eight times. I've had six months, two twelve months, two eighteen months, a two years, and two lots of three years. When you come to add on the time spent in custody awaiting trial plus the remands in custody afterwards for sentence, it's totalling up to about eleven years net actually inside, all told. The charges have been mostly the same sort of things, shop-breakings, warehouses and so on; one of them was carrying offensive weapons and also there was an assault on the police. There's not much point in going through the details of how they came about is there, one by one; nothing very special or interesting in any of them, the ordinary run-of-the-mill criminal stuff.

There were periods in between when I was out; never very long, I should think ten or eleven months now and again at the most. That was usually because I was having a lucky run, the Law wasn't catching up with me. What I'm telling you about from now on was taking place in fits and starts during the times I was out of the nick.

I suppose the best place to begin with is that girl I was telling you about, Betty. When I'd done my Borstal she was still hanging around the same places I was, we were living together off and on; eventually we ended up getting married. By the time I was twenty-five we'd had a couple of kids; whenever I got done for something she'd go back and live with her mother over in Homerton, then when I came out we'd set up somewhere of our own again.

After I'd got a life of my own with her, I got on better with my old man: I used to drop down to see him now and again, we'd perhaps go out for a drink together and a game of darts. Course we didn't have a lot in common because our ways of life were so different, he was a straight man who worked for his living. If he thought I was a no-good, he didn't show it; we were always friendly, he never asked me much about where I'd been if he didn't see me for a time. He knew it was most often in the nick, but he knew there was nothing he could do about it, so the subject wasn't discussed. He died I think it was while I was doing my first lot of three years; a good man, I was sorry about it, I felt bad about not having seen him for a while before he went.

I had a good idea what Betty was up to while I was away, I'd heard rumours round different places that she was messing with other men; in the middle of one of my sentences she sent me a 'Dear John' – you know, she was very sorry but she'd met this other bloke who was going to provide a home for her and the kids, he was a steady working feller and all the rest of it. A few weeks before I was due out, then I got another letter: she'd made a terrible mistake, it was me she loved after all, would I forgive her and take her back. Course that was because this bloke had got nicked himself, wasn't it, he'd just be starting on his sentence when I was ending mine. She came up to see me on a visit and I faced her with it, all the same when I did come out I went back with her because I was fond of her and I liked my kids.

Things weren't very good between us though, they couldn't be under those circumstances. I was messing about with a few birds myself too, stopping away from home when I felt like it. I got a surprise though when I was on remand in Brixton waiting trial, a bloke I knew came up to me on exercise, he said to me 'Here Charlie, do you know your missus is in Holloway?' I said 'Do me a favour, leave off will you!' but he said 'No, I'm not kidding you, it's true.'

It was too. She'd been working with a little firm on her own, keeping watch while they were breaking into a place; her and one of the blokes standing in a shop-doorway snogging, pretending they were a courting couple. Anyway in the end she got nine months for it, the kids had to be taken into care, it was a right shambles all round.

After that things between us went from bad to worse; sometimes we were together, sometimes we were separated. She'd be living with a bloke, I'd be living somewhere else with another girl, then we'd have another try with each other; that was how it went on all the time. What really finished me was when she finally took up with a lesbian and settled down more or less permanent with her. That was one thing I couldn't stomach, I wouldn't touch her again after that. I heard about it when I was in the nick, it properly turned me up it did, I was so disgusted I had a try at doing myself in, cut my wrist with a razor blade. That's the cut there, seven stitches they had to put in it for me; the little scar below it was where I started, it's what they call 'the hesitation mark'.

Anyhow, it didn't come off; like I say, they found me at it and stopped me, put a tourniquet on and whipped me over the hospital wing and gave me some pills to calm me down. Then I started thinking about it after a few days, I thought 'Well, why should I, why should I get myself into that state over her, it's not worth it, it's stupid, that's all it is, bleeding stupid.'

After I'd come out that time, I still saw her round about now and again, but I'd no feelings for her. Not of the kind I used to have anyway, I was still friendly with her but anything else there'd been had gone. Before long I got hooked up with another girl, a different sort of person altogether;

very pretty, blonde, but much quieter and more sensible. Her name was Shirley, she was a good bit younger than me, she'd be only just over twenty then and I was thirty-two. She was married, she had a couple of kids herself, but her husband was a right dead loss, knocked her about and all that kind of thing, she was very unhappy with him. We seemed to get on all right together, somehow we sort of fitted if you know what I mean, so in the finish she left her husband and kids and came with me.

There was one thing about Shirley, you knew exactly where you were with her. Each time I went in the nick, on the morning I came out she'd be at the gate waiting for me, and she was as honest as they come. I got a divorce from Betty, she got one from her old man, and we got married three years ago. Now we've got two kiddies of our own; as far as I'm concerned there'll never be anyone else like her, there's nothing in the world she wouldn't do for me if it was necessary.

I think she's proved that. She started on the game about a year after we was married; funnily enough it was my first wife Betty who originally got her at it. We'd nowhere to live at the time, I was going through a bad patch; I met Betty one day in a club and when I told her about it she said 'Well why don't you and Shirley come and live in the house where I am, there's a couple of rooms vacant downstairs?' So that was what we did. In fact it was Betty's girlfriend who was landlord of the place, she said we could stay there rent free until I was in the money again. At first Shirley didn't want to go very much, she'd got the idea Betty might bring the kids back there from her mother's and try and set up with me again. But I knew she wouldn't, she was too taken up with her lesbian.

So we moved in there: I was still thieving, but by then I'd done a lot of time for it, I had to be very careful what I got involved in. The next time I got caught it looked as though I'd most likely get a five or a seven with my record; I'd already been warned the previous time I was liable for preventive detention. I didn't have much money, and I couldn't get much either, only fiddling little jobs that didn't bring in much pay. One day Shirley said to me 'Where does Betty get all her money from? She never seems to be short.'

'I don't know' I said, which I didn't. I said 'Why don't you ask her?'

No more was said then, but a few weeks later I wanted to go somewhere and I couldn't, I was skint. 'What do you want?' says Shirley, 'A couple of quid?' And she takes it out of her handbag and gives it to me just like that smiling all over her face. 'Where do you get that from?' I said. 'Oh' she said, 'Never you mind, you go out and enjoy yourself.'

Course I should have guessed, shouldn't I; there could only be one way Betty was in the money, I should have tumbled. But it took me about a month before I did. Shirley kept on handing me out these pound notes whenever I needed them, fivers at the weekend, buying new furniture and clothes all of a sudden; she was taking me and Betty and her friend out to supper two or three times a week, giving me the money to get the drinks for everyone with, it was ridiculous. One night when we got back I decided it was no use dodging it, we'd have to have it out.

I said to her 'Where are you and Betty getting all this money from then?' She didn't say anything, just laughed. I said 'Betty's on the game isn't she? Has she got you at it too?' 'Yes that's right,' says Shirley: 'Well – have you got any better ideas?'

I hadn't, had I, only going on like I was, waiting for a big one I could be sure of pulling without getting myself back in the nick. We talked it over a bit, she said as long as it didn't make me think less of her she didn't mind. I said no, in a way it made me think more of her, which it did. The only thing that did worry me, I said, was that she might get too fond of it with some particular feller and go off and leave me; but she said there'd be no question of that, I was the only one she loved, I could rely on her always. And as far as I know, it's never come up, it's just a business transaction with her, that's all.

She only does it part-time, five afternoons; on average I'd say she earns about seventy or eighty quid a week, tax free. That's a lot more than I could bring in. She charges three quid for sex, two quid for a rub-off, or five pounds if they want a full hour. Most of it's middle-aged men or elderly, really they're pathetic they are. Having to pay for their

sex, I'd never pay for it myself. I don't know what sort of
wives they must have. Well some of them, actually I do;
there's one old bloke comes quite often, he's a lay preacher,
you see his photo up sometimes on hoardings outside
churches, he tours around. Quite a nice feller really when you
get to know him, now and again he stops for a chat. He says
his wife's an invalid, a cripple, they can't have sex together,
but he's told her all about Shirley and she says she's pleased
he's found such a nice girl. I don't know whether that's true
or not but the rest of it is: I've seen his picture myself more
than once on a poster.

Some of them though are a bit weird. There's a doctor
comes from one of the big hospitals, he brings a case with
him with a dark blue uniform in it and a little white cap.
Shirley has to put it on and then she has to swear at him, use
real foul language while he crawls about on his hands and
knees on the floor; all the time he's saying 'Yes Matron,
that's right Matron, I'm sorry Matron.' Nothing else, he
doesn't want any sex with it; quarter of an hour of that once
a week, he gives her three quid every time.

She gets her clients from an advert she puts on one of
those postcards in a newsagent's shop windows. She swit-
ches them around a bit, puts them outside different places
and uses different wording, 'Young lady seeks part-time
employment', 'Young lady gives French lessons', and the
phone number. It's surprising how people can tell what they
mean; those who are looking for that sort of thing, they
know straight off what it's all about. Those two I suppose
are plain enough, but there's others she uses like 'Three-
piece suite for sale, needs recovering', 'Roomy chest of
drawers for sale', 'For sale, playful Alsatian puppy' – and
you know you never once get someone ringing-up with what
you might call a genuine inquiry for what it says on the
card. They can tell somehow, but don't ask me how.

Usually I'm hanging about somewhere in the house out of
sight in case of trouble; unless Betty's in, then I might go
out. But there's hardly any trouble ever, most men who
come are a good class quiet respectable sort of people. They
pay for what they want, they get it and then they go. There's
two things I won't let her do though, that's French and
sadism, I don't want her knocked-about. She tells them

straight off if that's what they're looking for they'll have to go somewhere else.

No, it doesn't make the slightest difference to my feelings for her, or hers for me. We still have our ordinary sex-life together and we both enjoy it, because it's based on love. The other thing's just mechanical, she says it's boring and meaningless to her; it must be. I did have that worry in the early days she might one time have it with someone and fall for him, but I wouldn't think there's much chance of that when you see what they are; most of them are nearly past it, feeble and old.

I wouldn't roll anyone who came, I don't agree with that. A bloke loses his wallet or his cash and he wouldn't come again; he'd warn off his friends too, it'd soon get round. Anyway, why should I, Shirley's earning enough for a nice comfortable living; why spoil it and have the risk of someone being so annoyed about it they'd try and fix you with the police. If they report it, the very least you could expect would be the Law coming nosing round to see what was going on.

I think myself on the whole when I see these fellers who come, well there must be something wrong with the world somewhere when there's so many have to pay for sex. Well, if the need's there and the money with it, somebody might as well get a slice of it; I can't see why it shouldn't be me. I think in some ways prostitution must be a very good thing: I mean the number of sex cases would be fantastic, wouldn't they, if it wasn't for that?

To Never Come Out

Andrew Brown

—I suppose it ain't wrong always finking about it is it? When you're alone in your cell there ain't much else to do is there really, except fink of all these fings, go over 'em in your head and try and puzzle it out. I do it all the time, finking and finking: it keeps coming back to me all the time like that, on and on, very very clear. It's funny that isn't it? It comes straight into my mind, I picture everyfing, every detail of it: where I was, how it happened, the houses, the rooms, the furniture, the women, what I said, how she looked, what she said: every single little fing, all as clear as if it might be yesterday or even today.

—There was this little lane ran along the side of the garden, a sort of fence not very high it was made of those wooden boards one overlapping the next one, edge to edge, you know what I mean? It wasn't very high this fence, you could just see over the top of it. As I was going along I saw this woman there hanging out the washing down her garden. A middle-aged sort of woman, mousey hair all over the place, she had a brown dress on.

I called out over the fence, I said could I have a bandage for me foot, I'd hurt me foot. She said she hadn't got a bandage, there was some shops further down, if I went down the lane I'd come to the road, there was some shops along there. When I looked over the fence again at the bottom she'd gone; she'd gone back in the house. There was some bushes and trees and things, I climbed over the fence and dropped into the garden, then I started walking up the path through where the vegetables were, out on to the grass. She came back out of the house with some more washing; when she saw me she said 'What are you doing in my garden, go

away, what do you want, I told you I hadn't got any band-
ages.'

There was a sort of a shed, a big shed where you keep
garden tools and things, I caught hold of her arm, I said,
'Come on, come in here.' She started yelling. I said 'Keep
quiet, I won't hurt you, I'm not going to hurt you if you
keep quiet.' She said 'What do you want, do you want
money, I've got some money in the house, I've got a hundred pounds in there, I'll give it you if you want it.'

I said 'Not likely, you'll go and phone the Law or start
screaming for help.' She said 'No I won't, you can come with
me, I'll give it you and then you can go away, I won't shout
out.' I said 'I don't want money, you can keep your money.
Just keep quiet and then I won't hurt you.' There was a lot
of room in that shed, a big place it was; all garden tools and
a big lawn-mower and a lot of old sacks. I said 'Get down
on those, you'll be all right. I just want a bit quick and
then I'll leave you alone.' There was an – it was like a rusty
old file with a handle and a pointed end, it was on a sort of a
workbench. I picked it up, I said 'This is for fastening you
in when I've gone, but I'm not going to hurt you with it,
keep quiet.'

She didn't make any noise then, I had an intercourse with
her and then I put the file thing through like the hasp outside the shed-door. I knew if she shook it it'd drop out, I
run off down the garden and climbed over the fence again
back into the lane. She had sort of grey eyes and a tight
brown dress. I don't think she can have been as frightened
as she said she was after, because she definitely didn't make
a lot of noise.

—That would have been Wednesday. Then I think it would
be about the following Tuesday, in the afternoon; there
was this girl, she was sitting on a bench in the churchyard
fooling about with these boys. They went away and left
her, she walked off over a field and down a path through
some allotments. She wasn't very old, I should say she was
nineteen or twenty perhaps, something like that. When I got
up behind her I said 'Does your mother know what you've
been doing?' She said 'What do you mean?' I said I wanted
to have a bit too. She said 'You must be a nutcase.'

There was a shed by the path on these allotments. I pushed her in there, and I done her and then I run out.

—On the Friday there was this girl in this house, I think she was a French girl or an Italian girl, something like that. I'd broken in this house through the back door. I had a look in the kitchen, there was nothing there, nothing in the dining-room; I was in the lounge, in the front room, and she came in. I think she'd been shopping, she had brown trousers on and a coat and a shopping-basket. She said 'What are you doing here, why are you in this house?' I said I was looking for some money. She said 'Madam doesn't keep no money in the house, there is nothing here, go away or I'll call the police.'

I said 'Are you sure there's no money here?' I said 'What about upstairs?', and she said no, there was no money anywhere, they never had any money in the house. So I said 'Oh well if there's no money I might as well have something else then.' I gave her a push on to the sort of settee-thing. It had big cushions on, that material what do they call it, chinetz, Chinese, something like that, all flowers and stuff. She started to scream and carry on, she was kicking her legs and hitting me with her fists. I said 'Shut up, I'm not going to hurt you if you keep quiet,' but she wouldn't, I got her trousers off but she kicked me really hard, she was tearing my hair, everything. So I give up, I ran out through the house again, through the kitchen, I went out through the back gate.

—This woman was in the street, it was night, I asked her was there a bus running, then I pulled her in a shop door-way. I started kissing and cuddling her, I said 'I'm not going to hurt you, don't make a noise.' She was struggling, then over the other side of the pavement, it was a wide pave-ment, this car pulls up and a feller sticks his head out of the window. He calls out 'What's going on, is everything all right?' I said to her 'Tell him everything's all right, if he gets out of that car he'll get hurt.' She said 'Are you going to kill me?' I said 'No, I don't know; you tell him it's all right and then we'll see.' She called out it was all right so the car drove off, then I had an intercourse with her but I didn't hurt her at all, I didn't knock her about or anything like that.

—I knocked at this front door, when the woman answered it I said could she tell me the way to somewhere or other, I don't remember where it was. She said she couldn't and she closed the door so I said all right. Then I went round the back and opened the garden gate, there was some french doors there that was not fastened so I walked in. I couldn't see anything in the room, I went in the hall and in the front room and there was nothing there either. I thought she must have gone out somewhere. I went upstairs and looked in a bedroom or two but I couldn't see anything worth having, then I opened another bedroom door and she was standing there at the mirror. I think she'd just been getting changed, she was zipping her dress up at the back. She had brown hair and I think it was brown eyes, a well-built woman she was, and a bit of lipstick on, not much.

'What do you want?' she says. I said anything, I didn't mind. She had some jewellery, some rings on the dressing-table, she said 'Do you want these?' I said no, I never touched jewellery. I said 'Come on, get on that bed, I'm not going to hurt you.' She said 'You're not going to rape me, are you?' I said 'I don't know,' because I didn't. She said 'Look,' she said, 'I'm a married woman, I never let any man touch me except my husband.' I said 'Well, even married women do it sometimes with other men.' She said 'Yes, but I'm a different sort of married woman' she said, 'I go to church and all that.' She said 'Please don't rape me.' I said 'All right, don't keep on about it, don't keep saying it.'

I was sitting on the bed and she was sitting on the bed talking to me like that. We were talking to each other it must have been ten minutes I should think, she was telling me all this about her husband, he worked for a big firm, a sort of a manager, a persons-manager I think she said, would it be, something like that? I said it didn't make no difference to me, she might as well let me have it, in the finish I had an intercourse with her and then I went. She was crying a bit. It might perhaps have been because she didn't want her husband to find out, I think.

—There was this girl, she was riding her horse along the side of a field. I was standing by this gate, when she came past I got hold of her by the leg and pulled her off. I'd thought she was older, she looked bigger on the horse somehow. When I got her off I could see she wasn't, she was more like a girl really. I said 'How old are you?' and she said she was fourteen. I said 'Well can you prove you're only fourteen?' and she said yes she could, she had a sort of disc thing round her neck with a chain on it; it had her name and address on and her date of birth, everything. I couldn't work it out; she said it showed she was fourteen so I said 'Oh all right then, hop it.'

She said 'I've lost my pony, he's run off,' and I said 'Well I'll help you look for him,' so I did. We went over near some bushes to look for him, then some other people on horses came along in the distance. She started running towards them and shouting, so I went the other way, I doubled back along the path and climbed over a fence and ran away.

—This woman was pregnant, I think it was four months pregnant she said she was, about four months, something round there. She said 'You can't, I'm pregnant, I'm going to have a baby.' I said 'That's all right, I won't hurt you, it won't do no harm. If you struggle it might hurt, but if you keep still you'll be all right.' It was in her kitchen, she was cooking the dinner I think; there was another room off at the side, like a little sitting-room it was. I had the intercourse with her there. There was like a small bed in the corner, it might have been a child's bed I think, I know it wasn't very big. There was an attache-case up on a shelf. She was a Welsh lady, a high voice, black hair, I suppose she'd be about thirty. Not very pretty, not what you'd call pretty, at least I don't think so.

—It was a big house, it was a bungalow actually; I looked in all the rooms and there was nothing. Where I went in at the back door there was this kitchen with all that stuff, what is it, formica, all round. Then a big kind of sitting-room with the telly there, two of those wooden chairs, basket chairs, like one there and one there, and a stand with drinks on. In the hall there was a mirror and by the side of it a sort of

umbrella prop, and a thing for hanging hats and coats. A
door to the place where you eat your meals, then some more
little doors, one to a child's bedroom, one to the toilet; and
then the next one was the bathroom, I pushed that open and
she was standing there without any clothes on, she had a
toothbrush stuck in her mouth but nothing on. Middle-aged,
sort of greyish hair, a bit grey at the sides. I said 'Come on,
it's all right, I'm not going to hurt you.'

*   *   *

The offences were committed during a period of four weeks
during the summer, and all of them were within a fifteen-
mile radius of his home. At one time more than two hundred members of the police force were on active duty trying
to catch him. Public warnings were circulated, an Identikit
picture which bore no resemblance to him was issued, and a
description which was accurate was published in the press.
It described him as being in his mid-thirties, with a fair
complexion and dark hair, about 5 ft. 9 in. in height, and
of medium build. He was stated to be strong, savage and
cunning. 'This Man Is Dangerous' said one newspaper's
front-page headline; 'This Monster Must Be Caught,' said
another.

—My wife read it all in the paper. She said 'Ooh my God'
she said, 'I hope he doesn't come round here.' I said 'You
don't need to worry' I said, 'he won't come round here.' She
said 'How do you know he won't, he might. Anyhow' she
said, 'I'm keeping the door locked, I'm not letting anyone in
if they come knocking here.'

I said 'You don't want to worry yourself about things
like that, he wouldn't touch you anyway, you're pregnant.'
She said 'Well there's one here they write about, she was
pregnant too and he done it to her.' 'Oh' I said, 'that's only
newspaper talk, you don't want to believe all you read in
newspapers. Some of the things they've written there about
him, I bet he's not as bad as they say. I bet some of them
even got on the bed for him if they was to tell the full truth.'
She said 'Well I wouldn't if he came for me.' I said 'How can
you tell, you just don't know; you might, fear can make
people do things, can't it?' She said she wouldn't do that for

anyone, then we went on and talked about something else.

About half past eleven at night there was a knock on the door, it was the woman who lives in the ground-floor flat. She said 'Come quick, there's somebody outside in the garden, I'm scared it's that man they've been writing about in the papers.' I said 'Oh go back to bed,' I said, 'he won't come round here.' She said 'He might, it might be him, I know I can hear someone out there in the garden.' Her husband was on night-work, that was why she was scared. I said, 'Wait a minute then, I'll go and get a flashlamp, I'll come down and look for you.' So I did, I got the flashlamp, I told her to come in and stop with my wife while I went down; then I went out in the garden and had a walk round it, then I came back and told her it was all right, there was no one there, perhaps there had been but they'd gone away. She said 'Anyway I'm very grateful to you for looking, Andy, I'd have been scared to death if you hadn't done that for me.'

The next night I was over at my mother's, she said 'Did you read all that in the papers about the chap raping those women?' I said yes I had done and she said 'You were round some of those places this week, weren't you?' I said yes I had been, I'd been in some of them. She said 'You're not the feller, are you, you're not the one they're looking for?'

I said 'No of course I'm not.' She said 'If you are, you just stop it. If they catch that feller they'll kill him: they don't like rape cases, they'll string him up on a lamp-post or something like that.'

So when she said that I didn't do it any more. I stopped it then all together till the next fortnight they caught me. They caught me because I slipped; there was some chaps at work talking about it, they were saying how he'd done this that and the other they'd read about, he'd assaulted an old woman with crutches and someone else he'd threatened with a knife. I wasn't thinking, I said 'I'll bet you'll find a lot of that was made up, she didn't have no crutches, she wasn't an old lady at all. And I bet you you'll find in that other case there wasn't a knife either. It was probably something more like a rusty old file and he wasn't threatening her with it, he was using it to fasten the lock on the door after him or something like that.'

One of the workmen said to me 'How come you know so

much about it then? Do you know the chap who did it or
something?' I said 'No of course not, I'm just saying you
can't believe what you read in the papers that's all.' Anyway he must have phoned the police, they were round at
work I should think it was only ten minutes later; a whole
lot of them in a van, they said they wanted to take me down
the police station.

When we got there they kept asking me was it me and I
kept saying no. They were saying 'Look we're not going to
hit you or hurt you or anything like that, but you're a very
sick man, a very very sick man, now come on, you tell us
about it, it'll be much better.' I said 'I'm not a sick man,'
but they said 'Yes you are, you've been in a mental hospital,
we know about that, we know you're sick.' I said 'Well what
if I have been in a mental hospital, that was four years back;
they let me out, didn't they, they said I was all right, I'm not
sick.'

But they wouldn't let me go. They kept me there I think
it was all that day and all the next day. Then they gave me
an I.D. parade, they brought these women in to walk down
the line, see if they could pick me out. I think there was six
or seven all together; one or two said they wasn't sure, one
of them sort of winked at me, one tried to hit me. The others
they just said 'That one, that's him, that's the man.'

So then the police said 'All right then, now come on, you
tell us, you might as well tell us now. There's nothing to be
afraid of, nobody's going to hurt you, we're just going to
look after you and see you can't do no more harm. You're
not going to get hung, it's not murder or anything like that.'

Then I said all right I'd tell them, and I did. One of them
afterwards he said to me 'I don't understand it' he said, 'you
don't even look like it, you've never done violence before, I
just don't understand it at all.'

—I should think there was ten cases altogether; ten cases
but they didn't charge me with them all. Some of the women
didn't want to go to court and give evidence, the police said
they could manage with those that did. In the finish it was
only six charges, they said they'd got enough with those to
make them stick. Four rapes, two attempted rapes, and a
few bits-and-bobs; assaults and larcenies and things like

that, because I'd broken into houses and taken a bit of money lying around in some of them and things like that.

The Judge said it was the worst case he'd come across, one of the worst he'd ever heard of, even though I was one of those what do they call them, sithopatics is it? He said I not only knew what I was doing, I must have knowed it was wicked too. He gave me life four times; four lots of life he give me, and I think it was two sevens, two lots of five, and a two. I don't know what it all added up to, I've never tried to work it out. I know it means they say I've got to never come out.

*   *   *

The note was printed in block capitals on a sheet torn from an exercise book. 'Andy is O.K.' it said. 'We look after him in here and see he gets in no trouble in the nick. He only done in reality what lots think in our secret minds. He needs help for if he ever gets outside though.'

—No, I dunno who put that note on your chair, one of my mates I expect. What does it say, I'm a nut-case? That's what they usually call me, nut-case, shit-bag, things like that. Everybody's the same in here, you can call anybody anything, they don't mind; everybody's all the same anyhow, the different things they've done, no one's any better than anybody else. Not the screws though, they wouldn't call you things like that; if they see it's getting you down they tell the others to stop getting at you, to leave you alone. There's one screw, he says to me 'Don't you listen to them, boy' he says, 'You stand more chance of getting out someday than they do, I can tell you that.'

No, if you make your mind up to it, it doesn't worry you, what's the point? I'm glad I'm here though, I'd sooner be here than in a mental hospital. Some of them were egging me on, they said if I talked to you, you might get me taken out of prison and put into a mental hospital. I asked the doctor about it, he said you couldn't, he said it was only him and a lot of other doctors could do that. So I said all right, I'd talk to you. I wouldn't have talked to you if he hadn't promised me that.

Because I don't ever want to go into a mental hospital again, that's why. I never want to go back to one of those places, I'd sooner be in prison and do my time like everyone else. No, it's not they're cruel places; some ways they're better than prison, you can go out for walks in the garden, have socials and things. At least you could in the one I was at, and you don't have to work there if you don't want to. Here you have to work; I don't mind that though, I'd sooner work even though the wages aren't very good. I mean you can't do much with five and ninepence a week can you? I'd sooner be here, though: I think I ought to be here, I think prisons are better places than mental hospitals for people like me. I'd sooner be a nut-case in a prison than a nut-case in a mental hospital any day.

You don't feel you're forgotten in prison somehow, not so much as you are in a hospital. There you feel nobody knows you; they're all sick people, a lot of them just walk around all day and they don't talk. Everyone talks here, you've got lots of friends. People take an interest in you, ask you how you're getting on, did you enjoy your visit when your wife came, show us your picture of your kid and all things like that. If you don't make trouble for them they don't make trouble for you; the cons, the screws, they all try and help you all the time. Besides to be in a mental hospital you have to be silly, and I don't think I am silly, not all that silly anyway.

Fifteen years, twenty years, you push it out of your mind don't you? Life's a life; he gave me four life sentences but what's the difference whether he gives me one or four or eight? I've only got one haven't I, I can't do more than that.

This is a photo of my kid, my little girl. However long I've done, that's how old she is; she was born the week I got my sentence, that's how I work it out. I've tried to colour it a bit with some paints one of the chaps on the block lent me. I couldn't get it right, she hasn't really got orange eyes, they're more brown but there wasn't no brown in the box. Fair hair but not as yellow as that. That's my wife, that was taken last year in the gardens outside the new block of flats where she lives. It's the block of flats there, it was only built last year, the council gave it us; that's where we live on the fourth floor, I think it would probably be say those two windows there.

Yes she's a nice looking girl, she's got a nice nature too; one in a thousand I'd say she is, one in a million even. I write her every week and then she writes one back to me. This is her last letter, I got it yesterday, you can see what she writes. 'I love you too, me and our baby we always love you, and we both always will. You always been good to me Andy no matter what they say, please look after yourself.' She writes a good letter doesn't she? Better than the letters I write to her, I have to get someone to help me if I can't spell one of the words. I go and ask one of the screws and he spells it for me and then he says 'Now have you got that Andy? You spell it back to me to show me that you've got it.' So then I do, and that way I remember it.

I can't really spell at all hardly. I was never learned it; usually I get it from reading, that's how I know most of the words because I've seen them in a book. I used to do a lot of reading but I don't do so much now. Oh that one they call Hank Janson, do you know him, Mickey Spillane, ones like that. If they had big words I just jumped them and tried to guess. Not in here, they don't have those books in here; it was before I came in that I used to read them. In here they've got nothing like those, only cowboys and westerns and hard books I can't understand.

I can't think of much else about my wife really. Only that she's very nice; when she comes in to see me she's always dressed herself up nice and tidy. She laughs a lot with me, tells me funny things to make me laugh. Like something funny happened when she went to the Assistance people, something like that. Or perhaps one of her friends told her she ought not to bother with me any more, and she said to her it wasn't no bother thank you – anything of that sort, she can say some right funny things sometimes. And talk, talk, talk, you can talk to her for hours and never get fed-up. One of the screws said to me one day 'That missus of yours is a real nice girl' he said, 'It's always nice to have someone give you a smile when you bring her over the visiting-room.'

The first time I ever met her was on a street corner, she was the sister of another girl who lived down the road from us. She came walking along, it was a Saturday night, she said 'Hello' she said, 'You're Andy aren't you from number seven? What are you doing standing out here looking so miserable for?' I said I was miserable because I wanted to go to the pictures and I hadn't got anybody to go with, and she said 'Oh I'll go to the pictures with you if that's all you want to cheer you up.' I said 'Well you'll have to pay' I said, 'Because I haven't got no money to pay with either.' So she said well all right she would, and that was it, we went.

We got married four weeks after that, because we were in love. We found ourselves a one-room to live in, not far from where her family was and my family was. We found it on the Monday and we got married on the Saturday and we moved in there together on the Saturday night. We went to the pictures in the evening, then we went home to our room and we went to bed. I didn't know what to do because I'd never had a girl before, and she didn't know because she'd never been with a boy. We kissed and cuddled each other for a bit and then it was all right, we liked it, we used to do a lot of love-making after that.

Altogether we were married three years, right up to the time when I got into this bit of trouble. Well it was more than a bit of trouble, I should say up till when I got into this big lot of trouble. No, there was nothing else before, only one house-breaking I did about a year after we got married, that I never got caught for. We were hard-up for the rent because I was out of work for a bit. I told her I thought I knew somewhere I could go to get it off a friend of mine. I went up the other end of town and broke in a big house there, I found this money I think it was about thirty quid in a biscuit-tin on top of a cupboard, the first house I went into. I took it straight back to her, I said my mate had given it me, it was something he'd owed me a long time; and I said 'There'll be a bit left over after you've squared the rent, let's have a night out.'

We went into town and we went to the pictures – two pictures, a big one and then a Donald Duck place where they just had cartoons. We had our photo took in an arcade, then we went and had a meal, some hamburgers and chips and two cups of tea each, we bought a lemonade to take home with us and we went on some slot-machines. Oh yes and a white blouse in a shop window she said she liked the look of, could we afford it; it was twenty-seven and six I think, and we had just about enough left.

All the time we was married I was working except for about a month that time when I was off sick with the 'flu. I was a dustman working for the Corporation. That was always my job, I was doing that before we got married even, for about a year between when I came out of the mental hospital and when we was married. I liked it: on the dust we called it, that was what everyone called it. They'd say 'He's working on the dust', that means a dustman or a refuse collector I think they're called too. A dustman's best friend is the kids, they're always coming running up to you and saying 'Have you found any pennies, mister, give us any pennies will you that you've found?' So you do, you always give them a penny to get some sweets with. There's a lot of people think it's not much of a job but I did, I liked it. The money wasn't a lot, I think it was £11-8-0 a week about, but I don't smoke and I don't drink and I don't gamble so I didn't mind.

I didn't know if it'd be enough for getting married on though. When I was out with my wife having a walk in the park – this was before we were married, she wasn't my wife then – I said to her 'Would you ever think of marrying a dustman?' 'Oh yes' she said, 'I like dustmen, I'd marry the first one I saw.' So I said 'Well I'm a dustman' and she said 'Well you're the first one I've seen then aren't you, so I'd better marry you.' I told you she could say some funny remarks like that didn't I, very very quick she is, very humorous. And that was it, we got married the end of that week.

Well, the mental hospital I was in was a big one down in the south. I was there fifteen years, until I was nearly thirty. Not in the same one all the time, no; what I mean is, I was in institutions fifteen years, different mental institutions of one kind or another, always, all the time.

You see that's the difficulty, I don't remember things properly from far back, from childhood. Yes, I'll try.

—There was an accident. It was when I was seven or eight I think, round about there. I don't remember nothing at all

from before that, nothing, not where we lived or anything.
I think it was somewhere in the south but I don't know
where, you'd have to ask someone else. I've got two sisters
and eight brothers, that's eleven all together counting me,
and I was the first one, I'm the eldest of the lot. My father
and mother used to live in a caravan, they weren't gipsy
people but something like that, very poor people, tinkers
do you call them, wandering about?

And there was another one, at least my mum told me
once there was another one before me, but he died. They
were very cold and poor and they'd got nowhere to live
and it was in the winter, my father was carrying me and
she was carrying the other one, and he wrapped his coat
round me to keep me warm but the other one there was
nothing to wrap round him. He took a chill, he got pneu-
monia or something and died. He was older than me. So
really I was her firstborn she said. When I had my accident
she was very unhappy, she thought she'd lose me too. It
was in a yard somewhere, I was playing with a lot of
other kids, I got up on a big roof somewhere and I fell
through it, it was glass. This is what she told me but I don't
remember it myself really, I know I fell and cut myself,
cut all my leg, cut my face and my head and got a bang
on it, a bad bang she said. There's a scar there now, you
can see it, but it didn't affect me in any way. I was in hospital a long time; I don't know how long, I think she told
me once it was six months or a year, I know it was a long
time.

This had set me back, I had to go to a special school she
said, one that was for education subnormally or something,
I don't know the proper words. I can't remember the school,
I can't remember much of it at all; I think it would be in
Cornwall, I know it was a long way away and I never saw
anybody. Not my mum and dad I mean, I didn't see them
ever, they weren't there. It must have been a funny kind
of a school, not like a proper one because there was only
a few kids there; me and a few others, we never had no
lessons, we went for walks and things like that. They never
taught you spelling or sums or any of those things. I enjoyed it mostly, it was better than school from what I've
heard, because you could play all the time. It's a job to

puzzle it out though, where it was, what it was for. I think it was a kind of a home it might have been, just me and these two or three other kids and two voluntary ladies who looked after us.

Then I went back home, it would be when I was ten or eleven about. I remember that, I remember going back home, going to live with my mum and dad and all the others in a kind of a little house in a back-street place. They must have stopped wandering about then mustn't they? But I remember going back home because I didn't like it when I got there, I didn't like my dad, he was too fond of the belt. He was always laying into me with his belt. He said I might think he was hard but it was for my own good, he said one day I'd get myself into a big lot of trouble if I went on thieving.

He was a good father though, he kept us all fed, there was always food on the table. I don't think he had a job; he did something illegal to make his living at. No not screwing or things like that: what he did was he bred chaffinches and linnets, I think that's illegal isn't it, and he used to sell them to people in the market. I don't think you're supposed to do that but he did, he liked his birds, he had a lot of them in big wire cages in the back yard. He used to buy seed for them, he'd go without things for himself so long as they got their seed and their water.

What he used to give me the belt for was for knocking off, stealing, pinching things, apples and lemonade and sweets from shops, or handbags that me and some other boys used to take. We went in the parks, we had a big long stick, if we saw a courting couple on a bench or lying on the grass we'd creep up and get the woman's handbag with this stick with a sort of hook on the end of it, and then take the money out. The police were always coming round our house after me, he used to give me his belt every time when they'd gone. I kept running away, stopping out, not going home because I knew he'd give me his belt.

Then I went to a sort of a school for a bit near where we lived. I mean I was supposed to go to it, but I hardly ever did. I didn't like the lessons, I'd stay away playing all day or just running around. He used to give me the belt for that too when he found out.

When I was fourteen or fifteen perhaps it would be, I was taken to the court for being out of control and pinching things. My dad and mum said they couldn't control me, they'd got these other ten kids and they couldn't do nothing with me. In the court it was said I had a mental age of a boy of eight I think it was, a boy of seven or eight. Anyhow then I was sent to a special place for boys like me, a big like a school out in the country. I ran away from there I think it was eighteen times all together, I kept breaking into sweet shops and places and stealing. Eventually they said they couldn't do nothing with me and I'd have to go somewhere else.

The place I went to then was a kind of a place like where angels go to if you know what I mean, some of it was good and some of it was bad. It was an institution, I think it was called a Certified Institution or something, and you weren't supposed to be able to run away from there. But I ran away from there too, they kept catching me and taking me back the same as the other one, until they said they couldn't do anything with me either. So then I had to be sent to somewhere else where they had to have a special certificate to send you. That was that big mental hospital I told you about. That was a place you couldn't run away from. It was all right inside, it had big gardens and places for you to walk about, but all round it was this great big high wall that no one could ever get over.

I was there from when I was nineteen until I was twenty-nine. It didn't agree with me, I didn't like it, that's the place I was frightened they were going to send me back to that I thought you might be connected with. Most of all what I didn't like was that they were always picking on you. If you did something they didn't like they'd lock you up for a bit, then when they let you out you had to start right at the bottom and work your way up to all your privileges again one by one. Two weeks before you could have a walk in the grounds, two more weeks till you could play on the billiards table, another two weeks till you could sit in certain rooms, and all things like that. It was all the time like starting all over again, then back you'd go to the beginning the next thing you did wrong. There's a game isn't there, I don't know what they call it, you have a big board with

ladders and ropes on it, you go on a bit and then you go
down to the bottom again. It was like that. 'Ladders and
Ropes' is it? Yes that's right, 'Snakes and Ladders', well it
was all like that.

It's not like that in prison though; they give you three
days' loss of privileges, three days' loss of association and
so on; and when it's over, nobody holds it against you,
everything's forgotten. And you don't get into trouble for
things so much, well I don't anyhow, not here I don't get
into trouble hardly at all. I never fight or anything like that.

Nine or ten years I was in that mental hospital place, I
looked after the chickens they had mostly. All those funny
people there I told you about didn't I; they used to just
stand up stiff like that, all day they'd do it, and when you
went along the corridor the next morning there they were
again. You'd only see a doctor once in a while, if you had
a headache he'd give you an aspirin or something, but that
was all I remember.

One day they just came and they said 'You're all right
now, you can go.' I said 'Go? Go where?' and they said
'Anywhere, you're free to go, you can go home if you like.'
I think my dad had to sign a paper or something for me to
say he'd have me back at home. I said 'Well what have I
been doing in here all this time?' and they said 'Nothing,
you're all right now, you can go, you're cured.' It seemed
a bit funny to me.

Anyhow I went, and when I got home my dad said 'You'd
better get yourself a job at your age, twenty-nine.' So I did,
I got myself a job in three days, on the dust for the Corporation, and that was what I was doing ever since. I did a probation once, not long after I'd got home; that was for a shop,
I stole some sweets and a few bob, about twelve quid I
think it was. But they gave me the probation and let me go
on working, and there was nothing else after that.

No violence, no I've never done violence; only thieving,
knocking-off things, breaking into places when I was on
the run from those places. I'm not a violent man, my wife
would tell you that and my mum, I've never hit anybody
in my life. I think if I'd ever done violence they would have
kept me in that mental hospital place, but I never did, either
inside it or out, they told my dad I was perfectly safe to be

let out, except for keeping an eye on me about the thieving.

That was it about these rapes you see, I didn't do any violence with them, in fact I told them all, I said 'If you keep quiet I won't hurt you.' I expect that was what made them give in most of them, they were frightened I might knock them about. But I didn't, yet they never struggled very much; I can't make that out. No. I can't tell you why they let me go on and do it, that's too hard for me, I don't know what people are thinking. Perhaps if I was more intelligent I might; sometimes I think if I'd been more intelligent and had more of an education it would have gone better for me in the court.

Well what I mean is, I didn't know the words you see, and that's what made it go badly for me in front of the Judge. When they read out the charges to me I said what I shouldn't have done, I said 'Yes I fucked her. Yes I fucked her. Yes I fucked her,' and all like that, each one all the way through. Afterwards the screw said to me he said 'You shouldn't have said that, boy, that's not the right way to talk, that judge must have thought you were an animal or something. What you should have said is "Yes, I had an intercourse with her", not "Yes I fucked her", that's not a proper way to talk now is it?'

I didn't know no better did I? I suppose it's the way you're brought up. I've never had no manners. But I think that made it go bad for me, if I'd been better-spoken I might have got off lighter.

It was because I went to that mental hospital place, you got no intelligence there, no education, nothing. That's why I like these psychiatrists and things, they're intelligent people, they can talk to you and you can learn words from them. They give you jigsaw puzzles to do, they show you bits of them and they say what's missing and you have to try and guess what the piece is. I'm very good at them, it might be an elephant's trunk or something; I always know, I say straight off 'An elephant's trunk should go in that space there' or 'The lion ought to have a tail' or something like that.*

---

*In one section of the Binet-Simon I.Q. Test, at the age 6 level a card with simple mutilated pictures is shown and the subject is asked 'What part is gone?' or 'What isn't there?'

The psychiatrists never talk to me about this business, no. Just tests, things like that. There'd be no point in anyone asking me why I done it, would there, because I couldn't tell them, I dunno. Sometimes you sit in your cell and you think did I do those things, I suppose I must have, but it was such a long time ago now, it all seems like a dream. I done it because I enjoyed it I suppose, I wanted a bit and there was a woman so I had her. In court they said it was perhaps because my wife was pregnant, and I couldn't do it with her, she said it wouldn't be safe, it might hurt the baby. Could that be right do you think? Myself I think it was more likely because I'd been shut up all those years in that mental hospital place and I hadn't had it, and if I couldn't get it with my wife I had to get it somewhere else.

Someone asked me why I couldn't have gone to a prostitute and said 'Please could I have an intercourse with you?' But that wouldn't be right, and anyhow I'd be too scared. That's funny to say isn't it, it doesn't seem it could be right does it? I can't make head or tails of it myself. I do try, I try often when I'm lying in my cell going to sleep, I start thinking about these women; it's all very clear, I can remember every detail of it, the furniture in the room, everything. Then it sort of starts to drop off and I start thinking about my wife instead, that I love her, that I'd just like to be with her somewhere where we could be happy. I was happy, those three years we were married, I was very happy; she changed everything in my life, I'd been very lonely up till then. Don't make sense really does it, when you come to try and think about it? I go on trying, I expect one day I might be able to get to it. But there's no use hurrying about it, is there; after all I've got plenty of time to think, I've got more time than anyone.

All these doctors and psychiatrists and people, I shall still be here trying to think about it when they're all dead and gone.

*   *   *

The term 'moral imbecility' was recognized and given legal definition by the Mental Deficiency Act of 1913, and was changed to 'moral defectiveness' by the subsequent Act of 1927. Three grades were stipulated: idiots with I.Q.s of

20 or below, imbeciles with I.Q.s between 20 and 50, and feeble-minded persons who were those with I.Q.s between 50 and 75.

This third class did not bear the physical stigmata of the two lower groups; with a mental age between seven and twelve, they were defined as 'persons in whose case there exists from birth or from an early age mental defectiveness not amounting to imbecility, yet so pronounced that they require care, supervision and control for their own protection or for the protection of others; or, in the case of children, that they by reason of such defectiveness appear to be permanently incapable of deriving benefit from the instruction of ordinary schools'. In America the term 'moron' is used for this category.

Andrew Brown was diagnosed as being feeble-minded, or a 'high-grade defective' when he was fourteen. As a result he was detained in various mental institutions until he was twenty-nine, his frequent abscondings resulting eventually in his being confined for the last six years of this period in one of a maximum-security type. A very large proportion of those so designated prove capable of supporting themselves socially when they become adult, and cease legally to be within the category. They constitute less than 2 per cent of the population, and fewer than one in ten ever displays serious anti-social tendencies.

The introduction of the Mental Health Act in 1959 superseded all previous Acts. Under it moral defectives were redefined as either 'severely sub-normal' (previously the idiots and imbeciles), or 'sub-normal' (formerly the feeble-minded or 'high-grade defectives'). Under this Act those in the sub-normal category could not be compulsorily detained after the age of twenty-five unless they had been proved to be dangerous to others.

Therefore when the Act came into force Andrew Brown had to be discharged along with several hundred others in this same category. In common with most of them he was able to support himself socially. He obtained work almost immediately as a dustman and worked satisfactorily for nearly four years. His previous history of minor delinquencies had showed no tendency whatsoever towards violence, and there can be no question that his release was not perfectly justified. Further detention would anyway have been illegal.

There is however a fourth category of mental defect recognized by the Act of 1959 – that of psychopathic disorder. This is described as 'a persistent disorder or disability of mind (whether or not including subnormality of intelligence) which results in abnormally aggressive or seriously irresponsible conduct on the part of the patient, and requires or is susceptible to medical treatment'. But even when they are diagnosed as such, psychopaths cannot be compulsorily detained after the age of twenty-five either, unless they have demonstrated that they are dangerous.

Arguments as to what exactly 'psychopaths' are, whether they are even a demonstrably separate type and not merely those thrown into a kind of diagnostic dust-bin, have occupied doctors and psychiatrists for at least 150 years.

The American Benjamin Rush was aware of such mental states in 1812; and in 1835 Dr. J. C. Pritchard of Bristol was writing of those in whom 'the moral and active principles of the mind are strongly perverted or depraved; the power of self-government is lost or greatly impaired, and the individual is found to be incapable of conducting himself with decency and propriety'. At the end of the nineteenth century Krafft-Ebing spoke of them as suffering from 'a state of moral blindness, an insanity of altruistic feeling, a coldness of the heart'. And in 1939 the Scottish psychiatrist David (now Sir David) Henderson spoke of 'individuals who conform to an intellectual standard, sometimes high and sometimes approaching the realm of defect, who exhibit disorders of conduct of an anti-social nature, usually of a recurrent or episodic type, for whom we have no adequate provision of a curative nature'.

Twenty years later Henderson described an aggressive psychopath as 'someone in whom the fierceness and intensity of conduct seems often to be related to feelings of frustration which have their roots in the instinctive life of the individual. Action is almost in the nature of a reflex, it is a trigger-like reaction, with coldness, hardness, and an insensibility to the feelings of others, and an absence of remorse which relates the condition to a primitive level. It is sometimes a method of escape from a situation which has proved for the moment intolerable, an immature way in which the personality attempts to evade reality.' He added: 'The persons who constitute this group are obviously a very dangerous social class, and the majority of such cases are not susceptible to psychological treatment.' It has been estimated that they represent less than one-quarter per cent of the whole population.

And Sir David Henderson has also written this of the psychopath—

'The inadequacy or deviation or failure to adjust to ordinary social life is not mere wilfulness or badness which can be threatened or thrashed out of the individual so involved. It constitutes a true illness, for which we have no specific explanation. But it is extremely difficult to convince the public that aggressive conduct of a criminal nature can be studied scientifically; rather does the public find the so-called criminal a convenient person on whom to project its anti-social impulses. Whereas the criminal discharges his fear and aggression by attacking and punishing the peaceable citizen, the peaceable citizen discharges his fear and aggression by punishing the criminal.'

Andrew Brown stays where he is, doing four lives, two sevens, two lots of five, and a two. He likes prison; he is contented in it, he gets on well with others, he makes no trouble, he is quiet, mild, almost benign. A good-looking man, with dark hair neatly parted and combed into a wave over his forehead. Tractable, softly spoken, smiling often, writing each week to his wife to tell her he loves her, and waiting for the letter back which tells him that she too loves him. He likes liquorice sweets and budgerigars. Sometimes when he is talking and thinking, two lines of a faint frown show between his eyebrows, as he looks up out of the barred window at the sky with his blue, forget-me-not eyes.

An Appendix: Some Brief Remarks

None of the people who made these statements knows, or has ever known or had any connection whatsoever with, the persons in the main body of the book. Like them they represent no types and speak only for themselves

1 *H.J.C., aged 28, female, married.*

I was sexually assaulted by a male relative when I was eight: he was in his thirties. I didn't know it was happening until it happened, if you know what I mean. I'd been told all the usual business by my parents about never taking sweets from a stranger and all the rest of it: but this man wasn't a stranger, he was someone I knew and liked. That kind of physical contact from a totally unexpected source really did disturb me because it was so unfamiliar and rather frightening though I didn't know why. I can only describe it now as bringing something into the air that I'd never experienced before. I think I must say also that I did find it in a way which I couldn't understand as faintly exciting without knowing why. For a long time afterwards I never wanted to think about it and I pushed it right to the back of my mind: in fact I didn't mention it at all to anyone, not even to my parents, until when I was about twenty-two I told a girl that I shared a room with at college about it. I feel it would have been better if it hadn't happened, I don't think it helped much with the struggle of growing-up which you go through as a girl. For a long time during adolescence I had a feeling that there was something about sex which I didn't like; though of course I couldn't say it was due just to that incident. I've really only been able to think about it properly in the last few years. I'm sure it had no really serious lasting effect on me, in fact looking back on it now I feel kind of sad about him because I realize he was quite a nice person and it must have made him very lonely to be like that.

2 B.S.R., age 31, male, married.

When I was ten I was interfered with or assaulted or whatever it's called by a middle-aged man whom I knew only
vaguely by sight. I don't remember being scared, at the
time it just seemed a bit odd and peculiar and unexpected,
something untoward you might say. I found it faintly distasteful but I didn't feel frightened or outraged, nothing like
that, it was just I didn't like it or enjoy it but didn't know
how to get out of it, and it made me a bit nervous about
being on my own with men for quite a long time afterwards.
I was still at primary school and when you're a kid you
often 'tell' on people, and I did on him: the next day I told
my teacher because I had a vague kind of feeling that perhaps he'd go and tell the man off or something like that.
But instead he told the headmaster, and the headmaster
told both the police and my mother. The result was I was
taken down to the police station where a kindly policeman,
as I remember him, took me through the whole story to
find out exactly what had happened. I think it was that
which scared me more than anything else; somehow then it
had got much bigger and more difficult to understand. Although I didn't have to go to court, action was taken against
the man and he left the district. When I think about it now,
which I hardly ever do, it all seems to me to have been made
much more important than I think it really was, because it
had no terribly bad effect on me then nor has it ever had
any noticeable one since.

3 L.D., age 46, female, single.

When I was in my twenties a complete stranger once jumped
out at me in a deserted place in the dark and attempted to
assault me sexually. I was quite a strong well-built girl and
he wasn't very big, but all the same I was literally terrified.
Up till then I'd thought I was pretty sophisticated and tough,
I'd had several boy-friends and so on; but when something
like that happens your limbs seem to go like jelly. Even
though you probably are stronger than he is you feel almost
paralysed, you think your arms and legs aren't going to

work, you've got a sickening feeling that you're at a disadvantage. In my case I suddenly reacted with extreme
and violent anger, I was screaming and shouting at him like
an alley-cat, using the sort of language that startled even
me. He ran off and I went back to where I lived. I was
trembling like mad and it's funny now to recollect this, but
I couldn't bear to switch the light on when I got into my
room. I stayed in the dark having a long and absolutely
furious conversation out loud with myself, 'How dare he!'
and all that sort of thing. It took me about an hour to calm
down, and then I wanted to go out straight away and talk
to people, not about that but just ordinarily and be where
there was light and comfort and normality. It never crossed
my mind as it does now that there must have been some
kind of sickness in him that ought to be understood and
tolerated: then I was simply livid about it and I really was
threatening him with extreme violence when I was shouting
at him. It's strange, this was twenty-five years ago and yet
it still makes me feel a bit jumpy and nervous even now to
talk about it.

4 S. J. P., age 51, male, single.

Far from perverting me, the experience of what one might
call being 'had' at the age of thirteen by an older boy I
knew seemed to me the natural culmination of the way my
own emotional life had been developing ever since I was
conscious as a child of sex at all. I had no fear and no dis-
taste and not for one moment could I have said then, or
could say now, anything other than that I enjoyed it. It was
bound to have happened to me sooner or later and the only
surprise is that it didn't happen sooner. Of course I imagined
myself wildly in love with the boy concerned, you always
did at that age: one naturally tended to dramatize oneself
and the whole *ambience*. Nowadays I think there should
be a good deal less fuss than there is about the subject of
physical relationships between boys because I don't think
it's terribly important at all. Some of them change to
heterosexuality when they grow up, they marry and raise
families in the ordinary way, as indeed did that particular
boy I was involved with myself. I on the other hand have

remained homosexual; but it wasn't through that, I was homosexual already. I can't help wondering if there weren't boys like me what exactly the older ones would have done at that time when they were very virile indeed: they would have been having girls I suppose, and it could be argued that that would have been much more harmful: the consequences might have been a good deal more serious.

5 B.P., age 46, male, married.

I'm not kidding you boy, when I woke up and found this bloke trying to get into my bed I shot straight up in the air as though I'd been electrocuted, I leaped straight out of bed and ran though don't ask me where I was going, I was still half asleep. Later when I went back he'd gone so I just got back into bed after locking my door, and went straight off to sleep again. It's funny I should use that particular expression because that was it exactly; it was like once when I was trying to mend a fuse and got an electric shock which knocked me back half-way across the room. My reaction wasn't fear or disgust, much more utter and absolute astonishment that he should try it on with me. I'm not a queer, far from it, and I never have been; and I can remember being rather hurt, almost affronted you might say, that someone should take one look at me and think I might be that way inclined. The following day I told one of the other men about it, and he said 'Oh him, he tries that with everybody': and as soon as he said that it reduced it to a kind of acceptable normality, I thought 'Oh that's all right then, it's not me, it's him.' I still remember it vividly, but I've got to know so many queers since then and am so used to them that now I can only laugh at myself for being so utterly taken aback at the time.

6 P.K.D., age 52, female, married.

I really can't say that being indecently exposed to made much impression on me at all, I just thought 'Well how ridiculous, how absurd, the poor chap.' I think most women have experienced it at some time, and more than once: in fact any time I ever mention it everyone else always says 'Oh yes, that happened to me quite recently.' The first time it happened to me I was a schoolgirl, about six or seven, and at that time I merely thought it was a man who'd forgotten to fasten his trousers; I wasn't in the slightest bit concerned, I never even thought it worth mentioning to anyone. With the other man a few years ago I suppose I might have worried a bit more if the place hadn't been quite so public, because I suppose it does indicate someone who isn't normal and I might have wondered what he'd do next. But as it was the whole incident was so trivial my only reaction was to feel, as I say, rather sorry for him and wonder what possible satisfaction he could get out of it. The only time it ever crosses my mind now is when someone else mentions it in conversation, I never give it a thought otherwise.

7 J.H., age 23, female, cohabiting.

My bloke was done once for living on my immoral earnings and if you ask me I just think the Law was looking for something to put on him, I mean it was ridiculous; I don't think there should be any such charge, not for cases like that. If he's forcing you I suppose that's different, but if he's not then I don't see what it's got to do with anyone else. He doesn't earn his money legally either, he's a thief, but they don't do me for living on his immoral earnings. When he's got money he gives some to me, and when I've got some I give it to him, and how I earn it I reckon is my affair. No I don't mind doing it, it can be a good way of earning a living: I don't mind, he doesn't mind, so what's it to do with anyone else?

8 A.C.N., age 25, female, married.

When this happened to me, my reactions were of different kinds because they were at different stages in time. When it actually was happening I was frightened, petrified like an animal; and, realizing the inescapability of it, only wanting then to get it over.

Afterwards I was suffering from shock: I had been physically hurt, I was numb, but then the first feelings which began were those of self-questioning – whether I shouldn't have struggled harder, whether in some way I might even at the last have prevented it. But violence has always made me shrink: I have never been able to retaliate physically to it.

Finally I wanted to go and talk to somebody about it: a friend, I had to tell her. I didn't want pity, I wanted some kind of reassurance, someone who'd tell me as she did that there was nothing I could have done.

Very slowly over a long period of time afterwards it began to dawn on me when I could bring myself to look back on it that after all, I wasn't any different as a person to what I'd been before. It had happened, it was over, it was getting further and further into the past: but I was still me. Time does wipe it away, especially if you can avoid making a great drama out of it. For this reason I think that while it's necessary to tell somebody about it afterwards, it doesn't mean that it has to be the police. I'd say to anyone now who was an outsider knowing someone to whom this had happened: 'Don't insist the police must be told. Give the woman time to work it out herself, try if you possibly can to somehow reduce the temperature for her.'

9 F.L.D., age 77, female, married.

You would give anything at all, even your own life, to make things different: not to have the horror, the shame, the desperation. You try everything you can think of that might help, you want to do something, anything, that could in some way alter things. You pray, you hope, you believe that somehow, one day, it's all going to be all right. And over and over again all through the years you keep saying to yourself 'Is it me, is it my fault, is it something that I've done?' No one can ever take that feeling from you, that somehow it must be your fault, and it goes on and on, round and round in your head. You can't find any comfort or any happiness or any solution, when it's your own son that does these things.

Acknowledgements

During the preparation of this book many people have helped me with encouragement, advice or assistance, and often with all three. Though nothing in it may be taken in any way as either reflecting their opinions or even necessarily meeting with their approval, I should particularly like to express my thanks to the following:

Harold Harris of the Hutchinson Publishing Group; Anthony Sheil; Douglas Gibson and Pat Weafer of the Circle Trust; Hugh Klare of the Howard League; Dr. I. G. W. Pickering, Dr. Prewer and Miss Martin of the Prison Medical Service; Professor T. C. N. Gibbens of the Institute of Psychiatry; Anthony Gray of the Albany Trust; Dick Atkin of the Ministry of Social Security; Dr. Donald West of the Institute of Criminology; Mr. P. J. Woodfield and Mr. T. Lodge of the Prison Department of the Home Office; Miss D. Love, Mrs. R. Levin, Philip Bean and Barry Swinney of the Probation and After-Care Service; Dr. Anthony Storr; Dr. Albert Ellis; Mr. J. C. Featherstone, Miss Monica Furlong, Mrs. Vicki Moore, Alan Nicholson and Joe Whitty; and J. Brahms. I am also grateful to Messrs. Faber & Faber Ltd. for giving me permission to reprint the quotation by W. H. Auden from *For The Time Being* which they published in 1955; to the Oxford University Press for permission to quote from *A Textbook of Psychiatry* by Henderson and Gillespie, 8th edition (1956); and to W. W. Norton & Company Inc. of New York, for allowing me to quote from D. K. Henderson's *Psychopathic States* (1947). My wife Margery has not only given me her unfailing support, but has also patiently undertaken the endless typing and re-typing of the manuscript.

There are not many books which deal wholly or partly with the subject of sex offenders. The best for the general reader is undoubtedly Dr. Anthony Storr's *Sexual Deviation* (Pelican). Among others to which I have frequently referred have been Alan Benthams' *Sex Crimes and Sex Criminals* (Wisdom House), which despite its lurid appearance contains a lucid and enlightened introduction by Dr. Albert Ellis; *Sex Offenders* by Gebhard, Gagnon, Pomeroy and Christenson (Heinemann), probably the most extensive study yet produced; *Child Victims of Sex Offenders* by T. C. N. Gibbens and Joyce Prince, and *Cruel Parents* by T. C. N. Gibbens and A. Walker, both published by the I.S.T.D.; *New Horizons In Psychiatry* by Peter Hays (Pelican); Henderson and Gillespie's *Textbook of Psychiatry* (O.U.P.); Richard von Krafft-Ebing's *Psychopathia*

Sexualis translated by F. S. Klaf (Mayflower-Dell) which though comically at variance with modern insight and interpretation still remains a great pioneering work; Dr. Alfred Kinsey's *Sexual Behaviour in the Human Male* and *Sexual Behaviour in the Human Female*, both published by Heinemann; Michael Schofield's *Sociological Aspects of Homosexuality* (Longmans); Dr. D. Stafford-Clark's *Psychiatry for Students* (Allen and Unwin); Lars Ullerstam's *The Erotic Minorities* (Calder) which advances the argument that even Swedish tolerance of sexual deviation is far from permissive enough; Nigel Walker's *Crime and Punishment in Britain* (Edinburgh U.P.); and Dr. Donald West's *Homosexuality* (Pelican). The informed and compassionate publications of the Albany Trust have been most helpful. I have also referred to the annual *Criminal Statistics* and reports of the Prison Department, published by the Home Office; and to articles published over the past few years in the *British Journal of Criminology*.

Panther Science

The Language of Life
An Introduction to the Science of Genetics

George and Muriel Beadle   8/6

Genetics, a relatively new science, is concerned
with heredity and variations from it, and its
significance is that for good or for ill it may soon
be in a position to modify the biology of the
human being. Because it is a new discipline its
way of thought and its language have tended to
baffle most readers. This present book is one of
the first to deal with the vital problem of
communication.

'Dr. Beadle, a geneticist whose work earned
him the Nobel Prize in 1958, explained each part
of the subject to his wife who had no scientific
training, and it was she who actually wrote the
book. This has removed the major barrier of
language that exists between scientist and
laymen. The terms used are clearly explained,
helped by a free use of metaphor and a
simple style'
Times Educational Supplement

Panther Science

The Biological Time-Bomb
Gordon Rattray Taylor   8/6

'The first major exposition addressed to the general public of issues which are going to be very much with us in the next few decades ... The point at issue is simple to state, very difficult to deal with.
The pursuit of knowledge eventually brings the power to control the subjects that knowledge is about; and power can be used for many purposes. In the physical sciences mankind has already been brought face to face with this. Knowledge of the atom has given him the power to devastate the Earth with nuclear bombs. Taylor's aim is to show us that biological knowledge is on the point of presenting us with powers that are equally double edged'
C.H.Waddington in *Science Journal*

'Taylor's book with its remorseless assembly of the components of the biological time-bomb, already dangerously near the critical mass, should alarm us'
Ritchie Calder in *New Scientist*

Panther Science

Man and Monkey
Leonard Williams   8/6

'This magnificent piece of pioneering research
has a direct bearing upon all our lives'
Gavin Maxwell

Mr. Williams lives with his Humbolt's Woolly
Monkey colony near Looe in Cornwall. From his
close observations of his twelve unusual charges
(ranging from eight years to ten months) the
author draws some valuable and disturbing
conclusions about the nature of *human* society.
He believes that man in his present
over-urbanised state can learn much from the
monkey conduct of affairs: neurosis, violence, and
racialism are unknown to them. A thoughtful
reading of this important book might well help
along the road to the eradication of these evils
among human beings.

'Simply superb. I am full of admiration'
Konrad Lorenz

'Mr. Williams is a close observer, and what he
has to say about the social and sexual life of
his monkeys is fascinating'
Anthony Storr

Illustrated